★

Soldier Boys

★

Published by Melbourne Books
Level 9, 100 Collins Street,
Melbourne, VIC 3000
Australia
www.melbournebooks.com.au
info@melbournebooks.com.au

National Library of Australia
Cataloguing-in-Publication Entry
Author: Waugh, Maxwell Neil.
Title: Soldier boys : the militarisation of Australian and New Zealand schools for World War I
ISBN: 9781922129451 (paperback)
Notes: Includes bibliographical references and index.
Subjects: Military education--Australia--History.
Military education--New Zealand--History.
World War, 1914-1918--Participation, Juvenile.
World War, 1914-1918--Participation, Australian.
World War, 1914-1918--Participation, New Zealand.
Dewey Number: 940.40994

★

Soldier Boys

★

The Militarisation of Australian and New Zealand Schools for World War I

MAXWELL N. WAUGH

M

MELBOURNE BOOKS

Contents

'No one taught us in school how to light a cigarette under attack in the rain, how to make a fire with wet wood — or that the best place to thrust a bayonette is in the stomach, because it doesn't get stuck fast like it does in the ribs.'

— Erich Maria Remarque, *All Quiet on the Western Front*

Acknowledgements

It would have been extremely difficult, and even more time-consuming, to compile this book without the services of my former employer, Monash University in Melbourne. For this I am eternally grateful, in particular to the Dean of Education, Professor John Loughran, for accepting me as an adjunct research fellow in his faculty these past two years, which has enabled me to use the extensive research facilities available through Monash and other universities. Hence my sincere thanks to the library staff at the Clayton (including the invaluable services at the 'Rare Books' department) and Peninsula campuses.

I commend the various research services at the State Library of Victoria, such as the LaTrobe Reading Room, the newspaper archives and the Rare Books department, for the willing assistance given by the respective librarians and archivists.

My thanks to Dr Alan Gregory, archivist of Melbourne High School, for access to photographs and descriptions of the school's cadet units, and wartime copies of school journals.

In New Zealand I was fortunate to have the assistance of several librarians from the University of Auckland's Epsom Campus, who managed to find a number of wartime copies of *The School Journal* locked away in the archives there, and also at the Auckland Public Library, where a research librarian led me to a shelf of North Island school histories, which proved invaluable.

For the chapter on Villiers-Bretonneux I acknowledge the help of the guides at the Franco-Australian Museum in Villiers-Bretonneux and at the nearby elementary school.

My thanks to Dr Nigel Starck at the University of South Australia, for his encouragement in this venture, and his assistance in gathering material from the State Library and the Flinders University Library storage facility in Adelaide. I am indebted to Mr Lyall Kupke, Chief Archivist at the Lutheran Archives in Bowden, South Australia, and to Ms Jenni van Wageningen and Mr Greg Slattery, the respective archivists of Concordia Lutheran College and Immanuel Lutheran College in Adelaide.

I am indebted to my son, Nic, for enabling me to travel to New Zealand in 2012 for research purposes, and also to my daughter Alison who urged me on in times of despondency and, as always, willingly undertook the task of editing the manuscript.

I am appreciative of David Tenenbaum, Publisher at Melbourne Books, for accepting this book for publication, and to Editor Chloe Brien for her competence and patience in handling the corrections.

Finally, thanks to my wife Elizabeth, who endured countless hours of being without my company over the many years I have been engaged in this engrossing research.

Introduction

'In 1932 one sees the futility of 1914–1918 — the insane folly that cost millions of lives and disorganised the whole world ... God! What a damn fool I was to get into it. What a damn fool! What a damn fool!'

— Lieutenant Joseph Maxwell, VC, MC and Bar, DCM, the second-highest decorated Australian soldier in World War I, served in the AIF at Gallipoli and on the Western Front, and was a former compulsory senior cadet in Newcastle, NSW, 1912–14.[1]

Many patriotic Australians like to boast that in both world wars we have been able to achieve a sufficient level of volunteers to send overseas, without having to resort to military conscription. The only exception has been the Vietnam War, from 1969 to 1975, when several thousand 'national servicemen' were chosen through a 1 in 6 ballot.

However, this research argues that military training was certainly alive and well in the schools of Australia (and New Zealand), through its units of Junior (aged 12–14) and Senior (aged 14–18) Cadets, at first in a voluntary form from the late nineteenth century, but more importantly on a compulsory basis from 1910 to 1929, which includes the period of World War I. In this respect we were 'more British than the British', as there was no compulsory military training in the school systems of Great Britain or other British Empire countries during this period.

The vast majority of the youths and men who volunteered for the AIF during 1914 to 1918 did so willingly, because they had been well trained and indoctrinated in the public and private schools of this nation. Tragically, they soon found themselves being used as 'cannon fodder' in the killing fields of Gallipoli and on the Western Front, where 60,000 were killed in action or died of wounds, 150,000 were wounded, and countless survivors of the horrors of trench warfare were left to wrestle with their 'personal demons' for the rest of their lives.

It's no wonder that many thousands of young Australian recruits responded so readily to 'Mother England's call', for here was a ready-made army in waiting. They were an army of fit and disciplined patriots, thanks largely to the schools that helped prepare them for the terrifying, bloody and mindless conflict that was the Great War.

I vividly remember going to the cinema in Melbourne in my late teens (was it the Regent Theatre?) to see the black and white 1930 feature film *All Quiet on the Western Front*, and for the first time being profoundly moved by the terrors and the futility of war. After screening in Berlin, the film was promptly banned by the Nazi government, and copies of the book and film were destroyed in public burnings. In the rest of Europe, the US, and the world at large, the film was hailed as a classic motion picture, for which Lewis Milestone won an Oscar for Best Director. German audiences did not get to see it until 1952. Seeing the film led me to question why it was necessary for both sides to suffer such horrendous casualties at the Front for such little territorial gain, and why the Great War had to be fought in the first place.

Soon after watching the film I purchased a copy of Erich Maria Remarque's book of the same name from a second-hand dealer, and like most comparisons of this sort I found the book to be even more revealing than the film. Remarque had been a German soldier on the Western Front, was seriously wounded in the Battle of Flanders and repatriated to Germany for the duration. At the Front he had witnessed some of the terrible carnage of hand-to-hand fighting, with artillery shells and hand-grenades exploding all around, causing havoc and horrendous casualties on both sides. He vividly described the additional hazards of mud, snow, lice and rats in the trenches, diseases like trench foot and rheumatic fever, the cries and suffering of wounded soldiers and horses, the insane and the shell-shocked, and the general feeling of depression among those who had survived to fight another day. The book depicts the naivety of the new recruits who, fresh from school and with just six weeks battle preparation, are maimed and slaughtered because they ignored the warning signs of the flares, the shelling or the dreaded gas attacks. I will never forget the imagery of the German unit marching through the rain and the slush on the way to the front line, and the sight of open wagons carrying scores of roughly-hewn wooden coffins parked by the roadside, which the soldiers knew only too well would be available for many of them after their next engagement with the enemy.

But the part I recall most distinctly occurs soon after the beginning of the novel. Remarque portrays a school classroom, where a group of senior students has just graduated amid high spirits, with hats and textbooks being tossed into the air. Their teacher, Kantorek, joins in the festivities and takes pride in the fact that he has recently accompanied the class of twenty to the army recruiting office to sign them up for service at the outbreak of the Great War, in 1914. Tragically, only a handful survived the ordeal. Many of them later regretted they had succumbed to Kantorek's pressure tactics, as he had encouraged a few of the boys to enlist before they had reached the age when military service became compulsory. Had they resisted the teacher's prompting, each of the three of them could have had up to nine months of freedom before the onslaught. I can remember the repugnance I felt that the German education system had been used so blatantly to recruit the cream of their youth to fight in such a needless war.

It would be many years later, long after becoming a teacher myself, that I would discover that many thousands of Australian and New Zealand lads had been coerced into enlisting in this brutal conflict, through the respective state education departments and the private school system, in much the same way as their German counterparts. And I made sure that, as a lecturer in the History of Education at

Monash and Deakin Universities in the 1990s, my students understood how the school systems in Australia and in Germany were used to indoctrinate and train its youth for military service.

I write this book not as an avowed pacifist, because I realise that, like our involvement in World War II where the whole of Europe was endangered by the Nazi threat and Australia itself was in danger from Japan, there are wars that are simply unavoidable. But with most international conflicts we have been involved in, like the Boer War, World War I, Korea, Vietnam, Iraq and Afghanistan, they have nothing to do with Australia, and are supposedly justified only by our ties with Britain, and more recently with America.

Finally, I should mention that my abhorrence of World War I is fuelled by memories of my grandfather, Alfred Charles Waugh, who served as a Private in the 60th Battalion AIF, was wounded in the leg and shell-shocked at Ypres in 1916, before returning home in September of 1919. For as long as I can remember (he died at age eighty-five, when I was in my late twenties) my grandfather lived as a recluse in a room at the back of the family house in West Brunswick. Year by year he could be seen pottering around the back garden, with his white flowing hair and tobacco-stained beard, murmuring only salutary greetings as he saw us, or commenting briefly on the weather. To my knowledge he never ventured outside the front door of the house, or had visitors other than our immediate family, during that time. Such are the family recollections of the aftermath of the Great War that I bear to this day, and which provide just some of the motivation for my writing on this issue.

PART I

SCHOOL CADETS IN THE NINETEENTH CENTURY

1

Formation of Military Units in the Australian Colonies

After almost a hundred years of supplying a military presence in the Australian colonies, in the late nineteenth century the British Government decided that the full cost of maintaining its garrison would in future be met by colonial sources. With the withdrawal of the last British troops from Australian soil in August 1870 — the 2nd Battalion of the 18th Regiment (Royal Irish) — it was left to the respective colonial governments to be responsible for their own defences. This left them in a vulnerable position, with a large collective coastline to defend from potential enemies, such as France, Germany, Russia and Japan, all of whom had warships stationed in waters to the north and north-east.

> ... fear of attack by a hostile power was a mark of nineteenth-century Australian society. During the century there were some two hundred 'war scares'. France, Germany, the United States of America, China, Holland, Japan and Spain were all regarded, at some stage in the 1850s and 1860s, as a possible invader.[1]

A decade before the British withdrew, volunteer military units, such as the Victorian Rangers, the New South Wales Lancers and the Perth Mounted Rifles, were created. Almost 4000 volunteers had registered in Victoria by the end of 1860.

> ... drilling before and after work and on Saturday afternoons, and on public holidays, camping over Easter, and parading on the Queen's birthday. They bought their own uniforms and arms, and if mounted they supplied their own horses.[2]

In the Australian colonies, about 10,000 militia volunteers were in training by 1863. At about this time, the first rifle association was formed by volunteers in Sydney, and from 1862 annual shooting competitions commenced between teams from New South Wales and Victoria.[3]

Soon most of the colonies had a navy of several warships, like Victoria's iron-clad battleship, HMVS *Cerberus*, and South Australia's 920-ton *Protector*. Defence was one of the major reasons put forward in discussions between Australian colonies on the issue of Federation in the late nineteenth century. Following its Defence and Discipline Act of 1883, Victoria organised a regular militia and established a Department of Defence. Through their respective colonial militias, thousands of Australian volunteers were dispatched to serve in the Maori Wars (1863–1872), the Sudan War (1882–1884), the Boxer Rebellion in China (1900) and in South Africa's Boer War (1899–1902).[4] Soldiers from the newly created 'Commonwealth Military Forces' served during the last months of the South African conflict, after Federation in 1901.

The SS *Protector*, South Australian naval vessel, 1880s. J. K. Ware, *An Outline of Australian Navy History*, 1976

A fourteen-year-old naval cadet, c. 1890. W. James, *Admiral Sir William Fisher*, 1943, p. 10

The Mounted Rifles of the First Victorian Contingent, Melbourne, 1899. W. Calder, *Colonel Tom Price and the Victorian Mounted Rifles*, 1985

2

School Cadets — Some European Precedents

Switzerland

Unlike Australia, Switzerland has a long history of using schools to provide military instruction and drill for its youth as a means of defence. Surrounded by warring neighbours, the Swiss were renowned for their military preparedness. A system of military training in schools commenced in the early nineteenth century, where all boys aged twelve years and over had three hours of military drill per week during school hours. The result of this was that

> every man you see in a shop and field would start into a soldier if his bugle called; a soldier armed, equipped and ready for the march. The groom who feeds your horse may be a corporal; the doctor who prepares your draught may be a captain of the line. Every man is trained to face his duties when the trumpet sounds.[1]

Younger boys of six or seven learned the rudiments of military drill, 'for with a Switzer, drill begins as soon as he can stand erect and poise a stick'. Boys from the elementary and polytechnic schools could be seen marching to practice on the rifle range: 'boys on certain days march with pipe and drum, with glittering steel and mounted guns; the linesmen carrying rifles, the artillery wearing swords'.[2] Boys of 'riper' age carried out 'full battalion drill' and could win prizes for marksmanship, because 'to be a marksman in a village is to bear away the palm'.[3]

Cadets wore military uniforms and were issued with a miniature model of the regulation rifle. They were trained in the same rifle practices as the regular army and like them became 'a hardened marcher and a good shot'.[4]

All Swiss males were officially soldiers on reaching their twentieth year, until their forty-fifth year;

> But a Switzer is a soldier long before he enters his twentieth year and long after he has past his forty-fifth. At fourteen Switzers have been known to fight in line; and in the civil strife at Fribourg there were volunteers of seventy in the ranks.[5]

Even the Swiss schoolgirls were expected to train as nurses for the military:

> In every public school the girls are trained to take their part. They learn to staunch the flow of blood; they learn to dress a gunshot wound; they learn to nurse the sick ... They know some chemistry, and they are quick at sewing, binding, dressing, and such medical arts. If need be they can march in line, with knapsack on their backs, and keep up with their brothers night and day. In a defensive war they could be used as scouts, as messengers, as nurses and as teamsters.[6]

In the early years of the twentieth century, the Swiss model of universal military training for students was to be advocated in Australia.

Great Britain

Cadet units were raised in English public schools like Eton, Harrow, Winchester and Rugby in the 1850s, to supplement regular army units in the likelihood of war with Napoleon III, and because of concern over a Russian invasion around the time of the Crimean War (1854–1856).[7]

In Britain, the military cadet system was more directed towards the 'aristo-military class' of middle-class and upper-class public schools, unlike what developed in Australia, where schools that offered cadet training were more broadly based.[8] However, in the late nineteenth century, drill instruction became a major source of discipline in working-class state schools. Military activities evolved into an important means of recreation for working-class boys who left school to enter the workforce:

> Through the highly successful Volunteer forces, rifle clubs, ceremonial and drill units in factories, and brigades of shoeblacks and other useful street arabs and industrial apprentices … The scene was set for the dramatic waves of volunteering for the armed services in the Boer War and in 1914.[9]

In addition, youth movements like the Boy Scouts, Girl Guides and the Church of England 'Boys Brigade' became popular middle- and working-class youth movements. Special events like Empire Day and the Queen's/King's Birthday witnessed parades by these and other youth organisations, who 'provided the drill, the bands, the standard bearing, and the variety of uniforms necessary for such public ceremonies'.[10]

An estimated forty percent of all British males were in organisations like the Scouts (thirteen million in the Scouts and Guides) and the Boys' Brigade (two million) between 1901 and 1920, 'and the working class as a whole received a considerable infusion of middle-class values through them'.[11]

Germany

There seems to be no precedent of military cadets in the German school system prior to World War I, but there were cadet units attached to the various military academies and naval colleges throughout the country. In common with other European nations at this time, the schools were used by the government and the military to promote nationalistic fervour. For example, Sedan Day was a national holiday commemorating the German victory over the French army in the Battle of Sedan in September 1870, and patriotic ceremonies 'wherein song and play were geared to military themes' were held in the schools each year leading up to the event.[12]

Worthy of mention here was the *Wandervogel* (hiking birds), a German youth organisation founded in 1901 in Steglitz, a middle-class suburb of Berlin, where young boys (and later girls) roamed the countryside on weekends, singing folksongs, eating simple food around a campfire and sleeping in haystacks. The movement quickly spread to other middle-class areas, where young people wanted to escape the confines of urban living for a while and 'lead their own lives away from homes, parents and teachers'.[13] Other youth organisations took root at this time also, some sponsored by Catholic and Protestant Churches (who segregated the sexes more rigidly) and included some working-class youth as well, so that they became a 'rite of passage' for German youth as a whole. It is estimated that over half of all teenage boys in many large German cities were members of youth organisations, which was unprecedented elsewhere; 'in no British city did more than twelve percent join clubs, and in France and the United States the percentages were even lower.'[14] When World War I was declared, it was the members of these idealistic German youth groups (particularly the majority *Wandervogel*) who were among the first to rush to the recruitment centres to enlist.[15]

3

School Cadets in the Australian Colonies

Victoria

A form of 'semi' military drill without uniforms or rifles, which included physical exercises and marching, was taught in many schools from the 1860s, with precedents set in Great Britain.[1] At the Model School, one of Melbourne's earliest 'national schools' (non-church school), drill instruction was taught in the boys' school by the teachers.

The Model School Cadet Corps was founded in 1885, with uniforms of navy blue and red stripes, along with Francotte rifles and 'a bayonet in a black leather scabbard with a brass tip'. There were several detachments of cadets, with a minimum of twenty cadets in each. Boys who enrolled did so with their parents' or guardians' permission, were required to pay for their own uniform, and 'must be not less than twelve years of age, unless he were of a minimum height of four feet six inches and physically fit'. Arms and equipment were kept at the school under the care of the headmaster. From 1891, uniforms were changed to khaki.[2] Weapons instruction was given for thirty minutes before school closure on Tuesdays and Thursdays.

By the 1880s, many state and non-government schools in Australia had volunteer school cadet units equipped with rifles, largely because of the perceived threat to national security from Russia in the Pacific region. The heavy gun emplacements at the entrances to Sydney Harbour and Victoria's Port Phillip Bay date back to this period.

In Victoria, the new Minister of Defence and for Public Instruction,

Frederick Sargood, who was also a Lieutenant Colonel in the colonial military, brought together a number of school principals and teachers with a military background to discuss the formation of a volunteer cadet corps in Victorian schools, in order to familiarise boys with 'habits of discipline, regularity and obedience to authority'. On 5 December 1884, the first parade took place, with 840 boys from the newly formed Victorian Junior Cadet Corps, which was managed by both the Victorian Defence and Education Ministries. Major John Snee was placed in charge of the Corps, and soon cadet units commenced in a number of other Melbourne state schools, like Prahran and Brighton, some country schools in the areas of Geelong, Bendigo and Castlemaine, and in the private system, including Melbourne Grammar, Xavier College, Wesley College, Caulfield Grammar and Scotch College.[3]

Wesley College's cadets were first formed in 1867, and besides military drill the school had a rifle-shooting team that competed each year against other public schools for the James McEwen (of hardware fame) Cup. The Cup was eventually claimed by Wesley after winning it three times — 1873, 1874 and 1877.[4] The Geelong College Cadet Corps formed in 1885, and the fifty-one boys were commanded by three lieutenants, all masters at the college. The school rifle team competed at Williamstown Rifle Range 'with moderate success' for the Sargood Shield, which had replaced the McEwan Trophy as the prize for both public and government schools.[5]

Some of the boys at Xavier College 'grumbled' that unlike the other public schools in Melbourne, they were unable to have 'a grand send off' for ex-pupils leaving to fight in the Boer War, with prefect Bernard Page (later a military chaplain in WWI) the chief instigator. Subsequently, Major Alexander Lewis was contracted at £20 a year to drill a cadet corps in 1900, 'and the school's honour was restored'.[6]

Eventually, throughout the state, groups of twenty or more boy volunteers from twelve years of age could be seen being instructed in military drill and rifle shooting by a specially trained teacher or local army recruit, on a twice-weekly basis, often after school. Boys were required to measure no less than four feet and six inches in height, attend at least one hour's drill with arms each week, and no less than six battalion parades each year.[7] The instructors were paid two shillings, six pence by the government for each parade they conducted. As teachers existed on appalling salaries in those days, it is not surprising that many of the males were grateful of the opportunity for the extra after-hours payment they accrued as drill instructors. Cadets were also expected to attend a fortnightly camp at an army barracks in the January school holidays, where they were instructed in physical training, marching, rifle shooting, swimming and first aid. A three-day cadet camp at the Langwarrin Military Barracks in October 1889 attracted 1882 cadets from various parts of the state, but the event was marred by violent storms and the flooding of tents.[8] The introduction of military drill in the curriculum was seen as an important factor in providing discipline in schools, particularly for working-class boys.[9] Blue uniforms with red trimmings for the boys cost £1.50 each, towards which a seven shillings subsidy was paid by the Defence Department. There were some government funds available to assist families in necessitous circumstances towards the cost of cadet uniforms. Teachers, commissioned as lieutenants, received a uniform allowance of £2, and paid the remaining £3 themselves. Cadets were issued with a Belgian-made Francotte rifle with a .23-inch bore, a bayonet encased in a black leather scabbard, a leather waist belt, frog and pouch, and a cloth cape for wet weather.[10] All weapons were kept at the school, with the headmaster responsible for their safety.

By 1881, military drill was being taught in 186 schools throughout Victoria, with an overall attendance of some 11,437 students,[11] reaching its peak in 1892 when 17,210 boys were in training, taught by 338 teachers qualified in military drill, at a cost of £3930. However, as the 1890s progressed and the economic depression took its toll on government expenditure, the drill bonus for teachers was dropped even though the male teachers were still required to teach drill.[12] Uniforms were changed to khaki and the trousers carried a red braid stripe. In June 1900, a muster of 1202 cadets paraded at Victoria Barracks in Melbourne, with 7 and 8 Battalions commanded by Captain Duffy and Captain Walter Gamble respectively, the latter being a District Inspector with the Education Department. Gamble's superior was Major Thomas Brodribb, the Chief Inspector of schools and a strong supporter of the cadet movement.[13] The dominance of district inspectors in the Victorian school cadet corps was a major distinguishing feature compared to those of the other Australian colonies. This characteristic led not only to a closer link between education and military hierarchies, but also to 'greater military control over the everyday life of State Schools'.[14]

Classes for the instruction of cadet officers (usually teachers) in military drill were held annually at the Victoria Barracks, and were of one week's duration. More than 150 teachers had received military training in 1889.[15] To supplement their meagre salaries (male assistants were then paid as low as £100 per annum), teachers qualified in military training could earn up to £15 per annum in drill bonuses, with an extra £10 per annum paid for every fifty students above the set minimum. Besides the powerful incentive for monetary gain, military drill helped male teachers maintain order in the overcrowded classrooms of the day. Even students training at the Melbourne Teachers' College were required to do two hours of drill per week.[16] The Duke of Edinburgh reviewed 4000 Victorian cadets on the steps of Parliament House in 1901, and later in the visit took the salute at a march-past of 4900 boys at the Flemington Racecourse. A newspaper report described the scene as 'an immense procession of keen, soldierly lads, who bore themselves with the spring and alertness of trained troops'.[17] The Victorian Railways provided free rail passes to cadets attending battalion parades, rifle competitions, instructional classes and military camps.[18]

It is estimated that prior to the South African War (1899–1902) about 40,000 Victorian boys had received cadet training, and that 60 to 80 percent of the Victorian military contingent for the Boer War was comprised of former school cadets.[19] Major General John Charles Hoad, a former Victorian School Cadet officer, was appointed to command the 1st Australian Regiment in the Boer War.[20] In 1906, Melbourne High School (previously Melbourne Continuation School) was one of the first state high schools operating in Victoria. In that year it boasted that 'cadets had been hugely popular', and of the 140 boys enrolled 'all bar one' had voluntarily joined the school's cadet corps.[21]

Beechworth State School, Victoria, c. 1890. Note 'rifle room' and 'guard room' above doors. Courtesy Beechworth Primary School, Victoria

QUARRY HILL SCHOOL, BENDIGO.

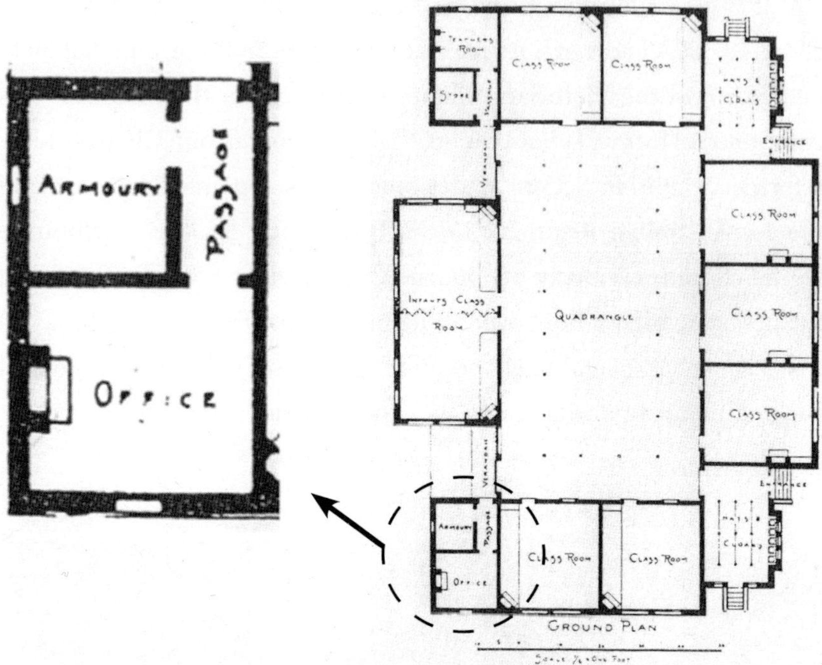

Victorian Department of Education archives, Treasury Place, Melbourne

His Excellency Inspecting the Cadets at Physical Drill.

Ours, Melbourne High School quarterly magazine, vol. 3, no. 2, 1909, p. 12

Sale High School Cadet Corps, Victoria, c. 1905. Ann and Peter Synan, *Sale High School Centenary Memories*, 2007, p. 4. Courtesy Sale High School

New South Wales

A form of school cadetship was first observed in New South Wales in 1834, through the teaching of military drill at the Australian College in Sydney, a Presbyterian grammar school.[22] In March 1866, headmaster Reverend G. F. Macarthur established a school cadet unit at St Mark's Collegiate School (later King's School) in Parramatta. It was modelled on the cadet corps established in Britain's Great Public Schools, in response to a French invasion scare. Macarthur assumed the rank of captain and was also chaplain to the volunteer forces of the colony.[23] The boys drilled 'for an hour before school and an hour after it, dressed not in grey at first but in clothes perhaps intended for the police'.[24] The Fort Street Model School was the first state school in NSW to be given permission to form a cadet unit in 1871, provided that the government did not have to supply uniforms for the purpose. Following much lobbying by teachers, approval was given in March 1871 for a Teachers' Company to be attached to the City Battalion in Sydney, under the command of Captain William Wilkins, former headmaster of Fort Street School and then Secretary of Education.[25] The NSW Government resisted pressure from its other schools to form cadet units until 1873, when over 2000 boys were registered. It is generally recognised that NSW was much more content to rely on British protection than Victoria, which preferred to depend more on its own military forces.[26]

Unlike Victoria, where trained teachers conducted each school corps and were supervised by several school inspectors that were also serving officers, the NSW military officers were the main trainers and there were periodic rivalries with some of the Education Department's power-brokers, the school inspectors. Captain Henry William Strong was chosen as commander of the cadet corps. He soon put himself offside with the inspectorate by insisting that he assume the responsibility for any teachers of military drill in the schools. Things came to a head in September 1877, when the *Parramatta Mercury* reported that a house inhabited by two women had been hit by rifle bullets of 'armed juveniles', and criticised the practice of allowing cadets to take weapons and ammunition home.[27] Such bad publicity and the lack of cooperation by many school inspectors led to a general decline in interest in school cadets in NSW into the 1880s. However, by the mid-1880s a renewal of defence scares occurred throughout the Australian colonies, spurred on by Germany's annexation of West New Guinea and West Samoa, French activity in New Caledonia, and fears of another war between Britain and Russia, and interest in military cadets was gradually rekindled.[28] This resulted in the formation of the NSW Public School Cadet Force in 1890, under the command of a Sudan war veteran Lieutenant Colonel A. Paul, and the unpopular Captain Strong was made a subordinate. Under the new management, the school cadet corps rose from a low of 1084 in 1881 to a high of 5842 in 1890. By this time, 55 out of 56 male teachers in training and 165 of the 432 male teachers in the colony were enlisted in the Training Battalion in NSW. Some country cadet units were inspired by the provision of an annual training camp in Sydney and there were periodic massed parades of up to 5000 cadets at important events. However, with the onset of the 1890s Depression, the camps were suspended for several years, and rifles and ammunition were restricted.[29]

Macquarie Fields Corps, King's School, New South Wales, c. 1871. Craig Stockings, *The Torch and the Sword: A History of the Army Cadet Movement in Australia*, 2007, p. 10

Summer Hill Public School, New South Wales, Cadet Corps, 1895. J. Burnswoods and J. Fletcher, *Sydney and the Bush: A Pictorial History of Education in NSW*, 1980

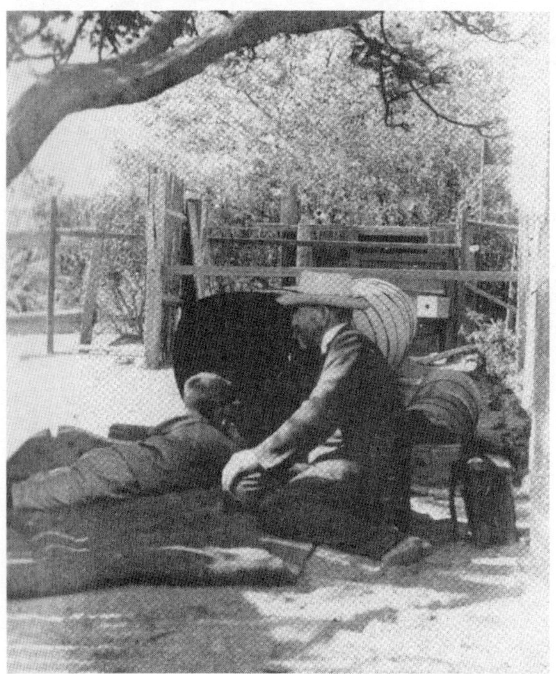

Miniature rifle range, Hillgrove Public School, New South Wales, c. 1908

Fort Street High School cadets, c. 1908. Courtesy Fort Street High School, Sydney

The other Australian colonies

In Queensland, a system of military drill had been in existence since the early 1870s, but had been instituted mainly as an enhancement to school discipline and management. Pupil-teachers were expected to pass an examination in drill during their training, as they were required to be familiar with words of command and their responses, such as 'attention', 'stand at ease', 'by the right, dress' and 'salute'.[30] A system of school cadets had only commenced in 1891, but by the end of that year, 597 boys had joined in both private and state schools. Several years before, District School Inspector John Shirley and the Commandant of the Queensland Defence Force had called for the introduction of cadets along Swiss lines. Sergeant-Major John Byrne was appointed drill instructor to the Education Department and began instruction in military drill to teachers and inspectors, and by December 1892, 290 of them had passed his course. From Byrne's drill classes the

Queensland Teachers' Volunteer Corps was formed, which involved 206 teachers out of a total male teaching force of 628. District Inspector Shirley claimed that the cadets and military drill would have to do for Queensland 'what conscription does in the European countries'.[31] By Federation, 3375 school cadets had been trained and 410 teachers had received military training in the QTVC.[32]

Cadet corps in South Australian schools had been in existence since 1862, when rifle-shooting competitions were reported in the *South Australian Government Gazette*,[33] though it was more prominent in Adelaide than in country areas. The standard of military drill was not high and displeased some of the school inspectors, who valued it mainly on 'hygienic' grounds. Largely through the recommendations of these inspectors, teachers began instruction in drill, mainly with the aim of increasing physical fitness among their young charges. Henceforth, inspectors' reports contained a section on military drill, and the efforts of teachers in this regard were judged accordingly. A certificate of competency in drill was issued to male teacher trainees who passed the examination. In some schools rifles were issued, and boys did rifle drill and battalion exercises. An annual demonstration at the Adelaide Show saw around 400 boy soldiers performing company manoeuvres and firing rifle volleys. Strangely, by 1886 the cadet system had all but disappeared from public schools in South Australia. This was largely due to a Select Committee of the South Australian House of Assembly inquiring into the state of the colony's defences. It found that there was no further need for government funding of school cadet units, so withdrew its organisational and financial support. Left to the initiative and enthusiasm of teachers, cadet activity began to wane. In its place the Colonial Commandant, Brigadier-General John Owen, instituted a 'limited' cadet force of fifteen to seventeen year-olds that was not based in schools. In choosing older boys he felt they would take their responsibilities more seriously, because 'if you drill boys when they are too young they get sick of it' and that too much drill 'rammed down their throats left them disgusted with it in later life'.[34] Inspired by the onset of the Boer War in 1899, a small battalion of 232 cadets was created from among the boys of Prince Alfred College and St Peter's College in Adelaide, officered by some Old Boys from both colleges who were granted volunteer commissions. The battalion had to be disbanded after 1901, however, when the new Commonwealth Government made no provision for the continuance of cadet units.

Following the granting of self-government to Western Australia in 1890, Colonel W. G. Phillmore, the colonial Military Commandant, encouraged the formation of a cadet corps, but several years elapsed before a system of Junior Cadets (in schools) and Senior Cadets (with volunteer army units) were formed in Perth and Fremantle, in 1897.[35]

A request from the headmaster of the Launceston Church Grammar School for a cadet unit in Tasmania was successful in 1883. The detachment of 45 to 50 boys was assigned to the Launceston Volunteer Rifle Regiment, and drilled by one of its officers and a non-commissioned officer (NCO). The Tasmanian Government voted the sum of £2.10 to equip each boy with a uniform, arms and other equipment supplied by the military.[36]

Senior Cadets at Bunbury, Western Australia. J. Barrett, *Falling In: Australians and Boy Conscription 1911–1915*, 1979, p. 232

Maryborough Grammar School Cadet Corps, Queensland, 1906. Craig Stockings, *The Torch and the Sword: A History of the Army Cadet Movement in Australia*, 2007, p. 47

Scotch College cadets at Launceston, Tasmania, target shooting with Lewis machine guns. Craig Stockings, *The Torch and the Sword: A History of the Army Cadet Movement in Australia*, 2007, p. 72

4

New Zealand School Cadet Corps

In colonial times New Zealand, like Australia, followed the British tradition of introducing a system of voluntary school cadets in a number of larger schools in the main centres. Military drill was first introduced into New Zealand schools in the 1850s, with records showing that drill was part of the curriculum for boys at Nelson College in 1857, and that a cadet corps existed as a co-curricular activity at Christ's College in 1873.[1] The private Christchurch Boys' High School established a cadet corps in 1883, two years after the school was founded.

Provision was made for military drill to be incorporated into the physical education program of public schools in the Education Act of 1877:

> In public schools provision shall be made for the instruction in military drill of all boys, and in such of the schools as the Board from time to time directs provision shall also be made for physical training.[2]

Both instructions were largely ignored until early in the twentieth century. Even though NCOs were made available in 1893 to act as drill instructors, only a few schools took up the offer. However, a survey in 1896 showed there were around 1000 cadets enrolled. A boost in interest occurred at the time of the Boer War, and in 1899 the parliament voted £400 for the purchase of dummy wooden rifles (thirty-five per cadet company). Defence Department NCOs began taking Saturday drill classes for teachers, and in Wellington 'some school mistresses shouldered wooden rifles and marched with the men'.[3]

Regulations gazetted in May 1902 stated that cadet corps would in future be under the control of the Minister of Education and would drill cadets over the age of twelve for up to one hour per week. A minimum of twenty boys was required for a cadet corps and if the numbers were insufficient, younger boys could be included provided they were over four feet and six inches in height. The Education Department would provide two shillings, six pence per child per annum towards the cost of uniforms, supply dummy rifles and one .310-calibre miniature Martini-Henry rifle for every ten cadets, and swords, waist belts and sashes for teachers. Major Lambert Loveday was appointed Commander of Public School cadets in 1901. By 1908 there were 185 cadet units, with a total of 15,183 cadets with 'boys uniformed in blue jerseys, knickerbockers, and glengarry caps'.[4]

Lieutenant Colonel Goring gave weekly instruction in military drill to about forty grade 5 and 6 boys in the Remuera Primary School cadet corps, using dummy wooden guns supplied by the Kauri Timber Company for one shilling each, and 'for a time there were two pupil lieutenants who also had dummy swords, a drummer and a bugler'. By 1912, the school boasted two companies of cadets, of 87 and 54 respectively, under the command of Captains McInnes and Tatton. A miniature rifle range was set up at the school in 1910 'using a Fletcher target and two BSA airguns'.[5]

New Zealand's Maryborough High School was one of the first public high schools to field a cadet corps. In 1902, its cadets featured in a drill competition and attended a camp to improve on musketry skills, using their Martini-Enfield rifles. At the Imperial competitions in 1907, one of their cadets proved himself to be 'one of the best six shooters in the Empire … at the 200 yard range with a six inch bull'.[6]

Among the private schools, the Wanganui Collegiate School was proud of being the 'top of New Zealand in the Empire shooting match for 1906' and the following year took possession of

> 180 belts, pouches and frogs (a frog was a belt attachment for supporting a sword or a bayonet), and a plentiful supply of ammunition arrived from the Defence Department.[7]

Wellington College's No.1 Company of forty-five cadets paraded at the memorial service for Queen Victoria in 1901, and later that year at the arrival of the Duke of Cornwall and York, the future King George V.[8]

Remuera Primary School Cadet Guard of Honour, New Zealand, 1900 (note the dummy rifles). C. Caughey, *Remuera Primary School 125 Years*, 1998, p. 16

2nd Lieutenant Joseph Hertzog, as a New Zealand cadet in 1908 and a soldier in 1915. Courtesy Ms Lynette Townsend, Tepapa Museum, New Zealand

Auckland Grammar School 'volunteer defence cadets', 1908. K. A. Trembath, *A Centennial History of Auckland Grammar School 1869–1969*, 1969, p. 169

PART II

EARLY TWENTIETH CENTURY DEVELOPMENTS

5

The Relevance of Empire Day

British origins

Many British, Australian and New Zealand senior citizens would remember the Empire Day commemorations in schools on 24 May each year, when after a patriotic ceremony of song, poetry, pageantry and a stirring address by a military officer or prominent citizen, the children were given a half day holiday.

This observance is said to have originated in Ontario, Canada in 1897, when a school head teacher received permission from the provincial Minister of Education for a 'Children's Day' of patriotic readings, addresses and activities to celebrate the birthday of the aging Queen Victoria on 24 May. After the Queen's death in 1901, the Canadian Parliament passed an Act to declare this day as a bank holiday, with schools expected to commemorate the occasion the day before.[1]

The concept of an Empire Day on this day is said to be the brainchild of Reginald Brabazon, an Anglo-Irish peer and the twelfth Earl of Meath. It was to be an occasion of loyalty by all subjects of the British Empire, as well as a means of revering the life of the late Queen. In 1902, spurred on by the Canadian example, the Earl of Meath persuaded the Secretary of State for the Colonies, Joseph Chamberlain, to write to his colonial counterparts about the suggestion of an Imperial Empire Day (as either a public or schools-only holiday) on this date each year. Subsequently, over the next few years 24 May was declared a public holiday in each of the British colonies, except Britain itself, due to the proximity of the existing Whit Monday holiday. Despite the Earl's protests, a holiday was not granted in Great Britain until 1916, when it was given as an acknowledgement of the Imperial war effort.[2]

Australian origins

Initial agitation for an Australia-wide campaign on this issue is credited to the Anglican Canon of Redfern, Reverend Francis Boyd, 'the antipodean Meath', who successfully lobbied the various state premiers and the conservative Prime Minister George Reid, who saw in the occasion an opportunity to promote an anti-socialist agenda. Annual Empire Day ceremonies were first introduced in Australian schools (government, Protestant and a minority of Catholic schools) in 1905, when songs, verse and concerts were held to mark the occasion. Specially composed songs such as 'A Song to the Flag' and 'We are Britons All' were sung, an 'Empire Day Catechism' recited, and children were encouraged to enter Empire Day essay competitions with topics like 'In what sense can an Empire prove itself to be great?'[3] It was common to see school assemblies with students, teachers and parents standing to attention to sing 'God save the King', and to hear a patriotic address by a local member of parliament or municipal councillor. At the conclusion of the event, each child usually received a memento, often in the form of a small card bearing the flag of the Union Jack, suitably inscribed.

There was, however, an ambivalent attitude towards celebrating Empire Day in Catholic Schools. In much of country New South Wales, for example, Catholic schools often joined with their state counterparts to celebrate Empire Day. In 1911, schools from both systems in Albury, Grafton and Dubbo celebrated together, while in Camden the Mayor attended the Empire Day function at St Joseph's Convent. But some of the Catholic parishes with predominantly Irish clergy, like those at Bathurst, were not so enthusiastic. Addressing the pupils of St Stanislaw's College, Father J. M. O'Reilly claimed,

> It is unfortunate that in Australia, patriotism seemed to be identified with the efforts of the British Empire League, and that the League taught children to love England instead of Australia.[4]

The aging Cardinal Moran of Sydney also shared these sentiments, exclaiming that many of the supporters of Empire Day 'were avowed enemies of the Catholic Church and were identified with those who advocated Primrose Day in England'.[5] A headline in the *Sydney Morning Herald* on Empire Day in 1911 proclaimed 'NO UNION JACK FLOWN' at the prestigious St Mary's Cathedral in Sydney, with the flags of Ireland and Australia unfurled instead, as symbols of Irish-Australian patriotism.[6]

EMPIRE DAY and all that . . .

AN HISTORICAL VIEW

BOB BESSANT

Senior Lecturer in Education
LaTrobe University

In June 1918 the following instruction to Victorian teachers appeared in the *Education Gazette*:

> Instructions for inculcating ideas of loyalty, service, and thrift . . . The curriculum as it stands is, in the main, adapted to teaching the underlying principles of a sane national sentiment. . . the important thing is that the atmosphere of the school shall be permeated with the spirit of loyalty and service . . .
> History. For the prescribed stories of notable deeds to be told in the third and fourth grades substitute stirring stories of heroic deeds in the present great conflict. . . Do not dwell upon the horrors inseparable from war, but emphasise the qualities that will make such stories immortal . .
> Geography. When dealing with the range and extent of the British Empire, the teacher should always make reference to British ideals of justice to subject races, and to the fact that the world over the British flag has come to be regarded as the symbol of true freedom and fair dealing.
>
> *Education Gazette* 20 June, 1918, p. 80

In the first three decades of this century such sentiments as expressed above were regarded as desirable values to be inculcated into the characters of the boys and girls of the State schools of Victoria. Loyalty, citizenship, patriotism, devotion to duty, self-reliance, sobriety, and good sportsmanship went with school syllabuses permeated with imperial geography and history, with British Empire patriots and heroes, stories of white explorers in darkest Africa and arid Australia bringing civilisation and Christianity to the ignorant and

The Education Magazine, Victoria, vol. 30, no. 5, 1973

Empire Day in the school magazines

Perhaps the most effective means of inspiring a sense of pride in the Empire to school children was through the monthly school magazines, such as *The School Paper* in Victoria, the *Children's Hour* in South Australia and New Zealand's *The School Journal.*

The May issues of these and other state school magazines contained patriotic narratives, poems and songs to coincide with the 24 May British Empire celebrations. Teachers were expected to plan much of their lesson material around this theme in the intervening weeks so that the children would be well prepared for this special event.

Most of the May 1910 edition of *The School Paper* for grades 5 and 6 contained material such as 'An Empire Catechism' which, like all catechisms, included a series of questions and answers to be learnt by the children by rote:

> Query. What do you mean by the British Empire?
>
> Answer. That portion of the earth's land surface which is under the authority of King Edward the Seventh.
>
> Q. What is the extent in square miles of the British Empire?
>
> A. About 12,000,000 square miles; of these only 121,000 square miles are in the United Kingdom.[7]

APPROVED BY THE DEPARTMENT OF PUBLIC INSTRUCTION, NEW SOUTH WALES.

...THE...

Commonwealth School Paper

FOR CLASSES V. & VI.

Registered at the General Post Office, Sydney, for Transmission by Post as a Newspaper.

Vol. II.—No. 4. SYDNEY. October 1, 1905.

FLAGS USED BY LIEUT.T PASCO, H.M.S. VICTORY FOR LORD NELSON'S SIGNAL AT TRAFALGAR

THE BATTLE OF TRAFALGAR.

[For the greater part of the period between the signing of the Treaty of Amiens (1802) and the Battle of Trafalgar (1805), England was in almost constant dread of invasion at the hands of the French. Napoleon Bonaparte had collected a large army of [illegible] men at Boulogne, and was only prevented from landing them on the English coast by the presence of the British fleet in the Channel. To make matters more serious for Britain, in 1805 Spain joined forces with France, and combined its fleet with Napoleon's men-of-war, which were locked up in Brest, Toulon, and other French ports. An attempt was made by a feigned French and Spanish attack upon our West Indian possessions, to induce the British Channel fleet to quit its regular station. This attempt failed, and so vigilant was the watch kept up by our great sea captains of the time—Nelson, Collingwood, and others—that the French flotilla of flat-bottomed boats, specially constructed to carry Napoleon's forces across the Channel, never ventured from under the protection of their chains and batteries. Nelson's great victory at Trafalgar practically annihilated the French and Spanish fleets, saved England from invasion, prevented India and Australia from falling into the hands of the French, made Britain

ISSUED MONTHLY BY THE DEPARTMENT OF EDUCATION, NEW SOUTH WALES.

THE SCHOOL MAGAZINE

OF

Literature for our Boys and Girls.

PART II - - FOR CLASSES IV & V.

[Registered at the General Post Office, Sydney, for Transmission by Post as a Newspaper.]

Copies of this Magazine may be purchased from Government Printer and all Booksellers.

Vol. II.—No. 4. SYDNEY. May 1, 1917.

THE UNION JACK.

In the year 1194 Richard I brought back to England from the Crusades a flag containing a red cross, known as the Cross of St. George, and he made it the battle flag of England.

As years went on St. George came to be recognised as the patron saint of England, and at last, as early as 1222, England's favourite battle-cry had become "St. George and Merrie England."

This flag, with its plain red cross upon a white ground, was flown on Edward III's ships at the Battle of Sluys in

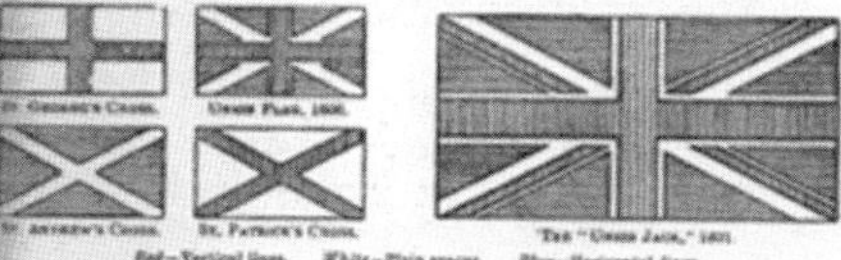

1340, and for fully three hundred years it was the Englishman's standard. The sea-kings of Elizabeth flew the old flag on their mast-head in those spacious days when her great seamen sailed round the world.

On 12th April, 1606, three years after the accession of King James of Scotland to the English throne, it was formally declared that St. Andrew's cross, a white saltire on a blue field, should be combined with this cross of St. George to form the Union Flag of Britain. Under this

[Price 1d.]

EMPIRE NUMBER.

Children's Hour

FOR READING AND RECREATION.

GRADE IV

TOP LEFT
The Commonwealth School Paper, New South Wales, October 1905, Mitchell Library, Sydney

TOP RIGHT
The School Magazine, New South Wales, May 1917, Mitchell Library

BOTTOM
The Children's Hour, Education Department of South Australia, grade 4, May 1918

OPPOSITE
The School Paper, Victoria, grades 5 and 6 Supplement, May 1910

Supplement to "THE SCHOOL PAPER—CLASSES V. AND VI.," *May, 1910.*

An Empire Catechism.

[The following are extracts from an "Empire-day Catechism," issued by the League of the Empire, a body having for its objects to further friendly intercourse among schools of the British Empire, and to help people of all classes and countries in the Empire to work together for their mutual benefit.]

Query. What do you mean by the British Empire?

Answer. That portion of the earth's land surface which is under the authority of King Edward the Seventh.

Q. What is the extent in square miles of the British Empire?

A. About 12,000,000 square miles; of these, only 121,000 square miles are in the United Kingdom.

Q. What proportion of the earth's surface does the British Empire cover?

A. About one-fifth, or 21 per cent.

Q. How does the extent of the British Empire compare with that of other countries?

A. The extent of the British Empire is greater than that of any other State. The nations outside the British Empire possessing the largest extent of territory are:—Russia, 8,000,000 square miles; United States, 3,623,000 square miles; Brazil, 3,220,000.

Q. What is the number of the subjects of King Edward?

A. About 400 millions (400,000,000). Of these only about 43 millions (43,000,000) live in the United Kingdom.

Q. What proportion of the inhabitants of the earth are the subjects of King Edward?

A. About one-fifth, or about 22 per cent.

Incorporation of school cadets in Empire Day ceremonies

Schools with cadet units attached, particularly after 1911, would also put on a display of military drill to the music of a brass (or at least a drum and fife) band, with an accompanying march-past salute to the flag flying overhead. Around the country thousands of cadets took part in 'Empire Day Rifle Shoots', competing for local, district, state or national trophies. Mass displays of military drill were performed at the Sydney Cricket Ground to mark the occasion in 1909, when over 7000 cadets from metropolitan schools paraded.[8]

A 'martial aspect' was noticeable at the Empire Day ceremony at the Fort Street School in Sydney in 1912, where 'four hundred fine-looking cadets formed a guard at the school entrance, drums were rolled, bugles blown, and there was a march past the Union Jack.'[9]

Instructions on how to celebrate Empire Day were given to head-teachers by the respective state education departments. In Victoria, this took the form of a notice in the monthly education gazettes, copies of which were sent to each school.

There were also occasions when Boy Scouts (and later Girl Guides) took part in Empire Day celebrations at schools or at other community functions. The Earl of Meath, later inducted onto the Executive Committee of the Scouting movement, was clearly advised of the distinction between Scouting and military cadets: 'We are a Peace organisation … the main reason being that a very large number of people will allow their boys to join the Boy Scouts, who are not in favour of general military service.'[10]

Empire Day celebrations in Australia continued into the early 1960s, when they gradually faded into obscurity, no doubt because of the increasing alliance between Australia and the US, and Britain's severance of preferential trade with Commonwealth countries prior to its entry into the European Common Market.

EDUCATION DEPARTMENT, VICTORIA.

THE SCHOOL PAPER.

FOR GRADES VII. AND VIII. (1913).

No. 160.] [Registered at the General Post Office, Melbourne, for transmission by post as a newspaper.] MELBOURNE. Price 1d. [FEB. 1, 1913.

By kind permission of the proprietors of *The Leader.*]

SENIOR CADETS, SPRING-STREET, MELBOURNE, "MARCHING PAST" HIS EXCELLENCY LORD DENMAN, GOVERNOR-GENERAL AND COMMANDER-IN-CHIEF OF THE COMMONWEALTH.

The School Paper, Victoria, grades 7 and 8, February 1913

6

Early Calls for Military Conscription in Europe

Germany and France

The beginnings of modern conscription in Europe are usually traced to Prussia in 1733, when military service in the royal regiments of Frederick the Great was made compulsory for much of the population, with quotas for each municipality being determined annually. France followed suit in 1793, when all Frenchmen from 20 to 25 years of age were liable for service. At first the French government permitted no exemptions, but eventually clergymen, divinity students, doctors, only sons of widowed mothers and workmen engaged in the manufacture of war materials could be excluded. Men with incurable medical conditions were also exempt, but those with curable diseases received only temporary discharge. However, men of means could purchase substitutes, so the burden of military service fell heavily on the 'peasants'.[1] Conscripts who feigned infirmity or deliberately wounded themselves could receive five years' imprisonment, with informers being rewarded. The Prussian system was modified in 1813, where instead of a designated number of conscripts, all able-bodied males were expected to submit to three years of service, and thereafter to be on-call in the event of a national emergency.[2]

Following the defeat of Napoleon, the French army no longer required universal training. They introduced a 'lottery' system instead, where twenty-year-olds drew lots to decide their fate — military duty or exemption. Changes to the lottery in 1872 meant that those Frenchmen dealt the 'good' numbers were conscripted to serve six months training, while those with the 'bad' would continue to complete five years.[3]

N. Stargardt, *The German Idea of Militarism: Radical and Socialist Critics*, 1994

Switzerland

The Swiss system of compulsory training was also held up as a fine example for other nations to follow. Switzerland had adopted compulsory military service after the French Revolutionary Wars of the late eighteenth century, when the Swiss Republic was overrun. Since the early 1800s, all Swiss boys from the age of twelve were taught military drill and rifle shooting at school: 'a soldier learns his business in the school; not only exercise and drill, but the use of arms, the habits of obedience, order, silence, the power to listen and to speak.'[4] Schoolgirls were taught the art of treating sick and wounded men. The girls were instructed how to dress wounds, and how to treat the sick.[5]

By 1872, there were over 100,000 'well drilled and armed' soldiers serving in Switzerland, and a similar number of trained reserves. All men between the ages of twenty and forty-five were expected to be part-time soldiers.[6]

Great Britain

Across the English Channel in the early 1900s, the British did not take kindly to the notion of conscription on the European continent, as the London *Economist* indicated:

> Our own pressgang for seamen was revolting enough, but the sight of a [French] impressment could not be compared with the distressing scenes at the Conscription ballot, when piercing shrieks accompanied the drawing of the fatal ticket from the urn.[7]

Unsurprisingly, the British people generally ridiculed the Imperial Defence Association's publication *The Briton's First Duty: The Case for Conscription* when it appeared in 1901. Not to be deterred, the newly formed National Service League, with Lord Wellington as president and G. F. Shee as secretary, proposed compulsory rather than voluntary service in the defence forces. Believing that the term 'compulsory service' was more palatable than 'conscription' in Britain, Shee published a pamphlet, *The Advantages of Compulsory Service for Home Defence*, in 1902, which advocated compulsory military training in school for lads between the ages of 14 and 18. Those between 18 and 21 should train between four and six months for the first year, and undertake refresher courses of several weeks each year afterwards. Although the League suggested that such service would be for home service and defence purposes only, the proposal was ignored by the government, who viewed the Royal Navy as the best means of defence for the British Isles. Henceforth, the British National Service League decided to attempt to introduce their concept through the British colonies first, and in particular Australia, which had already begun to show interest.[8]

7

Calls for Military Conscription in Australia and New Zealand

Agitation from Australian politicians

As early as July 1901, in the first Australian parliament, senior Labor member Billy Hughes proposed a form of compulsory military service that could be avoided only if the unwilling person paid a 'capitation tax' for someone else to serve in his place. Hughes advocated that Australia should follow the current Swiss model of compulsory national defence: 'I lay it down as a basic proposition that it is the first duty of every man to defend his country'. Hughes advocated that every male between the ages of 18 to 45 years should be given six weeks military drill, the first three being continuous and the remainder periodical.[1] Another Labor member, J. M. Fowler, also lent his support:

> I would like to see the system of training applied here as a matter of physical development, and as a matter of discipline, which is of immense value to children, and remains with them throughout their lives.[2]

Also endorsing Hughes' motion, but from the other side of the chamber, was Freetrader and President of the Melbourne Rifle Club William Knox, who thought that only those men who had proved to be effective with a rifle should qualify for citizenship: 'it ought to be compulsory upon every boy who is physically fit to learn the elements of drill and use the Francotte rifle.'[3]

Yet another Freetrader, Alexander Patterson, was equally supportive, claiming that 'compulsion in regard to matters of defence' was a citizen's 'fair share of the nation's burdens.'[4] Most other members, while in favour of military training for defence purposes, considered that a compulsory clause was not necessary and, like the Queensland Protectionist R. Edwards, believed that should the need arise 'every man in the country would be only too glad to come forward in its defence'. Edwards was also a strong supporter of volunteer cadet units, declaring that 'in a few years time we will have an army in each state ready to take the field at short notice'.[5]

Prominent Labor member King O'Malley was sceptical of the 'foreign invasion' mentality of many of his colleagues, claiming that the real threat was the current invasion of rabbits.[6] Not surprisingly, Hughes' motion for conscription was defeated in the House for the moment, though the issue continued to simmer close to the surface.

The Imperial Federation League of Australia

A meeting of The Imperial Federation League in Melbourne in April of 1909 heard Lieutenant-Colonel (and former Inspector-General of Victorian Schools) Thomas Brodribb give the address *Military Training for Our Schoolboys*. Praising the Swiss system of universal training in schools, Brodribb applauded the existing 'voluntary cadets' in Victorian schools, which he claimed had trained around 40,000 cadets by the time of the Boer War: 'of those soldiers who went to the South African War, I was told that 60% had been cadets.'[7] Brodribb went on to advocate publicly 'a few suggestions for the increase of the 'Force':

1. First, I would make military training of boys compulsory by law.
2. Boys aged 10–12 to learn company drill, etc., and military drill. No arms or uniforms required.

3. Boys over 12 to learn battalion drill, etc., physical drill with arms; rifle drill (including shooting); uniform to be worn.
4. A cheap rifle, something like the Winchester single shot (.22 bore) would be sufficient, to shoot at small targets at short ranges; no bayonet.[8]

Developments in New Zealand

In 1906, a decline in volunteer school cadet numbers was a real cause of concern to the newly constituted Defence League of New Zealand, which was an offshoot of the National Service League of Great Britain. They were troubled by the growing isolation of the country from England, and the proposed threat to national security from rogue countries like Germany, Russia, China and Japan. Beginning in Auckland, the Defence League quickly expanded and within two years boasted over fifty branches throughout New Zealand. Recruiting a number of journalists to their cause, the League was able to gain the support of the press, notably the influential *Auckland Herald*, and in addition published its own journal, *Defence*, where it outlined its constitution and aims:

> To ensure domestic peace and security from all possible invasion by obtaining the National adoption of the following safeguards:
>
> a. Universal defensive training of all boys up to the age of 21 years.
> b. The licensing of all men in the maritime and waterfront industries.
> c. Preference in all State employment and licensed industries to be given to British subjects who had fulfilled, or were willing to fulfil, specific military training requirements.
> d. All immigration to be confined to British stock who had agreed to undertake military training.

e. Rifle ranges to be established in the towns, and miniature ranges in the schools.[9]

The League supported the Swiss system of compulsory military training for boys, but not for those over twenty-one, where 'voluntary' recruitment into the NZ militia was recommended instead. They did advocate that all schoolboys be taught to shoot, and believed that 'the 3 R's be extended to include rifle shooting'.[10]

By purposely refusing to state how the schools would be used for military training, the League 'was able to confuse many people into the belief that it was merely advocating some form of rifle training'.[11] However, the League clearly declared its growing paranoia over the threat of foreign invasion, particularly from the 'Asiatic Menace', and even the threat to working-class jobs and living standards that 'Oriental immigrants' posed.[12]

8

The Defence Act of 1903 and the Establishment of the Australian Commonwealth Cadet Corps

Defence as a federal responsibility

One of the main issues in the push for Federation in the 1890s was the need for a Commonwealth military force as a means of national defence. At the turn of the century, an expensive and inefficient array of colonial military units of around 27,000 men provided an uncoordinated means of national protection.[1] These defence forces were taken over by the new Commonwealth Government in March 1901. But it was not until the 1903 Defence Act was passed that the individual school cadet units were amalgamated into a Commonwealth Cadet Corps, the Victorian contingent of which comprised ten battalions of around 6000 boys.[2] The Act empowered the Governor-General to establish a voluntary 'Military Cadet Corps' of boys aged 12 to 18. In an earlier Bill in the Senate, there was a proposal for mandatory military training of all boys aged 14 to 17, and although it received much support, particularly from the Labor Party, it was defeated 15 votes to 10.[3]

William Morris Hughes, the Labor leader, was emphatic in his support for the Bill. Although defeated for the moment, he was to continue to agitate for a compulsory cadet service in Australian schools.

Defence Department control of cadet units

The Defence Department now assumed control of the nation's cadet corps, and while the various state education departments were to be consulted over policy changes, they were expected to cooperate accordingly. Officers were to be drawn from among school inspectors, senior teachers or selected bureaucrats from the education departments and were to be considered as Officers of the Defence Force. Victorian officer training was conducted at Victoria Barracks in Melbourne on Saturday mornings. Teachers with a lieutenant's commission received an allowance of £2 towards a uniform costing £5.[4]

Boys aged 12 to 15 could enlist in the Junior Cadets at both primary and secondary schools, and out of school from age 16 to 18 in the Senior Cadets. Cadets were to have a minimum height of four feet and six inches, and would be required to drill for an hour per week during school hours, attend six battalion parades a year and undergo a course in rifle shooting. Arms were to be provided by the government, but the expense of the uniform was the responsibility of parents.[5] It was expected that the Commonwealth scheme would provide for 20,000 Junior Cadets and a further 3000 Senior Cadets, with a small portion of the latter trained as mounted units. From 1 May 1906, the volunteers were to be known as the Commonwealth Military Cadet Corps. Typical of the strong support around the country for the new Corps was a statement from Sir George Strickland, Governor of Tasmania, on the occasion of a cadet parade in Hobart in 1907: 'The cadets of today are the foundation of the future army of Australia, a branch of the great Imperial system of defence, on which the continuation of the British Empire is dependant.'[6]

The Melbourne *Age*, while it praised the reorganisation of Junior Cadets under a federal banner, claimed that the 'monumental blunder' in the scheme was that the cadet corps was limited to volunteers: 'The scheme to be of true service to the country should be compulsory and impose an equal obligation on every boy in the Commonwealth.'[7]

Each state Military Commander administered their cadet units through an Officer Commanding Cadets, who held the rank of major or lieutenant-colonel, assisted by an Instructor of Musketry, usually a captain or major.

With a coordinated Commonwealth approach to funding behind it, the cadet movement developed rapidly. By mid-1910, there were 24,216 Junior Cadets in 45 battalions and 10,225 Senior and Mounted Cadets in 16 battalions. Geographic location was the main method of organising cadet battalions in New South Wales and Victoria. For example, state school detachments of Senior Cadets in the Sydney area formed the 1st Battalion, and Sydney private schools constituted the 3rd Battalion. Similarly in Melbourne, state schools formed the 1st Battalion and private schools the 2nd and 3rd Battalions. Marist and Christian Brothers units comprised the vast majority of the 5th Battalion. State schools accounted for 83 percent of all Victorian school-based cadets in 1906, and at the prestigious Melbourne High School no less than 130 of the 131 boys in attendance were enrolled in the cadet unit. Invariably, cadet officers were drawn from the ranks of male teachers working in schools with cadet units attached, but were considered junior to serving officers in the Commonwealth Military Forces. School cadets could aspire to the ranks of NCOs on the recommendation of their unit officer.[8] Adelaide High School, the Melbourne high school equivalent in South Australia, boasted a cadet unit of at least forty-two students (including three cadet officers) when founded in 1908, all under the command of two regular army officers.[9]

By 1910, Junior Cadet units were found in 651 schools (582 being government schools) and 1206 teachers had passed their exams as cadet officers. Victoria boasted 204 detachments of cadets, 160 in primary and five in post-primary schools, and of 352 officers listed, 290 were teachers.[10] Schools with Junior Cadets were entitled to one teacher-lieutenant for the first thirty to fifty cadets, and another lieutenant for each additional fifty. For every 100 cadets a captain was assigned, and for 200, a major.[11] Eleven battalions were commanded by district inspectors. A three-week summer school camp of physical training for teachers was held at Geelong in January 1912, 'where 150 men received excellent training for three weeks under Defence department staff'.[12] In addition, 408 schools (110 of them in Victoria) had opted to have Commonwealth funded miniature rifle ranges in their grounds for rifle shooting practice.[13] Following complaints of rifles being left about schools indiscriminately, the Minister of Defence, Joseph Cook, commenced a program of placing rifle racks in schools. In 1909, the first year of implementation, it cost £1190, along with the sum of £3000 to construct miniature rifle ranges in the schools.

Mounted Cadet units

Mounted units were not officially part of the Senior Cadet system, and came under the direct command of the various state Officer Commanding Cadets. A minimum of eighteen boys between 14 to 18 years old and at least four feet and eight inches tall were required to form a mounted troupe. Boys had to be prepared to supply their own mounts, horse gear and uniforms.

By 1909, there were two squadrons in Victoria and New South Wales respectively, and one each in Queensland, Western Australia and Tasmania.[14] Senior Mounted Cadets who were seventeen years and over were eligible to transfer to other military corps, with the recommendation of a commanding officer. Similarly, it was hoped that 'Mounted Cadets would form a useful recruiting ground for the mounted branches of the service'. Squadrons of Mounted Cadets were assigned to Light Horse Regiments in NSW, Victoria, Western Australia, Queensland and Tasmania.[15]

By the outbreak of war in 1914, there were already twenty-three Light Horse Regiments throughout Australia, totalling 456 officers and 6508 other ranks. The recruits were mainly located in country areas and trained with their own horses and equipment.[16] Noted South Australian recruit Hugo Throssal, who won the Victoria Cross in the savage fight for Hill 60 at Gallipoli, joined the remote Jennacubbine Mounted Rifles 'where local farmers, school friends, and sporting team players rode and drilled together' soon after leaving Prince Alfred College in Adelaide, where he was a volunteer cadet.[17] His unit was amalgamated into the 10th Light Horse Regiment when war began. Hugo captained the local Wyalkatchem football team and was proud to lead all eighteen players to sign up together in the Regiment. By war's end 'seven of the players would be dead and many others would come home maimed'.[18]

Cadet William Thomas Grant of the Box Hill Mounted Cadets, Victoria, 1915. He later served in the 5th Battalion on the Western Front, France. Courtesy Colin Holden

Cadet camps

Annual camps were organised for Senior Cadets in various parts of the Commonwealth. The Australian Army military camp in Langwarrin, on the Mornington Peninsula, was a popular site in Victoria. For three days in August 1910, around 800 boys aged 14 and 15 from the 4th and 5th Battalions, from both private and government schools in Victoria, were camped in tents and training for twelve hours per day. The 4th Battalion comprised cadet units from Brighton Grammar, Hawthorn College, Caulfield Grammar, All Saints Grammar, Trinity Grammar, St Thomas' Grammar School, Ballarat Continuation School and Geelong Continuation School. Represented in the 5th Battalion were the Christian Brothers Schools in St Kilda, South Melbourne and North Melbourne, and also included the St Augustine's Orphanage Band.[19] On the second day of the Langwarrin Camp the boys were reviewed by Colonel Stanley, the State Commandant. As a reporter for *The Argus* wrote: 'They have been drilling and marching, deploying and skirmishing, manoeuvring and operating ever since daylight, and they are thriving on it.'[20]

In 1911, the Minister of Defence gave permission for a Senior Cadet detachment to represent Australia at the coronation of King George V in London. Fort Street High School in Sydney sent a contingent of thirty-three cadets.[21] Seventeen of them later enlisted to 'fight for the King' when war broke out three years later.[22]

Cadet camp at Langwarrin, Victoria, 1910. Craig Stockings, *The Torch and the Sword: A History of the Army Cadet Movement in Australia*, 2007, p. 53

9

The 1909 Defence Act Incorporating Compulsory Military Training

The visit by Lord Kitchener

Late in 1909, the British Field Marshall, Lord Kitchener, visited Australia at the request of the Commonwealth Government to investigate and advise on the nation's defence requirements. Over a period of two months he visited military camps in each state, and was given a lavish reception by politicians and military leaders wherever he went. In his report he stated that Australia's forces were 'inadequate in numbers, training, organisation and the munitions in war'.

Just prior to Kitchener's report, the Deakin Government had already enacted legislation in its December 1909 Defence Act, which required the compulsory military training of all boys 12 to 18 years of age, Australia becoming 'the first modern English-speaking country in the world to do so'.[1] A number of members of parliament had long advocated such an act, with the previous Fisher Government (Labor) demanding the 10 to 18 year old component of the Swiss model. Besides the mandatory training of Junior Cadets (12 to 14 years old) and Senior Cadets (14 to 18 years old), the Deakin government legislated for compulsory membership in the Citizen Military Forces (CMF) of all men aged 18 to 25. Junior Cadets were required to undergo military training for 96 hours per year for two years, and Senior Cadets 90 hours per year for four years. Following the completion of Senior Cadets, recruits served in the CMF until they reached twenty-five years of age.

The Act was to be implemented on 1 January 1911, with the first of the new trainees commencing in July 1911.[2] For Junior Cadets, training began during the first July that a boy reached the age of twelve. In that first year, about 92,000 boys around Australia commenced the training that was expected to produce fully trained recruits by the time they turned eighteen years of age.[3] State Railway Departments encouraged cadet corps by providing free rail transport to battalion parades, special functions, rifle competitions and military camps.[4] Exemptions were granted to boys who lived more than five miles from the nearest training centre (usually a school), the medically unfit, aliens and theological students. Persons convicted of 'disgraceful or infamous crimes' or to be of 'notoriously bad character'[5] were permanently disqualified. In 1911, of 155,132 boys registered, over one-third were granted exemptions, the vast majority on residential grounds. By the end of 1918, the proportion of exemptions would be reduced to almost one-fifth.[6]

The Bulletin cartoon. T. W. Tanner, *Compulsory Citizen Soldiers*, 1980, p. 164

Presentation of colours to Senior Cadets by Lord Kitchener in Melbourne, July 1909. *The School Paper*, grades 5 and 6, May 1910

Military districts

The existing six military districts, based loosely around state lines, were divided into ninety-three geographical battalion areas, from which each area would provide a CMF and a Senior Cadet battalion. At the time the army's quartermaster general, Lieutenant Colonel J. G. Legge, estimated that 100,000 lads would shortly be in training in the Senior Cadets scheme alone, and when fully operational would cost the government £161,000 per annum.[7]

Following the Imperial Conference in London in June 1911, a separate meeting of the Committee of Imperial Defence was held. The British Foreign Secretary, Sir Edward Grey, explained British Foreign policy in relation to the situation in Europe in some detail, and the Dominion leaders were left in no doubt as to the seriousness of the predicament. When the Australian contingent — Prime Minister

Andrew Fisher, Minister for Defence G. F. Pearce, and Minister for External Affairs E. L. Batchelor — later conferred, they unanimously agreed that a European war against Germany was inevitable by 1915, and that Australia's defence program needed to accelerate accordingly.

Front cover of *The Commonwealth School Paper*, New South Wales, December 1909

10

Compulsory School Cadets — Regulations

Junior Cadets

Under the Defence Act of 1910, instituted on 1 July 1911, the 'Australian Junior Cadet Regulations' meant that all male inhabitants aged 12 to 14 years who had resided in Australia for at least six months and were British subjects 'shall be liable to be trained as Junior Cadets'.[1] Boys were to present themselves to an area officer at a training centre for a medical examination at designated times and places, through notices displayed at post offices, or posted to headmasters of schools where Junior Cadet training was authorised. Exemptions were to be granted to boys who resided a distance of over five miles from a place appointed for training, usually a school. Permanent exemptions could be obtained if it could be proved that a boy was 'blind, deaf, dumb, maimed, insane or otherwise unfit for any physical training'.[2] By June 1912 a total of 54,137 boys aged 12 to 14, in all six states, had been medically examined, with 52,899 (97.7 percent) pronounced as fit for training.[3]

> On Wednesday afternoons we boys really drilled, much more seriously than on the Monday morning march to the flag-saluting; we drilled for half an hour and a fat Instructional Sergeant from the Defence Department came to supervise us. We drilled in platoons of our grades and 'Gussy', the young male teacher of Third Grade, was our commanding officer.[4]

The training for Junior Cadets was to begin when they turned twelve years old, and would continue for two years, largely as a 'classroom based activity' taught by teachers who were trained for the purpose by regular army instructors. For each financial year every boy would receive ninety hours of training, comprising the following:

PART III — TRAINING

(a) Physical Training — to be carried out on each school day for not less than thirty minutes, and the attainment of a certain standard of efficiency.
(b) Marching drill, elementary, and the attainment of a certain standard of efficiency therein.

Boys unable to attend schools where the prescribed cadet training was authorised (some states had not yet raised the minimum school-leaving age to fourteen years) were required to attend training under military instructors at designated places and times. This was not to interfere with the ordinary hours of schooling. Such training would entail:

Evening drills — From 1st October to 1st of April	... 42 hours
Upon weekly half-holidays throughout the year	... 48 hours
Total	... 90 hours[5]

All Junior Cadets were to be inspected by Officers of the Australian Military Forces or school inspectors, no less than once in each year of training.[6]

Penalties for evading training

There were strict regulations for compliance:

Evasion of Training

(1) Every person who in any year, without lawful excuse, evades or fails to render the personal service required by this Part shall be guilty of an offence, and shall, in addition to the liability under section one hundred and thirty-three of

this Act, be liable to a penalty not exceeding one hundred pounds.

(2) Every person who, being a person liable to training under this Part —

(a) fails, without lawful excuse, to attend a compulsory drill: or

(b) commits a breach of discipline while on parade, shall be guilty of an offence and shall, in addition of any liability under section one hundred and thirty three of this Act, be liable to a penalty not exceeding five pounds.[7]

Breaches of these regulations were heard in a Children's Court. Junior Cadets who committed minor breaches of discipline were usually punished by extra periods of training, not exceeding thirty minutes. Reflecting on his schooldays at Armadale State School in Victoria, Brian Lewis recalls, 'The twelve-year-olds of the grades higher than ours had legal obligations under the Defence Act. They were Junior Cadets and could be prosecuted if they missed their official drills.'[8]

In contrast to the Senior Cadets and the CMF, there were few evasions or prosecutions for Junior Cadets because their training was largely conducted within school hours.[9]

Allowances and equipment

A contingent payment of two shillings and sixpence per year for each Junior Cadet was paid to headmasters of approved schools:

PART VI — ANNUAL CONTINGENT ALLOWANCE

(2) The allowance may, in the case of schools, be expended on

(a) Maintenance of miniature rifle range

(b) Ammunition

(c) Printing, stationery, postage, etc.

(d) Care and protection of stores on charge

(e) Replacing losses or damage to equipment
(f) Clerical assistance in connection with the keeping of records[10]

While Junior Cadets were not required to wear uniforms to training, there is evidence that many of them did later at their own expense.[11] However, when using the miniature rifle range at designated schools they were issued with guns and ammunition:

PART VII — EQUIPMENT, SCALE OF MATERIAL

(1) All equipment including arms, ammunition, and all other stores issued for the use of Junior Cadets, shall be accounted for by the Area officer in whose area such cadets are situated. Arms may be issued by him on loan to Headmasters of schools at which Junior Cadet training is conducted.
(2) Area Officers shall at the time of issue obtain a receipt for such equipment from headmasters, who will be held responsible for the preservation of the same, reasonable wear and tear excepted. Arms and other equipment are not to be used for any unauthorised purposes.

(A) INSTRUCTION

Issue of .230" Francotte Rifles for use at Miniature Rifle Ranges — Junior Cadets

(1) .230" Francotte Rifles will be issued to Area Officers, in the proportion of 10 per cent of Junior Cadets, for re-issue on loan to Headmasters of such schools that have miniature rifle ranges. A year's supply of material for cleaning and preserving arms, in the same proportions laid down in regulation 33 will be issued at the same time.[12]

APPENDIX III — STANDARD FOR MINIATURE RIFLE SHOOTING

I. STANDARD

To be able to load and fire the authorised rifle without assistance, to know the essential rules in regard to safety, and to be able to hit a target so that three out of five test shots will be within a circle of 6 inches diameter, firing from about 25 yards' distance.

II. PRACTICE

To have fired not less than 20 rounds in the year under instruction from a master of the school, on a miniature rifle range with authorised rifles and ammunition.[13]

Purpose-built miniature rifle ranges, not exceeding fifty yards in length, were constructed in the playgrounds of many schools across the country, provided that the supervising teacher had qualified as a rifle range instructor. By June 1911, a total of 408 schools had had Commonwealth-financed miniature rifle ranges constructed in their grounds.[14] Initially, only .23-calibre Francotte rifles could be used, but later .22 Winchester and .303 Lee Enfields were introduced. Cartridges were to be handed one at a time to cadets prior to firing, and no talking was permitted except by instructors. No less than twenty rounds of ammunition per year were to be fired, and cadets were expected to load and fire weapons without assistance. A pass in rifle shooting required the target to be hit within a six-inch diameter, by three out of five shots, from a range of twenty-five yards.

Activities for Junior Cadets were largely carried out in schools, with thirty or more boys to be trained. The military District Commandant then delegated responsibility to local headmasters, who then delegated the task to teachers from within their schools. Contact between the military and teachers conducting cadet training was to be kept to a minimum. However, once a year all Junior Cadets were to be inspected by a representative of the Commandant and their state of proficiency reported upon. Education Department District Inspectors also reported on the state of the cadet corps when undertaking their annual inspection of each school.[15]

Senior Cadets

Boys aged 14 to 18 years were required to enlist as Senior Cadets. As age fourteen was the minimum age for school leaving at the time and the majority of pupils were at work by then, arrangements were made for such boys to attend training in the evening and on weekends. Universal secondary education in most Australian states had only recently been introduced. In Victoria, for example, several 'agricultural high schools' had been opened in rural towns, and four 'continuation schools' in more urban areas, as early as 1904.[16] Legislation for the establishment of 'high schools' only came into effect in 1910, just as the Commonwealth was introducing its Defence Act of 1910, incorporating compulsory training throughout the country.

Senior Cadets, like their Junior Cadet counterparts, were required to undergo a medical examination at designated dates and times, prior to their enlistment on 1 July in the year they turned fifteen. Besides being designated medically unfit, other exemptions were granted, for being:

1. not substantially of European origin or descent
2. theological students (while they remain such students)
3. persons who reside outside areas in which training is carried out that would involve great hardship
4. (a) persons who have been convicted of any disgraceful or infamous crime, or
   (b) to be of notoriously bad character[17]

By June 1912, there were 120,648 eligible boys given an army medical examination, of whom 111,433 (92.4 percent) were pronounced medically fit. Some 66,557 boys were given temporary exemptions because they resided too far from a training facility.[18]

Organisation

For the purpose of Senior Cadets, the Commonwealth of Australia was divided along state lines into six military districts. They were formed into ninety-two battalions across the country, with each battalion under the command of a regular army major or captain. Within each battalion there were a number of companies, usually of eight to ten in strength.

Commonwealth of Australia Cadet Statistics for 1912

Military District	No. of Cadet Battalions	No. of Cadet Companies	No. of Cadets	No. of Training Localities
1st Queensland	12	121	12,006	60
2nd New South Wales	32	334	33,346	151
3rd Victoria	29	285	28,123	121
4th South Australia	9	91	8712	47
5th Western Australia	6	40	3911	38
6th Tasmania	4	33	2976	29
Total	92	904	89,074	446[19]

The 904 companies in the Commonwealth of Australia comprised:

1 captain
2 lieutenants
1 colour sergeant
4 sergeants
4 corporals
2 buglers
106 privates
120 total[20]

Cadets were required to wear military uniforms while 'on parade', which were issued free by the military authorities. Uniforms were not to be worn on any other occasion.

Each cadet was also issued with:

1 rifle
1 protector fore sight
1 sling
1 pouch
1 waist belt

A Record Book was also given to each cadet, which contained records of service, attendances at parades and camps, and any disciplinary action taken against him. The Record Book contained thirty-six regulations, which included instructions relating to uniforms, weapons and equipment, exhortations on obedience, and the treating of women with respect. Rule 36, the final rule, left no doubt of what was expected of them in a time of armed conflict: 'Australia gives us freedom. Let us guard her well, train for her sake in peace, and die for her, if need be, in war'. Failure to produce a Record Book on request 'constitutes a military offence'.[21]

In addition, each cadet company received:

1 x .303 rifle per every 10 cadets
150 rounds of ball ammunition for each cadet
2000 rounds of .303 ball ammunition per company[22]

Annual Musketry Courses for Senior Cadets in 1912 attracted 30,026 participants throughout the Commonwealth.[23] Senior Cadets were required to serve in either naval or army units:

> All those liable to be trained as Senior Cadets shall be allotted to the Naval or Military Forces, and shall be trained as prescribed in elementary naval or military exercises and in musketry, and shall be organised in naval or military units.[24]

A Combined Parade of 18,642 Senior Cadets from Sydney, and suburbs involving six brigades of Army Cadets (17,915) and a contingent of Naval Cadets (727), took place at Centennial Park in Sydney on 30 March 1912, in the presence of the Governor General. In congratulating the cadets and their officers, His Excellency remarked:

> The numbers, organisation and good order maintained on this parade demonstrated the good results achieved after only nine months of Universal Training.[25]

Boys approaching the school leaving age of fourteen years were encouraged through the schools to enlist as recruits for the training ship HMAS *Tingara*. Approved candidates were sent to Sydney with fares and expenses paid.[26] Teachers were asked to advise parents and guardians 'contemplating a naval career for their sons' that they would be signed up 'to serve therein up to the age of 18 and for a period of seven years thereafter'. Trainees must be a minimum height of five feet and two inches, with a chest of thirty-two inches. The pay range would be seven shillings per week on entry, rising to two pounds and nine shillings on becoming a Chief Petty Officer. In addition, candidates 'must be of good character, able to read and write and understand the first four rules of arithmetic'.[27] The following year, 1913, approaching school leavers were notified about 'Cadets Wanted' for the Royal Australian Naval College at Geelong in Victoria, with details listed in the grades 7 and 8 *School Paper* and the *Education Gazette and Teachers' Aid*.[28]

Senior Cadets could also qualify as honorary commissioned officers (lieutenants), but had no authority to command in the Defence Forces unless they had served for at least three years in that capacity. Lieutenants in the Senior Cadets could gain promotion to captain after serving for two years at that rank.[29] The annual training of cadets was composed of:

> 4 whole day drills (not less than 6 hours)
> 12 half day drills (not less than 3 hours)
> 24 night drills (not less than 1½ hours)[30]

Absentees (other than due to illness) would be penalised as follows:

(a) absent with leave — 1 extra parade
(b) absent without leave — 2 extra parades[31]

There was also provision for variety in the mix of the three drill categories, providing the total was no less than seventy-two hours for the year. The training would comprise:

Physical Drill
Infantry Drill (up to that of a battalion)
Military Field Training (in companies)
Musketry[32]

Workforce employers of Senior Cadets were warned not to 'prevent or attempt to prevent any employee from cadet training or camps — penalty £100'. Trainees were warned 'not to evade service without lawful excuse — penalty not less than £5 or more than £100 (depending on the means of the family)' or 'confinement in any prescribed institution of place for time missed'. Trainees so convicted became 'ineligible for employment of any kind in the Commonwealth Public Service.'[33]

The Bulletin cartoon in Tanner, T. W., *Compulsory Citizen Soldiers*, 1980, p. 122

Issued with M.O. 1/1911.

REGULATIONS AND INSTRUCTIONS

FOR

UNIVERSAL TRAINING

UNDER THE

DEFENCE ACT, 1903-1910.†

PART I.—GENERAL.

AREAS.

All male inhabitants of Australia (excepting those who are exempted by this Act), who have resided therein for six months, and are British subjects, shall be liable to be trained, as prescribed, as follows:—

(a) From 12 years to 14 years of age, in the Junior Cadets; and

(b) From 14 to 18 years of age, in the Senior Cadets; and

(c) From 18 to 25 years of age, in the Citizen Forces; and

(d) From 25 to 26 years of age, in the Citizen Forces:

Provided that, except in time of imminent danger of war, service under paragraph (d) shall be limited to one registration or one muster-parade.

This Act shall not, so far as concerns the obligation to render personal services for purposes of training, apply to any person who reaches the age of eighteen years in or before the year in which this Part commences.

C.675.

THE SCHOOL PAPER

FOR GRADES V. AND VI. (1913).

MELBOURNE.

TOP LEFT
Australian Defence Act 1903–1910 to introduce compulsory training for Junior Cadets and Senior Cadets throughout Australia from 1911 to 1929. Courtesy State Library of Victoria

TOP RIGHT
A 'compulsory' cadet from Collingwood, Victoria, 1912. Craig Stockings, *The Torch and the Sword: A History of the Army Cadet Movement in Australia*, 2007, p. 63

BOTTOM
Senior Cadets on parade in Collins Street, Melbourne, in 1913, about to be reviewed by the Governor General. *The School Paper*, Victoria, grades 5 and 6, January 1913, p. 1

C.M. Form N. 6

MILITARY FORCES OF THE COMMONWEALTH.

JUNIOR CADET TRAINING.

Military District Third

Certificate.

This is to Certify

I. That J Lynch has attended School of Instruction for Junior Cadet Training of 88 hours instruction held at East Melbourne from 3rd January '13 to 16th January '13

II. That J Lynch attended Practical Examination in Junior Cadet Training held at East Melbourne on 18th & 20th January '13 and qualified as a

Instructor in Junior Cadet Training

in the undermentioned Subjects:—

Subject.	Percentage of Marks obtained.	Result.*
(a) Physical Training	76	Passed.
(b) Marching Drill	72	Passed.
(c) Miniature Rifle Shooting	66	Passed.
(d) Swimming	–	Passed.
(e) Running Exercises	76	Passed.
(f) First Aid	75	Passed.
Aggregate	365	Passed.

P C Raper Capt Brigade Major, A.I.Staff, 15th Brigade

Military District of Victoria

Place Brunswick

Date 17-2-1913

P1286 V&R.

TOP

Sergeant-Major Thomas (left) instructing Puteney Grammar School (SA) cadet unit, 1911. W. R. Ray, *Puteney Grammar School 1847–1972: A Record*, p. 9

BOTTOM

L. Blake, *Vision and Realisation: A Centenary History of State Education in Victoria*, 1973, p. 1286

TOP
L. Blake, *Vision and Realisation: A Centenary History of State Education in Victoria*, 1973, p. 1282

BOTTOM
Compulsory military training attendance book for Cadet H. N. Griffiths, Fort Street High School. Courtesy Fort Street High School, Sydney

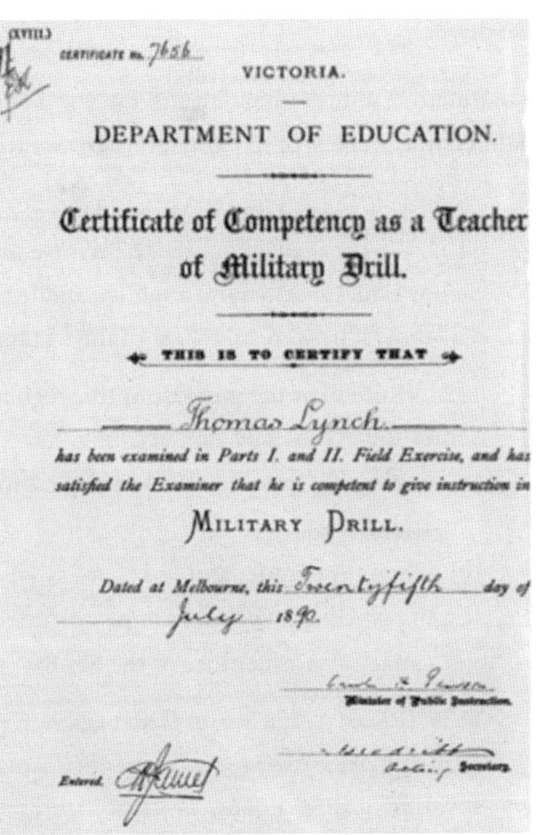

(XVIII.)

CERTIFICATE No. 7656

VICTORIA.

DEPARTMENT OF EDUCATION.

Certificate of Competency as a Teacher of Military Drill.

THIS IS TO CERTIFY THAT

Thomas Lynch

has been examined in Parts I. and II. Field Exercise, and has satisfied the Examiner that he is competent to give instruction in

MILITARY DRILL.

Dated at Melbourne, this Twentyfifth *day of* July 1890.

Minister of Public Instruction.

Acting Secretary.

Entered.

AUSTRALIAN MILITARY FORCES

6th Battalion, 4th Infantry Regiment.

Major J. GREEN, Commanding Officer

Area 4B-b—Senior Cadets

PROGRAMME OF PARADES

Quarter ending 31st December, 1920

Note your Company & Platoon

Name of Cadet H. N. Griffiths

No. .... Section, No. 20 Platoon. "C" & "D" Coys. (Fort Street School)

Address ....

"C" & "D" Coys.

(Fort Street School)

Date.	Time.	Nature of Parade.	Signature of A.O. or S.S.M.
Oct. 8	1.30 p.m.	Comp. Whole-day	
„ 14	3.30 p.m.	Comp. Half-day	
„ 21	3.30 p.m.	Comp. Half-day	
„ 28	3.30 p.m.	Comp. Half-day	
Nov. 3	1.30 p.m.	Comp. Whole-day	
„ 9	1.30 p.m.	Alt. Whole-day	
„ 16	3.30 p.m.	Comp. Half-day	

Discipline

Australian Military Regulations for the Defence Forces were clearly defined and to be strictly adhered to by Senior Cadets:

DIVISION 5 — DISCIPLINE

1122. (R615) shall, as nearly as circumstances permit, apply to a Senior Cadet as if he were a soldier, and to an officer of the Senior Cadets as if he were an officer of the Military Forces.

1124. (R659) For the purpose of this regulation a member of the Senior Cadets shall be 'on duty' —

(a) during the whole period of any continuous training which he attends; and
(b) when on parade; and
(c) in respect of every act done or omitted to be done by him in his capacity as a member of the Senior Cadets

1125. (R660) … If a Senior Cadet when in uniform or on parade, or in any place used for military purposes, has in his possession any intoxicating liquor, or cigarettes or tobacco in any form shall be guilty of an offence, and on conviction shall be liable to a penalty not exceeding five pounds. Possession … shall not constitute an offence against this regulation if his parent or guardian has previously notified, in writing, to the Area Officer his consent to that possession.

1133. (R665) A member of the Senior Cadets shall not be tried by a court-martial.

1134. (R666) A member of the Senior Cadets shall be liable —

(a) To arrest during the whole period of any continuous training which he attends; and
(b) To suspension — in each case as if he were a member of the Citizen Forces not on war service.[34]

Serious punishments could be meted out for training evasions by

Senior Cadets, with fines ranging from £3 to £100, in default military detention, usually in an army barracks.

Each Senior Cadet was subjected to an Annual Inspection by a regular army officer to ensure:

(1) efficiency in discipline, training and interior economy
(2) whether arms, clothing and equipment are in good order, and books and records properly kept
(3) ability in handling his rifle with care necessary to prevent danger to himself and others[35]

11

Officer Training for Teachers

Regular army instructors were used to train the teacher-officers so essential for the cause. Both male and female teachers were encouraged to enter the training course, which would run for fifteen working days over six-day weeks. Trainees were required to be under fifty years of age and physically fit. Each training course was comprised of physical training, squad drill, miniature rifle shooting, first aid and organised games. Attendance was required between 9.30am and 5.30pm each day. Qualifying certificates were awarded to those who obtained a pass of 60 percent, and a 'pass with honours' required at least an 80 percent score. Trainees were given time off to attend a course of instruction and pay of up to ten shillings a day for travelling expenses. A 'drill bonus' of up to £15 per annum was paid to teachers who passed the training course, which would have been quite an incentive for many teachers, considering that at the time most of them were paid an annual salary as low as £100.[1] Male teachers under twenty-six years of age who qualified could substitute the instruction of Junior Cadets for their own universal training requirements if they later joined the CMF.[2]

In the nine months ending on 30 June 1912, there were fifty-three training courses attended by state and private school teachers, in both metropolitan and country locations throughout all states. There was a total of 55 school inspectors, 1592 state school teachers (including 245 women), and 70 male private school teachers. Passes were awarded to 1048 of the males (76 percent) and 71 of the females (29 percent). Female teachers attending one of the Adelaide courses during 1912 fared much better, with 41 out of 44 (93 percent) passes.[3]

After 30 June each year, headmasters of schools were required to complete a circular 'C. M. Form N. 1', the 'Junior Cadet Record' for each cadet at his school. It contained a record of a cadet's medical examination and the annual training performed. A duplicate copy was to be given to each cadet. 'C. M. Form N. 6 Certificate for Junior Cadet Training' was to be issued to cadets who passed the course. Both forms would accompany a cadet, when on reaching the age of fourteen he was required to register as a Senior Cadet.[4]

In his review of 'The Training of Junior Cadets' on 1 March 1913, Lieutenant C. R. Collins of the Citizen Military Forces, Physical Training Instruction Staff, expressed his confidence in Universal Training throughout Australia:

> When, at the age of fourteen, the boy passes into the hands of the sergeant-major, he is physically fit to do the work required of him. He knows and appreciates the value of discipline. He can march, and knows how to handle a rifle.[5]

Rifle drill for Victorian Teachers of Military Drill, Geelong. *Education Department of Victoria Annual Report, 1911–12*

Victorian Teachers Military Drill Class, Geelong, 1913. *Education Department of Victoria Annual Report, 1911–12*

Wanganui Collegiate School, New Zealand, 1918, Cadets with their Army Training Officers. Bruce Hamilton, *Never a Footstep Back: A History of Wanganui Collegiate School 1854–2003*, 2004, p. 12

12

New Zealand's Defence Act of 1909 and the Subsequent Defence Amendment Act of 1910

Besides the intense lobbying by the New Zealand Defence League for compulsory military training for the nation's youth since 1906, the Liberal Prime Minister, Sir Joseph Ward (a self-declared member of the League) decided to introduce legislation in the House of Representatives for a scheme of Universal Military Training. This followed his recent visit to London for the Colonial Conference early in 1909, where the Imperial General Staff urged all participants to 'adjust their organisation for home defence, as to admit of the dispatch without delay, of forces they desire to send to the aid of the Mother-Country or any part of the Empire'.[1]

Ward's Bill for Universal Training was along similar lines to Australia's Defence Act of 1909, whereby:

1. All boys aged 12 to 14 years were to receive military training of no less than 52 hours annually in the Junior Cadets arranged by the Department of Education.
2. Boys aged 14 to 18 years (the vast majority of whom would have been in the workforce) be given training in 'musketry and elementary military exercises' for 6 whole days, 12 half days and 24 evening parades annually in the Senior Cadets arranged by the regular Territorial Force.
3. Youths aged 18 to 21 years would form the General Training Section, consisting of 12 half day parades and an annual camp of 14 days.

4. Men aged 21 to 30 years would comprise the Reserve and undergo 2 muster parades annually.[2]

Passage of the Bill was swift, as there was very little hostility towards it. Many members could see some value in combatting 'the alleged decadence of contemporary youth'. The Minister for Defence, James Allen, prepared (unsuccessfully) to lower the minimum age of Junior Cadets to boys of eight years of age. Suggesting the Act did not go far enough, the *Auckland Star* opined that 'schoolgirls should have been liable for training also'. The Bill known as the Defence Act 1909 was passed in near record time, in December 1909, with the expectation that within six years New Zealand would have a reserve of trained manpower of around 50,000, 'and in ten, twelve or fourteen years — 100,000 men'.[3]

With Lord Kitchener paying a visit to New Zealand in March 1910, on his way home from a tour of Australia, the government decided to defer the implementation of the Act until after his scheduled review of the country's defence forces. Kitchener referred to his 'Memorandum on the Defence of Australia' and uncovered the same deficiencies in the New Zealand's defences: 'the lack of adequate training, numbers, organisation and suggested several amendments, including that the age restriction on the General Training Section be extended from 21 to 25 years'. Despite the farming lobby's objection that this would cause a shortage of agricultural labour, the government agreed to the suggestion, resulting in the Defence Amendment Act 1910. Further delay followed when it was discovered that there were insufficient experienced army officers in the country to commence the scheme, until a number of instructors could be brought out from England, on loan from the British Army. Registration of trainees commenced in February of 1911, and the scheme was finally underway by the beginning of June that year.[4] By the end of July 1911, 29,991 Senior Cadets (aged 14 to 18) and 21,838 'Territorials' (aged 18 to 25) had commenced their training.[5]

At Auckland Grammar School under the new Defence Act, 'the cadets took on a more serious hue', with the existing nine companies of sixty boys being doubled and a smaller company of Junior Cadets added to the ranks under commanding officer Captain Walker. The school was expanding its program:

> There would in future be half-day parades as well as more than twice the number of lunchtime drill sessions, while the cadet syllabus would extend to the layout of camps, sanitation and hygiene, in addition to the class-firing at the Penrose range on Saturday mornings.[6]

Artillery Section Cadets, Hamilton Boys High School, New Zealand. B. Buckland and P. Pollard (eds.), *One School Two Stories 100 years On: Hamilton Boys High School, Hamilton Girls High School*, p. 32

13

Reactions to the Introduction of Compulsory Military Training

Support

The vast majority of Australians would be proud of the long tradition of opposing the conscription of young men to fight overseas in its declared wars. Despite the close voting in the controversial 'conscription referendums' of 1916 and 1917, only volunteers served in World War I.

However, it is not generally known that in the school and workforce systems, in both Australia and New Zealand, compulsory military training at home was the norm from 1911 until 1929.[1] Not even in Great Britain, let alone the other British Empire countries at the time, such as South Africa and Canada, were the youth subjected to military conscription.

As in all wars, there were many people who were conscientious objectors and opposed the killing of others on humanitarian grounds. Certain minority Christian sects like the Quakers, Jehovah's Witnesses and the Christadelphians were renowned for their pacifism, but there were also pacifist individuals from mainstream churches, like the Anglicans, Presbyterians, Methodists and Roman Catholics, and smaller denominations like Congregationalists, Baptists and the Churches of Christ.[2] In addition, there was strong opposition from some trade unionists and others with socialistic, humanistic or rationalist beliefs.

But for the most part, the Christian churches were strong supporters of the government and its military preparedness, both before and during

World War I. In the 1911 census, the vast majority of the Australian population identified with one of the main Christian denominations, with only 0.024 percent claiming to have no religion.[3] Perhaps the most influential and patriotic clergyman was the Reverend W. H. Fitchett, headmaster of the Methodist Ladies College in Melbourne.[4] Fitchett had published *Deeds That Won the Empire* in 1897, a book that was widely read in schools. The first edition sold 10,000 copies in four days, and by 1914 a 29th edition had been published. It was also stocked in bookshops around the British Empire, vying with authors like Carlyle and Conan Doyle, and there was even an American edition published. A standard prize for schoolboys in English public schools, the book was also recommended to the scouting movement by Lord Baden-Powell.[5] At sixpence a copy, over 100,000 of them were sold throughout the world.[6] Although Fitchett claimed in the preface that the book was 'not written to glorify war', it was generally accepted that it had the opposite effect, as the preface indicates:

> War belongs, no doubt, to an imperfect stage of society; it has a side of pure brutality. But it is not all brutal. Wordsworth's daring line about 'God's most perfect instrument' has a great truth behind it. What examples are to be found in the tales here retold, not merely of heroic daring, but even finer qualities: of heroic fortitude; of loyalty to duty stronger than the love of life … of the patriotism which makes love of the Fatherland a passion.[7]

Australia's remoteness from the rest of the Western world, particularly Great Britain, was a cause of concern for many citizens. Japan had been the victor in the recent Russo-Japanese War and was looking to extend its influence in Asia.[8] The rapid growth and mobility of the Japanese warships had made it the most powerful fleet in the Pacific. Britain was at the time preoccupied with the growth of German industrialisation and military hardware, and its growing naval threat in the North Sea. This increasing sense of isolation and military insecurity fuelled the fears of many Australians, and led them to demand stronger defence alliances with Britain and closer co-operation with other British Empire colonies, such as New Zealand. Organisations such as the Australian National Defence League were formed for this purpose.

Founded in Sydney, the League was a cross-party organisation whose President, Sir Normand MacLaurin, was a prominent Sydney medical doctor and Member of the Legislative Assembly. At its first meeting, on 5 September 1905, the following charter of the League was formulated on the motion of Sir Julian Salmons MLC, and seconded by the Honourable W. H. Hughes, MP:

> To take such measures as may be necessary and proper to secure:—
>
> (a) Universal compulsory training (military or naval) of the boyhood and manhood of Australia for the purposes of National Defence, the military training to be on the lines of the Swiss system, and the naval training on the lines of the British Royal Navy Reserve, modified to suit local circumstances.
>
> (b) An adequate and effective system of national Defence[9]

Not surprisingly, the Australian National Defence League strongly supported the Australian Government's 1910 Act for the introduction of compulsory Junior and Senior Cadet Corps.[10] The League promoted its views avidly through its quarterly magazine *Call*, posting it free to all members of federal and state parliaments, newspapers, judges, mayors, landowners of over 5000 sheep, and leading clergymen. For the 1910 federal election, the League publicised a list of over eighty candidates who adhered to its strong advocacy for home defence.[11]

Since its inception in 1891, the Australian Labor Party had mixed feelings about compulsory military service, despite the strong agitation of their leader, John Christian Watson, and the member for Lang in NSW, William Morris Hughes, both of whom were members of the

Australian National Defence League. By 1908, the Federal Labor Party came out in support of the proposition, which became party policy until 1919. In introducing the motion, Watson paid tribute to Hughes:

> The scheme which had been laid down by the Deakin Government was very largely on the lines of that mapped out by Mr Hughes, to whom a great deal of the credit was due in this connection.[12]

It was, of course, the Fisher Labor Government who invited Lord Kitchener to review Australia's armed forces, and who so willingly pre-empted his recommendation to incorporate the compulsory military training of our youth in the Defence Act of 1910.

Opposition

However, there was also strong opposition to the concept of compulsory military training by many left-wing unionists, including those associated with the International Workers of the World, and other 'socialist' organisations. The Melbourne weekly newspaper *The Socialist*, one of the early vocal critics of the new legislation, featured the front page headline 'Conscript Boys of Australia' and warned Australian youth:

> Your parents have been told that their boys between the ages of 14 and 18 must be drilled, and marched, and taught to carry firearms, in order that when they grow up they may know how to fight as soldiers, and shoot down or bayonet the lads of other countries ... Now is the time to protest against the folly of this compulsory military training in organised murder.[13]

In 1910, two Adelaide Quaker laymen, John Hills and Percy Fletcher, launched the anti-conscription Australian Freedom League. It quickly spread to the other states, and by the time war was declared four years later it had a membership of over 55,000.[14] *Freedom*, the organisation's magazine, declared to its readers:

> The present compulsory military training scheme is a great deal more than the thin edge of the wedge ... it will unavoidably lead to a fully-fledged continental conscription system ... NOW IS THE TIME TO PROTEST.[15]

A similar organisation, the Anti-Militarist League, was also formed in South Australia, at a meeting in the Socialist Hall in Adelaide in November 1911. With a charter to 'kindle the flame of anti-militarism' among Australians, the League regarded human life as sacred, and the taking of life as unjustified. A member at the gathering, Mr O. Bennett, declared that soldiers killed 'in the interests of capitalists, and militia men would be used to suppress workers'. A unanimous resolution passed at the end of the meeting protested 'against the action of the Federal Government in compelling the youth of Australia to act against their better nature and train as members of the defence force'.[16]

A meeting of the Federal Convention of the Women's Christian Temperance Union in Adelaide in 1912 reiterated their previous stand taken in 1895, in calling for the disbanding of the then voluntary cadet scheme: 'not only were lads subjected to temptation in camp, but the system engendered in the minds of the young people, a war spirit quite contrary to the teaching of Christ'. Acting on a resolution of the South Australian branch of the WCTU, the meeting, which claimed to represent 'all shades of political and religious opinion', called upon the Federal Government to repeal the compulsory clauses of the Act. They said that it caused 'a serious infringement of civil and religious liberty, a menace to home influence and a cruel, needless and unwarranted burden upon the manhood and boyhood of our land'.[17]

While there was a sizeable number of eligible young recruits and their families who opposed, and in many cases defied, the compulsory provisions in the 1910 Act when it came to be implemented in July 1911, the vast majority of the call-up complied. In the initial call-up in 1911, no less than 92,000 boys between the ages of 12 and 17 years, began their compulsory military training, which was designed to produce fully trained recruits for the Australian Army after four years of service in the Senior Cadets.[18]

Initially, there was a slow response to cadet registrations and the Minister for Defence, George Pearce, showed a degree of restraint towards protesting organisations and individuals. After the first year, however, although pleased with the general approval of the population towards the Act, the prosecution of non-compliants intensified.[19] In the first two years of operation there were 130,000 Senior Cadets and 50,000 Junior Cadets in training nationwide,[20] and by the beginning of World War I in August 1914, a further 40,000 had been added to the ranks.[21] There were in addition several battalions of the Light Horse Regiment that contained cadets, and a small number of boys were selected — competition was fervent — for training as senior naval cadets, with 3000 accepted in 1911, and from then on around 1000 more annually.[22]

There is no escaping the fact that for the four years the Defence Act of 1910 was in place before the outbreak of the war, there were 27,749 prosecutions, which resulted in 5,732 boys serving periods of detention or imprisonment.[23] Given that many of those prosecuted were repeat offenders and that some of the prosecutions were for minor offences, the percentage of boys prosecuted could have been around eight to nine percent.

It took almost twelve months before the penalty provisions for non-compliance of the Act came to be enforced, as many magistrates took a while to become fully cognisant of the legislation and many first offenders were let off with a warning. The Melbourne *Argus* reported on four Senior Cadets from Shepparton in Victoria, who absented themselves for a whole day parade in January 1912 by 'going instead to view the fire brigades' demonstration on the recreation reserve'. Captain Nugent told the magistrate that, as they were regarded as 'good boys' and as it was their first offence, they were cautioned 'to teach them and other cadets a lesson', and were discharged.[24]

By the end of June 1912, twelve months after the Act was declared, it was announced that 17,000 cadets were liable for prosecution. For the next two years, the backlog of cases ensured that prosecutions around the country averaged 265 per week.[25] Concomitant to this situation, the opposition to the Act gathered strength from year to year, until it virtually diminished overnight with the outbreak of the Great War in 1914.

But with the new Military Regulations for the Universal Training of Senior Cadets on 25 July 1913, the penalties for non-compliance were strengthened. Under Section 135 there was provision for the following fines:

1. £100 for evading all drills in a year
2. £5 for missing a single drill and in addition to or in lieu of any penalty he may be committed to the custody of any prescribed authority[26]

From the commencement of compulsory training, there were many complaints that the Senior Cadet system disadvantaged the lads in the urban working-classes. The main contention was that boys fortunate enough to attend private schools, and the newly emerging high schools, were allowed to be trained as part of the school routine by slightly lengthening the school day and/or shortening the time for 'games', and so avoid evening and the alternate Saturday afternoon parades that the working-class majority had to endure.

> The boy of poor parents, however, who leaves the elementary school at 14 years of age, has to put in his drills at night and on Saturday afternoons. At night, after he leaves work, he drills, often in bad weather, in badly lit streets, or in the squares and parklands … An arrangement that allows the boy of wealthy parents to drill apart from the working lad on the public drill grounds, knocks equality out of this Act.[27]

One of the earliest batches of defaulters to be charged occurred in Adelaide, in October 1912. The *Adelaide Register*, under the headline 'Cadets in Trouble', reported that fifty-one boys 'of tender age' appeared at Port Pirie Court before magistrate Mr J. Mitchell, charged with not having attended the necessary drill parades. The young defendants all pleaded guilty and had a variety of excuses for their non-compliance. Claude Farrell, aged sixteen years, had a shortfall of 47.5 hours. In his defence, Farrell claimed to work at the smelters, and as the sole support for his widowed mother could not afford to take time from his work to attend drills. He was ordered to pay twenty shillings costs and 'commit himself to the care of the military authorities'.[28]

At the same trial another boy, David William Fitzgerald, with a shortfall of 44.5 hours, said he lived about four-and-a-half miles out of town and had no horse to bring him to parades. Working from 'daylight to dark' on a farm, he was too tired to drill after finishing work. His father testified that it was impossible for his son to attend the drills, as it was too far for him to walk to Port Pirie. The magistrate was not at all sympathetic, told the boy's father to 'get him a horse then', and imposed a fine of £5, with fifteen shillings in court costs, in default six weeks in the reformatory.[29] All told, about half the boys were fined £5 with 15 shillings costs, and the remainder had to pay costs and were ordered to make up the missing time.[30]

In Paddington in Sydney, on 22 September 1913, there were 31 trainees summoned to appear before a magistrate, but only 16 appeared. One lad testified that he was the sole support of his mother and his sister, and could not attend drill on Saturday afternoons. While admitting the boy had extenuating circumstances, the magistrate declared 'the circumstances could not be used as an excuse under the Act' and ordered him to make up the extra time.[31]

A much more deserving case appeared before Magistrate Mr Love, at the North Sydney Police Court on 29 August 1912. Charles Osborne, a Senior Cadet from nearby Chatswood, pleaded for an exemption from military training:

> **Osborne:** I would sooner go to jail than do the drills.
> **Magistrate:** It is very unwise to speak like that.
> **Osborne:** I mean it. I have a good character from my employer. I do my work faithfully, and I have long hours. My father is dead. My mother died only four months ago. I and my brother are the sole support of the family … I have eight brothers and sisters, all under 16, to look after.
> **Magistrate:** It may be hard but I have to administer the Act.
> **Osborn:** I am trying to better myself, and I wouldn't be able to carry out my studies if I had to drill. If the court orders me to do the drills I won't do so. I will put up with the consequences.
> **Magistrate:** That is a matter for yourself. You are ordered to make up the 28 hours deficiency, and I will give you three months to do it. You will also have 24 hours in which to pay the 6/- costs.
> **Osborne:** I can't pay them.
> **Magistrate:** I won't discuss the matter.[32]

Exemptions on religious grounds were not easy to get, as Reverend Alfred Madson, a Methodist Minister, and his fourteen-year-old son found on being summonsed to the Collingwood Court in Melbourne for not registering as a Senior Cadet. In his defence, Madson stated:

> the Act requires me to act in opposition to what I regard as one of my most sacred convictions … then I rely on the Constitution, which declares I be allowed the fullest religious liberty.[33]

When asked again by the magistrate, 'Will you register your son?' the defendant declined to do so. After receiving a fine of £2, Madson asked, 'Can you make the alternative, imprisonment?' The magistrate replied, 'No. The imprisonment may be considered on another occasion.'[34]

A conscientious objection was also denied to a Melbourne Rationalist, Joshua Ratcliff, who was charged for preventing his two boys from registering. Objecting to militarisation in all its forms, Ratcliff exclaimed for all in the court to hear, 'Compulsory military training resulted in the physical and moral degradation of the country!' He was fined £12.50 on both cases.[35]

The Socialist opposition in Melbourne

One of the strongest of the groups opposed to compulsory military service was the socialists, particularly in Melbourne. This group ran a strong opposition campaign through its weekly penny newspaper *The Socialist: An Exponent of International Socialism*, from the time the Act was first announced until the outbreak of World War I, after which it was heavily censored by the Government.

Less than two months after the announcement of the Act *The Socialist*, in a front page article titled 'Conscript Boys of Australia', supposedly addressed to its younger readers, wrote:

> We wonder if many of you Australian lads have thought about this business of the compulsory military training to which the Government is subjecting you. Your parents have been told that their boys between the ages of 14 and 18 must be drilled, and marched, and taught to carry firearms, in order that when they grow up they may know how to fight as soldiers, and shoot down or bayonet the lads of other countries ... Now is the time to protest against the folly of this compulsory training in organised murder. Now is the time to make up your minds NEVER TO TAKE THE MILITARY OATH which deprives you of your will and conscience.[36]

The Australian Freedom League was given a regular column in the paper, and used it to advertise its meetings and promote its pacifist views. A resolution at the League's September 1912 meeting 'urges upon the Federal Government the necessity of abolishing the compulsory clauses of the Commonwealth Defence Acts ... and the power given to the Military Board to control education under the Junior Cadet regulations'.[37] By mid-1913, the League had claimed there had been over 10,000 prosecutions under the Act, 'all I believe are of the working class'. The article continued:

> Lads with certificates of ill-health from able, highly respected doctors, have had these proofs of their ill-health set aside; lads who have lost time from bad illnesses have been ordered into military custody to make up their drills; lads working on night shifts have been punished because they have not put in their drills during the day when they ought to have been asleep.[38]

Once prosecutions of defaulting cadets gathered momentum, *The Socialist* began supporting individuals and groups of defaulters. Using initials instead of the full names of the defaulters, the paper referred to Senior Cadet 'C. M.' of South Melbourne, who was sent to Queenscliff Fortress for not registering, even though 'he worked in a foundry and had to rise at 5am each morning and the drills interfered with his work'. The boy's mother wrote to his employer, asking for his job to be kept open when he returned from imprisonment. As the employer declined to do so, she claimed 'the lad will be amongst the unemployed on his release'.[39]

Through its column in *The Socialist*, the Australian Freedom League reported on cadet prosecutions from its branches in other states. It claimed that in Queensland 'forty-seven lads were sent to Lytton Fort for continuous detention for various periods ranging from one to forty-five days'.[40]

Trade union opposition

The mining community in Broken Hill in New South Wales contained a strong socialist element in the trade unions located there, particularly the Amalgamated Miners' Association. Not surprisingly, Broken Hill became a centre of much opposition to the Defence Act of 1910. Of the several hundred cases of defiance to the legislation, there were two that received Australia-wide recognition. Senior Cadets Alfred Francis Giles and Victor Yeo were the sons of miners, and were ably supported by their families and the socialist community in Broken Hill.

In the case of Alfred Giles, whose father had been prosecuted by the local Barrier Court for preventing his son for registering as a cadet, the lad was taken into custody at his workplace, taken to court and sentenced to two weeks imprisonment, during the first half of which he was on bread and water rations. Despite strong representation by the Miners' Association, the lad was forced to serve the full sentence in gaol. On his release, Alfred was presented with a gold medal 'for his brave stand' by the Barrier Branch of the Amalgamated Miners' Association.[41]

Victor Yeo, aged fourteen, was the son of an ex-British Army artilleryman opposed to war service on humanitarian grounds. Vivian Yeo, Victor's elder brother, had already served a fortnight's jail for refusing to attend drills and had gone into hiding. Young Victor was fined £5 in November 1912, or alternatively two months in prison. He chose jail and began his sentence in January 1913. Following public outcry over a fourteen-year-old serving a prison sentence, Josiah Thomas, Federal Member for Broken Hill, intervened and had Victor released on a bond after serving twelve days of his sentence. He said, 'There was a good deal of public resentment shown by Broken Hill people.'[42] In August of that year, Victor again appeared before the court, this time for failing to report for a medical examination. He received a sentence of one month's imprisonment. For much of the time, Victor was confined to his cell for twenty-two hours per day, and was often restricted to a diet of bread and water. After serving twenty days, Senator Millen, Minister of Defence, bowed to public pressure and ordered the boy's release.[43]

The Defence Department enlisted the help of headmasters of schools to provide the names of youths, past and present, who were eligible for training as Senior Cadets and 'may be evading service'.[44]

Opposition on religious grounds

Another case in Victoria concerned a sixteen-year-old Brighton lad, Thomas Roberts, whose family belonged to the Society of Friends (Quakers) and objected 'to all forms of militarism'. Thomas was subsequently sentenced to three weeks detention at Fort Queenscliff, where he refused to do signalling drill. On 6 June 1914, he was court-marshalled and sentenced to seven days solitary confinement.[45] Together with another defaulter, nineteen-year-old Harry Flintoff, an apprentice cabinet maker who later became a Methodist home missionary, Thomas was locked up in a cell to serve out his solitary confinement.[46] Incensed by their son's treatment, Susanna and Fred Roberts wrote to newspapers, ministers of religion and politicians across the country, and even to the American Secretary of State, who replied that 'it did not appear to be a matter in which the United States had any jurisdiction'. Thomas completed his sentence, but such was the public furore that the Federal Government forbade solitary confinement for recalcitrant military cadets in future.[47]

Walter Krygger, a seventeen-year-old boot shop assistant in Northcote, a suburb of Melbourne, chose not to register, as he was 'a Christian and followed the teachings of the Bible'. Despite his mother's outburst — 'there's no encouragement for boys to be Christians' — in the courtroom, Walter was sentenced to eighteen days detention at Fort Queenscliff. In a letter to his mother, Walter complained about the food and the vile swearing, 'the soldiers being as bad as the boys … I am in amongst a lot of Devils'. Refusing to drill, Walter was dragged around the parade ground by Corporal Willie Bartrop, and later attacked by another youth who 'dug his fingers into my neck, screwed my arm almost out of its socket … then he punched me in the face twice and knocked me into the ground'.[48]

On a more minor issue, in October 1911 the Melbourne *Argus* carried the banner 'Cadet Drill at Easter — Clergyman Urges Resistance' and quoted Canon Garland of Holy Trinity Church, South Brisbane, condemning the Federal Government for

> requiring compulsory attendance of cadets at encampments and drills at Easter time … Easter Day was the greatest Lord's day of the year … he counselled parents to refuse to allow their boys to attend drills on the days mentioned, or indeed on any Lord's day.[49]

In Melbourne on 16 June 1912, Reverend Leyton Richards, Minister of the Independent Church in Collins Street, preached a sermon. In the presence of several federal members of parliament, he called for the abolition of compulsory military training because 'if democracy is to prove its fitness to supplant old-time autocracies and tyrannies, it can never be by creating a new tyranny in the name of Defence'.[50] Richard's sermon provoked numerous letters of support and condemnation to *The Argus* in coming days, one of which, under the subheading of 'Being Prepared', was written the following day:

> I am only a woman, and a decided lover of peace, but I would like to ask Rev. Richards what he suggests we would do when this peace-loving, helpless island continent of ours is attacked by foes (as it surely will be in the future), if to have trained soldiers is a

crime? When England has both hands full with wars of her own, what is to be done? … allow me to warn all men of Mr Richard's type from living in a fool's paradise.[51]

Prosecutions ease as World War I begins

From the start of training in 1911 until July 1915, there were 33,942 prosecutions for drill absconders, keeping in mind that some of this number were prosecuted on two, three or more occasions, though there were no records kept of the number of multiple offenders. As the aggregate of each year's number in training over this period was 636,000, this represents about 5.3 percent of trainee prosecutions per year. The highest year for convictions was 1913, when the total was 10,158 or 7.8 percent of boys in training. The rate had fallen to 5.38 percent in 1914.[52]

Figures for the first five months in 1914 showed the drop in prosecutions and convictions for Senior Cadets nationwide:

State	Prosecutions	Convictions	Cadets in training
Queensland	201	190	11,688
NSW	1318	1224	30,647
Victoria	1129	949	27,409
South Aust.	481	435	8524
Western Aust.	231	227	4291
Tasmania	174	166	2895[53]

From the comparatively few boys brought to court, and the high level of compliance afterwards, it was clear that resistance was minimal and obedience notable. There were lads who successfully evaded the entire training process, but by the middle of 1914 the authorities claimed that most of the 10,000 'missing' youths had been traced and that very few were escaping their obligations.[54]

TOP
Objections to compulsory military training, 1914. Mansfield Collection, Latrobe Library, State Library of Victoria

BOTTOM
Socialist, Melbourne, 7 August 1914, p. 1

Australian Freedom League.

Compulsory Military Training

An

Analysis and an Exposure.

1914.

The Kingston Press, 38-42 Oxford Street, Sydney.

CLOUD AND CRISIS.

The Socialist

An Exponent of International Socialism.

PUBLISHED WEEKLY. [Registered at the General Post Office, Melbourne, for Transmission by Post as a Newspaper.] NINTH YEAR.

No. 420. 4/- per year. MELBOURNE, FRIDAY, AUGUST 7, 1914. ONE PENNY.

Ground Arms! For Humanity's Sake.
[With acknowledgments to Q. "Worker."]

Single Tax and Socialism.

An ardent Single Taxer has enough optimism for a hundred. By the abolition of taxes, and the imposition of a fine for possessing the best land, he tells us that all monopolies will be destroyed, that "Capitalism" as an evil will no longer exist, and that "every individual will be able to enjoy the fruits of his own labor." This state of affairs will, we are told, produce the millennium. Thus Single Taxers profess to be amazed why people should be so unreasonable as to desire Socialism, which promises nothing at once, which does not profess to give the individual *all* the fruits of his own labor, which is, they say, utterly "unscientific," and irrational. They profess to offer an immediate, simple, "scientific," and equably-distributed reform, calling Socialism an irrational, revolutionary, unworkable state of society because it does not fit in with certain rules of political economy enunciated by non-Socialists.

But is it right that this alleged irrationality of Socialism should cause us to regard the Single Tax as a panacea? The Single Taxer prides himself on reverencing Henry George's "Progress and Poverty" as "any ordinary man" reverences the Bible. Is Single Tax perfectly complete, consistent and rational? Surely not. In advocating complete freedom of trade and land-values taxation it professes to benefit society as a whole. Perhaps it may do so, but will the benefit thereby conferred be enough to produce a millennium? Will it not be the case that monopolies will be still encouraged by the unwillingness of the Single Tax reformers to reform the evils of manufacturing, trading, and investing Capitalism? They say that they are unwilling to do this because "Capitalism" in the "scientific" sense has absolutely no evils;

JOIN

The Australian Women's Peace Army

(Affiliated to the International Committee of Women for Permanent Peace).

TOWARDS PERMANENT PEACE.

Equality of Rights and Opportunities for Men and Women of ALL Nations.

Australian Headquarters: The Guild Hall, Swanston Street, Melbourne.

President: Miss VIDA GOLDSTEIN.
Hon. Sec.: Miss CECILIA JOHN.
Organiser: Miss ADELA PANKHURST.

MEMBERSHIP FEE: Voluntary, with Entrance Fee of 1/-

PLATFORM.

1. **Abolition of Conscription** and Every Form of **Militarism.**
2. **Women** to be given Equal Political Rights with Men in all Countries where Representative Government Exists.
3. **Education of Children** in Principles of Anti-Militarism and Internationalism.
4. **Self-Government** Not to be Refused to Any People.
5. **Respect for Nationality.**—No Territory to be Transferred without the consent of the men and women in it. The right of conquest not to be recognised.
6. **Foreign Policy** to be Subject to Democratic Control.
7. **General Disarmament** to be aimed at by the Governments taking over the manufacture of the munitions of war and controlling International traffic in them.
8. **Trade Routes** to be open on equal terms to the shipping of all nations.
9. **Investments** to be made at the risk of tne Investor, without claim to the official protection of his Government.
10. **Secret Treaties** to be void, and the theory of the **Balance of Power** to be abandoned.
11. **Our Social System** to be remodelled on a basis of co-operation, so that production and distribution shall be controlled by the people for the people.
12. **International Disputes** to be referred to an International Court of Justice, in which men and women of all classes shall be represented.

JOIN THE WOMEN'S PEACE ARMY NOW!

Mansfield Collection, Latrobe Library, State Library of Victoria

The Bulletin,
29 August 1912

The cells at Fort Queenscliff in Victoria, used to confine conscientious objectors to Senior Cadet training, like Tom Roberts and Harry Flintoff in 1914. J. Barrett, *Falling In: Australians and Boy Conscription 1911–1915*, 1979, p. 186

SATURDAY DRILLS.

TO THE EDITOR OF THE ARGUS.

Sir,—I think all will admit that a boy must have some form of recreation, but as things are at present he has practically no time on the first six days of the week for such a luxury. A large number of Saturday afternoons are required for drill. I myself have attended statutory parades for the last three Saturdays, which I think is "a bit over the odds."

As aforesaid, a lad must have some sport, and at present the only time in many weeks is the seventh day, which, I am sorry to admit, is becoming quite a sporting day. I agree that there ought to be some drill, but by no means the number of parades that now have to be fulfilled by us.

Another grievance is the uniforms we are given. In the instance of myself, I have been given a 6¾ hat to wear, whereas my natural size is 7¼. Needless to say, it looks absurd, as I believe I do also when wearing it, judging by remarks from street children. Yours, &c.,

OVER THE ODDS.

April 30.

2 May 1914, p.10

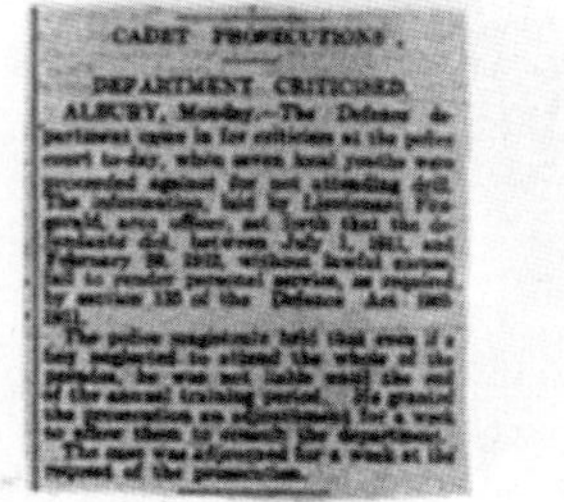

CADET PROSECUTIONS.

DEPARTMENT CRITICISED.

ALBURY, Monday.—The Defence department came in for criticism at the police court to-day, when seven local youths were proceeded against for not attending drill. ... section 135 of the Defence Act 1903-1911.

The police magistrate held that even if a boy neglected to attend the whole of the parades, he was not liable until the end of the annual training period. He granted the prosecution an adjournment for a week to allow them to consult the department.

The case was adjourned for a week at the request of the prosecution.

26 March 1912, p.4

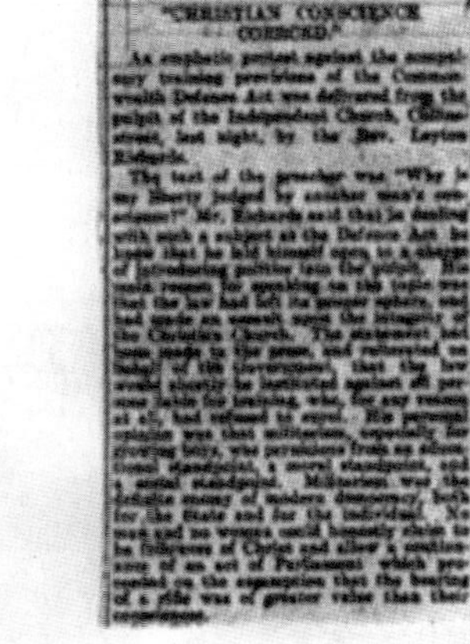

COMPULSORY TRAINING.

PROTEST FROM THE PULPIT.

"CHRISTIAN CONSCIENCE COERCED."

An emphatic protest against the compulsory training provisions of the Commonwealth Defence Act was delivered from the pulpit of the Independent Church, Collins street, last night, by the Rev. Leyton Richards.

The text of the preacher was "Why is my liberty judged by another man's conscience?" ...

18 June 1912, p.8

COMPULSORY SERVICE.

QUAKERS REFUSE COMPLIANCE.

PRIME MINISTER'S REPLY.

3 March 1914

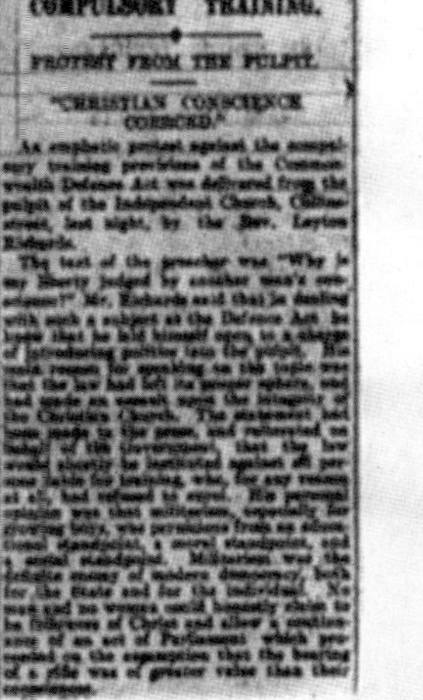

COMPULSORY TRAINING.

ADDRESS AT THE TRADES HALL.

During a meeting held by the Trades Hall Council yesterday evening, Mr. J. W. Barry, secretary of the Australian Freedom League, gave an address on "The Compulsory Clauses of the Defence Act and the Workers."

Mr. Barry said that all over the world the classes were rising against militarism, because it was used to oppress the worker, and was not employed on his behalf. The time had come when the Compulsory Defence Act should be wiped off the statute book. Those who formed what was called the citizen defence force were not citizens at all, but boys from 14 to 18 years of age. Under clause 51 of the Defence Act the Military Board had power to make any regulations it chose, and these had all the force of laws. The Labour party, had it chosen to do so during last session of Parliament, could have smashed clause 51. Why had they not risen against it? All the sacrifices made necessary under the act fall to the poorer classes. The full force of labour organisations should be employed to aid all those lads who were making a stand against the conditions imposed by the system.

8 August 1913, p.14

DISOBEDIENT CADET.

ORDERED IMPRISONMENT.

TERANG, Wednesday.—Carl Hauff, a cadet, was proceeded against by Lieutenant Pollard at the police court to-day, before Mr. Read Murphy, P.M., and Mr. J. Bradshaw, J.P., for having on March 28, at drill, refused to obey orders and with having behaved in an insulting and disorderly manner. Hauff was sentenced to two days' imprisonment and to pay 20/- costs.

2 May 1912, p.10

The Argus headlines showing prosecutions for Senior Cadets evading compulsory parades

The Bulletin, 31 August 1911

Cartoon showing a dissenting cadet in solitary confinement in a police cell. *Sunday Times*, Perth, 26 July 1914

BRISBANE COURIER

TRAINEES PROSECUTED.

FAILURE TO ATTEND COMPULSORY PARADES.

DETENTION AT LYTTON FORT.

The Central Summons Court yesterday was crowded with smiling youths who had been ordered to attend to answer charges of not having attended the requisite number of compulsory parades. Lieutenant-Colonel R. A. Moore, P.M., was on the bench. The prosecutions were brought by the Seventh Infantry (Moreton) Regiment, which was represented by the adjutant (Captain T. V. Brown).

The majority of the defendants pleaded guilty without offering any excuse, and one humbly asked if he would be allowed to pay a fine instead of "taking out" his days at Lytton. "I'm afraid not, my boy," Colonel Moore said. "You see, money's no object. It's your presence that is wanted."

Another stated that he had learned from the Press that married men were exempt from service. He had been wedded, and had consequently believed that he was quite correct in not attending drill. The adjutant, who was prosecuting, explained that there was a regulation which exempted trainees who were the sole support of widowed mothers, providing their occupation was interfered with by drill. Defendant tendered a newspaper, in which Colonel Moore discovered there was a statement to the effect that trainees who were the only support of their "relatives" were excused. "Oh!" he exclaimed, "I think you have stretched your imagination somewhat. It is not very clear from this that a married man is excused. I'm sorry, but I can't do anything for you."

A young man named Thos. Vincent Maguire appeared to answer three charges of having absented himself without leave from drill. He pleaded guilty to each.

"This man," explained the adjutant, "has been heard to state that he would do no drill except at Lytton."

Colonel Moore: Why doesn't he join the permanent force, then?

Defendant: I have a certificate!

Colonel Moore: Not a medical certificate, surely? You look too well altogether for that?

Defendant: I was in the hospital for four weeks!

Colonel Moore: During this drill period?

Defendant: Well—er—I couldn't exactly say.

The Bench was here informed that the offender was a boxer, and was in the habit of exhibiting his skill at the Stadium frequently.

Defendant admitted this, but said he was very desirous of obtaining a medical certificate.

A CONSCIENTIOUS OBJECTOR Tom Roberts, as a 16-year-old Quaker, was sentenced to 21 days detention at Fort Queenscliff in June 1914. A week's solitary confinement was also imposed on him by the army. The resultant uproar led to promises that the latter punishment would not be used again. Photograph, taken about 1918, from Thelma Bell.

LEFT

Brisbane Courier, 8 May 1914, p. 6

RIGHT

J. Barrett, *Falling In: Australians and Boy Conscription 1911–1915*, 1979, p. 189

14

Reactions to Compulsory Training in New Zealand

Support for the legislation

Arguments for compulsory military service had already been voiced at the inaugural meeting of the National League of New Zealand in its Manifesto of August 1906. Founding President Mr W. B. Leyland declared:

> The League is connected to no party. It appeals to every citizen who realises that peace is among the greatest human blessings, and that security within our borders can only be ensured by our being able to defend ourselves from attack.[1]

The objective of the National League stated that 'universal defence training, either ashore or afloat, of all boys and young men until the age of twenty-one, with encouragement of continued training'. Rifle ranges were to be provided in every New Zealand township, with 'sufficient rifles to be kept in the country to arm every capable citizen'. The League was to organise 'an educative lecture system illustrating the fearful consequences of invasion, etc.', publish a periodical to its membership, placing League literature in the hands of every elector, 'particularly by arousing the intelligent patriotism of the young', and if necessary, secure by referendum 'an overwhelming majority for universal training'.[2]

Implementation problems

Although Army Headquarters did not anticipate any compliance difficulties once the compulsory training was underway in July 1911, there were a number of problems in the implementation of the scheme. Administrative planning put the small New Zealand Army staff under great stress, particularly in the outlying country districts. Parade grounds needed to be found or upgraded, and some additional drill halls had to be erected. Poster material needed to be displayed around the country calling for military registration and medical examinations for prospective trainees, and in some areas military personnel were obliged to undertake house-to-house canvasses to help ensure compliance.[3]

The last day for registration had been designated as 30 June 1911, by which time it was anticipated that around 40,000 enrolments from those aged 14 to 25 would eventuate. However, despite all the effort, the government was surprised when just over 30,000 recruits had registered by the due date, leaving a large number who had failed to meet their obligation. Such a low registration level alarmed the government and it was determined to take action against the offenders. The original Defence Act of 1909 contained penalties for non-compliance, which included fines of up to £5, as well as depriving offenders of employment in government services. Failure to pay fines could result in the courts ordering a period of imprisonment in a civil prison, which was the usual practice, showing no distinction between military and civilian offenders.[4]

Once prosecutions commenced, it was inevitable that some of the youths were sent to civilian prisons for non-payment of fines, the result being that some young offenders were imprisoned alongside common criminals. Naturally, this act caused outrage in some sections of the community and greatly embarrassed the government.

Concerted opposition to the Act

While most sectors of the New Zealand community accepted the transfer of a voluntary system of military training to a compulsory one, there were pockets of resistance from the outset. At first the main centre of hostility was Christchurch, where the Editor of the *Christian Herald*, Louis B. Christie, founded the Anti-Militarist League in June 1910. Eighteen months later, there were sixteen Anti-Militarist League branches throughout the country.[5]

Although there was no Labor Party yet in existence in New Zealand, there were several Labor candidates among the ruling Liberal Party. The anti-militarist Socialist Party was operating, with memberships mainly from miners of the West Coast and the waterside workers of Canterbury. In Wellington and Christchurch isolated socialist groups expressed opposition, but there was no single voice in the Labor movement against compulsory military training: 'Socialists saw compulsory training as something to be opposed in New Zealand, because it was opposed by socialists everywhere.'[6]

Socialists who identified with the Marxist I. W. W. (International Workers of the World) saw it as 'an attempt to consolidate the class basis of society, by the creation of a military caste' and the professional soldier was seen as 'an agent of the employing class and a traitor to his own.'[7]

A National Peace Council of New Zealand (modelled on the English National Peace Council, established in Bristol, England, in 1905) was formed by Charles Mackie, a Baptist lay preacher in Christchurch, who called upon the people to passively resist the government. Together with the New Zealand Socialist Party, Christie and Mackie, and their respective protest groups, they formed a joint National Peace Council and Anti-Militarist League, and undertook an organising tour of the South Island as a prelude to a national campaign.[8] Rapidly expanding throughout 1911, the Peace Council was estimated to have a membership of over 30,000 in sixteen branches, with most of its views being published in the *Maoriland Worker*.[9]

Besides being hostile to compulsory military training, they also protested against 'the introduction of the spirit of militarism into New Zealand's schools'. Two strong supporters of the Peace Council in Canterbury, Mrs Sarah Page and Mrs Ada Wells, worked tirelessly with members of the Women's Christian Temperance Union in an effort to abolish the Junior Cadet system in schools. Many of the women 'had an aversion to the sight of their sons in military uniform at the early age of twelve', and also objected to the oath they were regularly required to repeat — '... to obey the orders of the General and the officers set over me' — as the boys were too immature to understand what they were saying.[10]

Their public agitation on this issue eventually proved successful, when the government's Defence Amendment Bill of October 1912 abolished the 'compulsory' Junior Cadets in the schools, returning to a 'voluntary' system.[11] Other amendments in the Bill included that the imprisonment of non-fine payers would in future be served in military rather than civil prisons, which could not exceed twenty-eight days, exemption from military service was to be allowed on religious grounds, and that fines for offences under the Act could be forcefully recovered from an offender's wages.[12]

The first imprisonment for the non-payment of a fine under the new Act occurred in the Magistrates' Court in Wellington on July 1911, when a youth, William Cornish, received a sentence of twenty-one days jail. The outraged Editor of the local *Maoriland Worker* wrote at the time, 'Nothing can justify the jailing of "anti-boys" and their handcuffing, fingerprinting, and broad arrow garments and hard labour.'[13] Imprisoned youths were in some cases well-respected members of local communities, 'many of them Bible class leaders or regular churchgoers ----- they were all very young ---- youths from 18–21 years'.[14] It was often left to army officers to search private houses for defaulters, and to appear in the law courts as prosecutors. In the public eye, the army soon became identified as a prosecuting agency, and also came under attack from the anti-militarists.

A group of young men of military age in Addington formed an impromptu group, calling themselves the 'We Won'ts', which soon became formalised as the 'Passive Resisters' Union', with James Worral and Reg Williams as joint secretaries. The youths vowed to 'resist coercion, conscription, and compulsory military training under all circumstances, in defiance of all pains and penalties that may be imposed'. Other branches were formed in Wellington, Auckland, Millerton and Runanga. In all, 217 eligible trainees in the PRU pledged to refuse military drill in 1912.[15]

Membership of the Passive Resisters' Union was unique in that it was comprised solely of youths and young men liable for service under the Act, who pledged themselves to defy it. With a membership of mainly socialist leanings, the Union published a provocative monthly paper, *Repeal*, though it took until 1913 before the group was fully organised: 'Its members were rather hot-headed in their opposition to the Defence Act, and in consequence, were continually running foul of both the civil police and the authorities.'[16]

In June 1913, a number of Union members in Petone descended on the local police station, and persuaded the sergeant in charge to release a jailed defaulter in order to allow him to participate in a football match. 'The "hero" was carried onto the playing field amidst scenes of enthusiasm.' [17]

During that same month, eight young defaulters were taken to the military barracks on Ripa Island, in Lyttleton Harbour. Prior to being transferred from the Lyttleton Police Station to the island by barge, the boys were taken in charge by the military authorities 'and marched to the wharf with fixed bayonets, while the waterside workers and others on the wharf cheered the offenders'. When the boys were eventually released, a crowd of 2500 unionists assembled at a Christchurch theatre welcomed the 'Ripa boys' and held the largest anti-conscription meeting to that date. Thereafter, the boys often travelled around the country to anti-conscription rallies and told of their experiences in prison.[18]

When the outspoken Australian Quaker J. P. Fletcher visited New Zealand in March 1912 on behalf of the Australian Freedom League, he commended the efforts of the Peace Council and the Passive Resisters' Union in resisting the Defence Act. Claiming that he found the 'opposition to military training more militant in New Zealand than in Australia',[19] he was undoubtedly referring more to antics of the 'Union' rather than the 'Council'.

Lord Baden-Powell, founder of the Boy Scout movement, had mixed feelings about the idea of training military cadets. He conducted a seven-week visit to New Zealand and Australia promoting scouting in 1910. While commending the Australasians on their preparations for defending themselves, he took pains to identify his scouts as 'peace scouts', and although recognising that boys needed to be taught 'discipline', he rejected the idea of teaching them military drill: 'I have long since found out that drill does not make a soldier. It is necessary to develop the intelligence of the men, and to instill in them a sense of "playing the game" before exposing them to drill.'[20]

The *Christchurch Press* reported in May 1912 that at times up to thirty percent of Senior Cadets were not attending[21] and that many of those who were present were often intentionally disruptive. One of the problems was that in some areas, many of the cadets were without uniforms and rifles up to two years after the Defence Act was enacted, and consequently did not take their drill seriously: 'When they were fully equipped they did show great improvement, but it was not until 1915 that discipline was satisfactory.'[22]

Perhaps the difficulties in enforcing the legislation led to insufficient trainees in the New Zealand Territorials (militia) early in the war, because the lack of volunteers after the war dragged on past Gallipoli, and brought about the introduction of military conscription for overseas service in 1916. This was in line with similar legislation in Great Britain.

Despite the prosecutions, opposition to military conscription continued to grow in New Zealand. Prosecutions in 1911 totalled 28, in 1912 it was 3187, and in 1913 it was 7930, a total of 10,245 convictions in the first three years of operation.[23] In the 1912 batch, of the 3187 summons issued under the Defence Act, 1923 cadets were convicted. Fines were applied in 1437 instances, with some 120 boys choosing a prison sentence in lieu of the fine.[24]

Opposition groups complained of discrimination in the way prosecutions under the Act were carried out, with claims that the working classes were being targeted because of their concerted resistance: 'West Coast boys had been persecuted and imprisoned whilst thousands elsewhere have not been prosecuted.'[25] There was also criticism of the enormous cost of the scheme, with the government spending around £600,000 annually (Lord Kitchener had estimated £400,000) and a further £250,000 annually on naval defence: 'the country is now spending 8 shillings and 11¾ pence per head on defence in comparison with Australia, which is spending 7 shillings and ¼ pence.'[26]

Opposition against the scheme continued to mount, with country politicians pointing to the inconvenience caused to young farmers attending the weeknight parades and weekend drills, complaining that 'there is often more time taken up in travelling than drilling'. Some of the military officers also came under criticism, as was the case in Palmerston North, where 'officers were quartered in the best hotels and spent a large portion of their time playing golf, whilst the "other ranks" had been under canvas'.[27]

With the newly constituted New Zealand Labor Party in power by early 1914, and the strength of the opposition to compulsory training rising steadily, if it hadn't been for the outbreak of World War I later that year the whole scheme may have been under threat:

> By the middle of 1914 compulsory military training had become very much a party political question. Liberal opinion was setting itself against it, and the Government was very much on the defensive ... the outbreak of war saved the scheme, and of course, provided its military justification.[28]

PART III

THE WORLD WAR I PERIOD

15

Initial Responses of the Schools to the Outbreak of WWI

Victoria

In the September 1914 issue of the *Education Gazette*, the Education Department of Victoria went to some length to advise its teachers about discussing 'the war' with the children in their care. Under the title 'Calmness in Time of War', state school teachers were urged to do their part to 'influence the majority of the homes in the state through the children'. They were advised that the daily life of their communities should 'proceed naturally' without excitement being stirred up by teachers, particularly with the younger children:

> Emotion is more infectious than disease. The children infect the homes ... Calmness needs to be practised by teachers more than by other persons. Teachers can do good by example. Talks to the older children on patriotism, illustrated by present events, would be effective, and the lessons on history, civics, geography may be made interesting by dealing with current matters.[1]

In common with schools in other states, Victorian schools were asked to raise money towards a 'patriotic fund' to support soldiers currently embarking to war destinations, which during September 1914 had already raised the princely sum of £2,091. 2s. 4d.[2]

Schools were urged to involve their local communitiesin fundraising efforts for the welfare of their soldiers, with suggestions including:

1. Pianoforte and violin solos of a patriotic nature by scholars and teachers.
2. Patriotic unison and part songs by the children. These can be learnt and practised during school hours.
3. Recitations and selections from Shakespeare of a patriotic and school interest.
4. Patriotic solos by teachers and children. (What school has not its lady vocalists, its choirmen and choirboys?)
5. Exhibitions of physical drill, musical drill, Morris dancing, maypole, etc.
6. Sale of work done by girls in their spare time and at home, eg. plain needlework, knitting, crochet, lace, fancy needlework, table centres.
7. Sale of articles made by girls at a cookery centre, or at home, or those given by friends.
8. Sale of work in paper and cardboard done by the boys, eg. hair-tidies, letter-racks, hatpin-holders.
9. Sale of work done by boys at manual centre or at home, eg. small models, paper-knives, key-labels, book racks.
10. Sale of photographs taken by photographic members of the staff.[3]

Barely three months after the commencement of the war, the *Education Gazette* published a speech entitled 'Education and the War' by the Right Honourable J. A. Pease, MP, Minister for Education in England. Pease's speech began by posing the question 'What can we do for our country?' He proceeded to answer it, mainly by justifying Britain's actions in entering the war:

> We can keep the system of education going. Many teachers and students have been summoned to military duties, whilst others are asking themselves whether duty calls them to go or to stay. The teachers can do more than anyone else to help their scholars … The scholars can be shown that we are involved in war by stern

> necessity, that we are fighting in the cause of peace. At the present moment a blow has been dealt, and I sincerely believe through no fault of ours …[4]

Each of the state departments of education had a monthly journal available to scholars in grades 3 to 8, for the price of one penny. The Victorian issue (it was also reproduced for schools in Tasmania and Western Australia) was called *The School Paper* and contained short stories, poems and songs designed to interest young readers of varying ages. It often contained material about the Australian bush, pioneers, heroes, morality, and current patriotic events, like British Empire Day. In the September issue for grades 7 and 8, there appeared the banner 'Britain at War', and an extract from the speech in which King George V declared war on Germany in August 1914. A large photograph of the King accompanied the script. In the article, George V expressed his appreciation for Australia's support in Britain's conflicts, both past and present:

> to my people of the overseas dominions for the generous, self sacrificing help given by them in the past to the mother country, confident in the belief that in this time of trial, my Empire will stand united, calm, resolute, trusting in God.[5]

The same issue of *The School Paper* carried a three-stanza poem, 'The Call', credited to 'Oriel' in the Melbourne *Argus*. It reiterated the King's sentiments, particularly in the chorus lines:

> Coo-ee! It's the mother country calling.
> Coo-ee! Her sons shall make reply;
> The children of the free,
> From sea to surging sea,
> Now hear the call,
> They'll stand or fall,
> Prepared to do or die.[6]

A photograph with the inscription 'Lord Roberts inspecting the Australian Mounted Cadets in London' accompanied the poem.[7] The contingent of about twenty-five Australian Light Horse Senior Cadets had been touring in England, during the school holidays in 1914.

EDUCATION DEPARTMENT, VICTORIA.

THE SCHOOL PAPER.

FOR GRADES VII. AND VIII. (1914).

No. 179.] [Registered at the General Post Office, Melbourne, for transmission by post as a newspaper.] MELBOURNE. Price 1d. [SEPT. 1, 1914.

BRITAIN AT WAR.

Britain declared war against Germany on the 4th of August. In anticipation of this declaration, the Ministry of the Commonwealth of Australia, fully confident that its action would be in accord with the wish of the people, had offered, on the previous day, the Australian fleet and 20,000 men to the mother country. From Canada, New Zealand, and other parts of the Empire, offers of help were also sent to the British Government. The King promptly acknowledged these offers in the following memorable words:—

Photograph by W. & D. Downey, London.]

HIS MAJESTY KING GEORGE V.

(The uniform is that of an Admiral of the Fleet.)

"I desire to express to my people of the oversea dominions with what appreciation and pride I have received the messages from their respective Governments during the last few days. These spontaneous assurances of their fullest support recall to me the generous, self-sacrificing help given by them in the past to the mother country. I shall be strengthened in the discharge of the great responsibilities which rest upon me by the confident belief that, in this time of trial, my Empire will stand united, calm, resolute, trusting in God.

GEORGE, R.I."

150 THE SCHOOL PAPER—GRADES VII. AND VIII [SEPT. 1, 1914.

WHAT ARE WE FIGHTING FOR?

Pa'tri-ot'ic (*pa*, "a" as in *ale*; or *pat*, "a" as in *an*), actuated by love of one's country.

In-tel'li-gent, having a clear knowledge about things.

Loot'ing, plundering or sacking (a conquered city or the like)

Tyr'an-ny, unjust or oppressive government; government without law.

Sac'ri-fic'ing, suffering to be lost.

Dis'ci-pline (*plin*, "i" as in *ill*), training, whether physical, mental, or moral; drill.

Ar'ro-gant, proceeding from undue claims or self-importance; proud; overbearing.

Pol'i-cy, settled or definite course or method followed by a government or an individual.

Re-sist'ance, act of resisting or of standing against force or pressure; opposition; hindrance.

Av'e-nue, passage; way or opening.

Dom'i-na'tion, government; overbearing rule.

U-surp', take by force and without right.

Prem'i-er (*prem'i-er* or *pre mi-er*), first in position, rank, or importance; principal; leading.

Su prem'a-cy, highest power or authority.

Ad-min'is-tra'tion, rule; government; putting laws in force.

Con-cil'i-a-tor-y, kind in manner; tending to win good-will.

Boast'ful-ness, boasting; self-praise.

Cri'sis, time of difficulty, danger, and suspense.

Trus-tee', one who manages anything in trust for another.

Cow'ard-ice (*is*, "i" as in *ill*), want of courage to face danger; base fear of danger or hurt.

Ri'val-ry, competition; act of becoming, or state of being, a rival.

1. This is a time when our boys would like to be men, and our girls to be women—the boys to fight, and the girls to nurse. Must they stand idly by in this day of trial? By no means. There is not a boy or girl in Australia who cannot help in some way. Some will do extra work at home while father or brother is absent with the troops; others will deny themselves pleasures to give their pence to a patriotic fund; some girls will learn first aid and nursing, and others will help to make clothing for the soldiers.

FIELD-MARSHAL EARL KITCHENER, SECRETARY OF STATE FOR WAR.

From his advice to the soldiers of the Expeditionary Force:—"Fear God; honor the King; abstain from liquor and looting; be courteous to women; be sure that your conduct justifies the welcome and trust awaiting you."

2. At a time like this, too, we must look forward. In a few years, the boys and girls of to-day will be the men and women of Australia. What kind of men will the boys be; what kind of women, the girls? Every boy can redouble his efforts, in school and playground, to become a man who will be a strength and a credit to Australia, and to the race from which he is sprung; every girl can strive her utmost to become a good woman, an intelligent citizen, and a capable home-maker. Without good homes, no nation can be strong; and so the girls can help quite as much as the boys. Every boy and girl, too, should try to understand what we are fighting for in this war.

3. The Briton of to-day is the child of forefathers who fought for centuries against king and noble to win freedom. The passion for

LEFT

King George V speech at the declaration of WWI. *The School Paper*, Victoria, grades 7 and 8, September 1914, p. 145

RIGHT

At the outbreak of WWI, Field-Marshall Kitchener gave this speech to the children of the British Empire. *The School Paper*, Victoria, grades 7 and 8, September 1914, p. 150

(AUSTRALIA).

THE SCHOOL PAPER.

FOR GRADES VII. AND VIII. (1916).

No. 197.] [Registered at the General Post Office, Melbourne, for transmission by post as a newspaper.] MELBOURNE. Price 1d. [MAR. 1, 1916.

BROTHERHOOD.

Dep'ot (*dep'o*), here, station where recruits are assembled. (It is the French word *dépôt*, printed in English without the accents.)

Re-pos'es ("o" as in *old*), rests; takes his ease.

Per'illed, imperilled; put in peril.

An-ces'tral, handed down from one's forefathers.

Stake, property or interest involved.

Pa'tience, power to wait and endure calmly.

Clam'or, noise; din.

By the courtesy of the proprietors of *The Argus*, Melbourne.]

SCENE AT THE TOWN HALL, MELBOURNE, EARLY IN FEBRUARY, 1916.

"Fast they come, fast they come;
See how they gather!"—SCOTT.

1. The rich man who reposes
In his ancestral shade,
The peasant at his plowshare,
The worker at his trade,

2. Each one his all has perilled,
Each has the same great stake,
Each soul can but have patience,
Each heart can only break.

TOP
Cover of *The School Paper*, Victoria, for grades 7 and 8, May 1916, showing recruitment for the AIF at the Melbourne Town Hall. Courtesy Education Department, Victoria

BOTTOM
The School Paper, Victoria, grades 7 and 8, September 1914, p. 146

The other states

One of the first indications of support from New South Wales occurred immediately after war was declared, when the headmistress of North Sydney Girls High spoke at the Monday morning school assembly and made a 'special appeal to alleviate suffering' to the girls. Later that week, the pupils had raised an initial £20. In September, the school's Old Girls Union held a concert, at which the senior girls sold their homemade sweets, which contributed another £60. Next, the girls decided that every pupil be levied one penny a week for the Belgian Orphans' Fund, which raised £10 by the end of November.

Girls at the Presbyterian Ladies College in Croydon promptly formed sewing groups after school hours and at weekends, 'knitting and sewing for lonely soldiers or homeless Belgians'.[8] The concern over Belgians was highlighted by British military propaganda in the press and in billboard posters, claiming that German soldiers were bayoneting Belgian babies and raping their mothers and other young women, 'and what they do to the women no man can repeat even to another man'.[9]

Following Victoria's lead, the NSW Education Department commenced a Patriotic Fund in August 1914. Within the first two months, over £200 had been received from weekly collections in 1560 schools.[10]

The Government of Tasmania launched a Children's Twenty Thousand appeal for the purchase of war savings certificates, supported by children, parents, friends, and teachers, which was over-subscribed within a year. Fundraising was also organised through the schools for 'purchasing comforts' for the Military Base Hospitals in Hobart and Launceston. School needlework classes knitted items for the Australian Red Cross.[11]

In South Australia, the Children's Patriotic Fund was established in government schools, with funds raised through self-denial boxes, war savings stamps, concerts, fetes and penny drives. Money raised from any form of gambling, including raffles, was not permitted in the schools, as 'games of chance could never be condoned, not even for the war effort'.[12]

While individual schools were quick off the mark in fundraising in Western Australia, it took until May 1916 before a coordinated effort was made to form the State Schools Patriotic Fund. This was said to have raised about £100,000 by the end of 1919.[13]

Boy Scouts from Queensland helped man Red Cross rooms, military hospitals and the YMCA, and were busy making splints, crutches, walking sticks and sandbags. One troop even wound and packed over 50,000 roller bandages.[14]

His Excellency Governor Sir Henry Galway, inspecting a cadet guard of honour at the Christian Brothers of Wakefield Street School, South Australia, 28 November 1916. R. B. Healey, *The Christian Brothers of Wakefield Street 1878–1978*

TOP
Farewell to 'old boys' off to WWI. R. N. Gibbs, *A History of Prince Alfred College*, Adelaide, p. 162

BOTTOM
Sydney Grammar School Rifle Team, 1916. Courtesy Sydney Grammar School Archivist, Mr G. Cooper

FAREWELL
TO
ST. PETER'S
AND
PRINCE ALFRED COLLEGE
OLD BOYS
LEAVING WITH
AUSTRALIAN EXPEDITIONARY FORCE.
Town Hall, Adelaide, September 10, 1914.

Chairman:
HIS EXCELLENCY THE GOVERNOR, SIR HENRY GALWAY, K.C.M.G.

Joint Committee:

St. Peter's Collegians' Association—
[illegible]

Prince Alfred Old Collegians' Association—
[illegible]

16

Ex-Cadets and Trainees Among the AIF

'... quite a few of us were products of the Compulsory Military Training Scheme, so that we already knew how to shoot, and ride, and live under camp conditions. I feel that those recruits were the backbone of the First AIF in 1914. The men who landed at Gallipoli were not entirely untrained, as they might otherwise have been. It was the leadership and communications that failed there, not the men.'

— Personal quote from the autobiography of Air Marshall Sir George Jones, who first served as a Private in the 9th Light Horse Regiment at Gallipoli in 1915.[1]

Following the declaration of war on Sunday 3 August 1914, Australian Prime Minister Joseph Cook's offer of a first contingent of over 20,000 troops was gratefully accepted by the Imperial Government in London. This contingent of 22,373 officers and men, bound for training in Egypt, sailed in troopships from Albany, Western Australia, on 1 November 1914, under the command of General W. T. Bridges.

It is not known just how many of these soldiers had received either voluntary or compulsory military training as cadets prior to enlistment. As the cadet corps were already attached to the various battalions of the Citizen Army, they went off to war in these units. C. E. W. Bean, Australia's Official Military Historian, claimed 'the Senior Cadets — aged fourteen to seventeen — filled a recognised place in Australia's defence system. The cadet officers and boys who were trained in 1910–14 immediately played a great part in the First A.I.F.'[2]

Former pre-WWI army cadet and AFC pilot, Air Marshall Sir George Jones. Photo courtesy his niece, Ms Brenda Lovell

The revered Australian commander, Brigadier General Harold (Pompey) Elliott, also applauded the value of the compulsory training system to the armed forces: 'It was that very scheme ... that had produced the trained officers and NCOs who turned the men of the 7th into potential soldiers so quickly.'[3]

Private school cadets

What is known is that when the First Expeditionary Force was being enrolled in August 1914, no less than seventy-one ex-cadets from Scotch College in Melbourne were farewelled at a dinner at the college, given by the Old Scotch Collegians' Association, prior to their departure.[4] One former Scotch College recruit, Corporal J. D. Burns, school vice-captain in 1914, later joined some of his schoolmates at Gallipoli. He was killed by a sniper in the trenches there, in September 1915. Burn's legacy, the renowned three-stanza poem 'For England', written while undergoing training at Broadmeadows Army Camp early in 1915, appeared first in the school's magazine, *Collegian*, later that year:

> For England
>
> The bugles of England were blowing o'er the sea,
> As they had called a thousand years, calling now to me;
> They woke me from my dreaming in the dawning of the day,
> The bugles of England — and how could I stay.[5]

At Scotch College in Launceston, Tasmania, the headmaster employed a Boer War veteran, Sergeant-Major William Welsh, to train the school cadet corps. He inspired the boys with his 'war stories and drumming into them the importance of fighting for one's country if called upon', as he had been in South Africa. He also 'showed them how to handle the heavy .303 rifle, to fit and use a bayonet, pitch tents in the bush, march and advance into battle'.[6]

In Melbourne, Wesley College initially contributed 78 recruits, and by March 1915 their number had swelled to 87.[7] On arrival in the Dardanelles, one of their number, Captain Harry Carter, had written a letter to Mr L. A. Adamson, his school headmaster. Adamson read the letter to the school assembly on Empire Day, 14 May 1915:

> Dear Mr A.,
>
> Please accept all good wishes from self and Old Wesley Collegians under my command. We land in an enemy country after midnight, perhaps under fire, have to land in pontoons and small boats, but the boys have 200 rounds of the best each, and are happier than they have ever been since leaving Australia. It is impossible to realise that anything unusual awaits us in a few hours.
>
> On behalf of the boys, again wishing you and the 'school we knew' every success.
>
> I am
> Yours sincerely,
> [signed] Harry Carter
> April 24, 1915, 10 p.m.[8]

Harry Carter survived the Gallipoli campaign, but was killed in action at Glencourse Wood on the Western Front the following year. The whole 1910 Champion Cricket Team enlisted, six gaining commissions, four of whom were later killed. Of the Head of the River crew of 1911, all nine, including the coxswain, enlisted, with four of them deceased by the end of the war.[9] By May 1918, no less than 914 Wesley 'Old Boys', or former students, had enlisted. Of this number, 117 were confirmed dead.[10]

Much school pride was exhibited, with news of King George V presenting a Victoria Cross to Captain Robert Grieve, an ex-Wesley Collegian, who gallantly led his men in disarming a German gun that had caused heavy casualties to his battalion in the trenches.

Old Boy, the Xavier College magazine for ex-pupils, kept count of their number enlisting in the AIF, which by the end of August 1915 totalled just over 300. At the college, military drills and parades increased, with Thursday afternoon drilling now from 3.30pm to

5.30pm. A large map of Europe in the school hall was regularly updated to show the progress of the fighting, and cadets commenced their own 'personal scrapbooks' of the war. Before the end of 1914 more than forty ex-Xavierians had enlisted, one of whom, Captain Joseph Peter Lalor (grandson of Peter Lalor of Eureka fame), died on his first day at Gallipoli from shrapnel wounds, 'surrounded by six Turks shot to death, and a seventh killed by the sword'.[11]

On the night of 10 September 1915, when the next batch of volunteer Old Boys were about to embark for the front, they sang with gusto and some tears one of the school rowing songs, 'Black and Red', but on this occasion with 'a more direct and immediate meaning':

> But raise again o'head
> Our standard Black and Red,
> And if 'tis stained with gore,
> We'll love it all the more,
> As if our ranks we close,
> Once more to face our foes,
> We'll fling them back defiance proud and strong.
> (chorus)
> As we march, boys, march for Kew
> All prepared to die or do ...[12]

At the Annual Speech Night in November 1915, the headmaster of Camberwell Grammar announced proudly that nearly one hundred of their Old Boys had enlisted, with most of them engaged in the Gallipoli campaign. Among them, Lieutenant Alfred Derham had been awarded the Military Cross, and Captain Frank Kerr the Distinguished Service Order. The headmaster could have also added that another of the college Old Boys, Keith Murdoch, war correspondent with the Melbourne *Herald*, had been highly critical of the action in the Dardanelles. He had travelled on to London to voice his concerns, which shortly contributed to the recall of the British Commander, General Sir Ian Hamilton.[13]

The Old Geelong Grammarians boasted that of the 417 of their number who served in the AIF, ten percent of them won the Military Cross for bravery, and that 'every Old Boy who went off to war did so with their blessing'. A high proportion of the boys were natural soldiers;

> ... boys bred in the bush and used to riding, shooting and taking physical risks. Tough characters — made even tougher by boarding-school life — many were fearless, even reckless in the face of danger.[14]

From August 1914 to May 1917, about ten per month of ex-Geelong Grammar boys enlisted 'with an acceleration early in each year as school leavers joined the ranks'. A study of the school rolls between 1908 and 1918 revealed that less than forty boys had not volunteered for military service during this time.[15]

The 1914 firsts football team from Caulfield Grammar presented themselves as a group to the recruiting sergeant near the end of the season. Fourteen of them were enlisted, 'four of whom were subsequently killed'.[16]

Some Senior Cadets from the Melbourne University Regiment would have been present among the fifteen members of the university's VFL team who enlisted at the outbreak of the war, 'and this body was not re-raised post-war, leaving a little-known gap in the roll of today's "industrialised" League'. This group was part of the university's mobilisation of 34 officers and 771 soldiers 'who passed their way up to the front', where 180 of them were later commissioned in the field.[17]

Newington College in Sydney boasted 580 ex-students in the AIF, with 'those who had distinguished themselves at the school the most ready to enlist'. Among these were 13 out of the 17 scholarship holders since 1905, and 72 of 118 prefects, as well as '13 from the 1912 1st XV [rugby] and 10 of the 1914 1st 11 [cricket]'.[18]

Among the 'old and present boys' from Catholic colleges in NSW, St Joseph's College 'led the way with over 400 recruits'; St Ignatius Riverview produced 274; Marist Brothers in Darlinghust 230; and Christian Brothers in Waverley 155, 'including a Victoria Cross winner who enlisted straight from school'. The headmaster of King's School claimed volunteers from 'well nigh all of the Old Boys for a quarter of a century past'. Among the 1714 from Sydney Grammar, one questionable Old Boy, R. E. G. Cunningham, enlisted at the age of fifteen, was repatriated home two-and-a-half years after being badly gassed at Passchendaele.[19]

An early batch of volunteers for the Expeditionary Force, farewelled in the Adelaide Town Hall on 10 September 1914, were a group of thirty-five 'old collegians' from St Peter's College and Prince Alfred College, who were presented to the Governor of South Australia, Sir Henry Gallway, and the two respective headmasters in front of a packed audience from the two school communities. In his keynote speech, which was 'brimful of patriotism and Imperial sentiment', His Excellency the Governor alluded to the glorious deeds of Australian soldiers in the South African War and to Britain's present needs. After this, 'the audience sang the national anthems of England, France and Russia with great feeling, and cheered the Allies, especially Belgium, with echo'.[20]

Prince Alfred College School Cadet team from Adelaide, in Brisbane for the Third Australian Cadet Competitions 1914. R. N. Gibbs, *A History of Prince Alfred College*, p. 161

Government school cadets

By the time World War I began, there were not many government secondary schools in existence, as the vast majority of students left primary school (which then included years 7 and 8) at the age of fourteen years to join the workforce, including those who were to begin apprenticeships. Besides Melbourne High School, then co-educational, the main secondary schools were located in regional Victoria and usually called 'agricultural high schools' at first, like Ballarat, Sale, Warnambool and Wangaratta. Geelong and Bendigo, like Melbourne High, were for training teachers and initially called 'continuation schools'. Similar to the public schools, each of them had compulsory cadet corps from at least 1911.

Ballarat Agricultural High School, with a 'strong militaristic tradition', had many successes in the 'South Street', the Ballarat 18th Brigade, and the Stawell Military Sports competitions in the years 1912 to 1914. At the outbreak of the war, no less than fourteen ex-students were studying at the recently established Duntroon Officers' School in Canberra, 'more boys than at any other school in Victoria'. Some thirty-five percent of the school's eligible students or ex-students responded to the first call for army volunteers, with most serving in the 8th Battalion of the AIF.[21]

Joseph Hocking, Principal of Melbourne High School, wrote personally to the forty Old Boys who were among the first enlisted, expressing 'cordial congratulations from the staff, students, and the Old Boys' and Old Girls' associations', and pledging 'that the school will try to do its duty at home, while you are doing yours abroad'. Early in the conflict, an effort was made by staff and students to send a copy of the school magazine to each Old Boy serving overseas, and was met with a positive response: 'This correspondence allowed the Old Boys at the front to engage in peacetime nostalgia, and it also allowed them to gather information of other school friends killed at the front.'[22]

One of their number, Lieutenant William Dawkins, wrote to his brother Lewis, then a student at Melbourne High, that 'war is a thing that no one should miss'. Less than three weeks after landing at Gallipoli, the twenty-two year old Dawkins was killed by a shell burst.[23]

A student at Wollongong High School, greatly concerned by the number of his ex-classmates on the Gallipoli casualty list, wrote: '... my class at school contained 44 pupils. More than half of them went away to war — 11 were killed and many wounded.'[24]

In the late 1960s, Melbourne military historians L. L. Robson and J. Dawes surveyed over two hundred veterans who were encouraged to write about their experiences in World War I, for their book *Citizen to Soldier*, published in 1977. As many of the correspondents asked that their accounts be used anonymously, the authors decided not to quote names after the responses, instead listing the names of all contributors in the appendix. A number of the veterans included anecdotes of their cadet training prior to service in the AIF. In answer to the question 'Why did you enlist?' some examples follow:

> I first became interested in the east Brisbane State School cadets as a pupil ... I was between 10 and 12 years old. I well remember my very first uniform, the trousers being about 2 inches too long, which was the cause of much merriment.

> Boys 14 to 18 had to serve as Senior Cadets ... the training time was 2 nights a week, and one half day each two weeks. This training was the making of our bunch. It took us off the streets and with the help of our instructors and officers we formed a rifle club, cricket and football teams. I can safely say that the majority of the A.I.F. had nearly four years training before they went into action. That is what made them superb fighting men.

> For years I had been indoctrinated in military matters as well as the glories of the Empire and an intense loyalty to the crown.[25]

In New South Wales, Old Boys from the prestigious Fort Street High School could be seen dressed in uniform, visiting their old school before leaving for the war. Some of the current senior students also enlisted, such as cadet Lieutenant Carl Ferns, who left on the troopship HMAS *Berrini* to take over German New Guinea in September 1914.[26] At the conclusion of the 1915 school year, six students 'volunteered from the classroom'[27], reminiscent of the schoolroom scene at the beginning of Erich Maria Remarque's *All Quiet on the Western Front.*

Numerous old Fortonians wrote to their beloved headmaster H. J. Kilgour from the battlefield about meeting up with ex-school chums, as Gunner Stokes reflected: 'Bill Lyon and myself were mentioning the Old Boys we have met here and came to the conclusion that Fort Street was doing all the fighting for England.'[28]

As Trooper L. Sandels wrote to Kilgour in 1915:

> I met so many old schoolmates over this way … I met one (Dinning) the other day while watering my horse at a trough. A new captain came to our unit, and I at once recognised him as a lad who once sat near me while Mr Selle tried to drum the meaning of tangents and co-tangents into us … and I am sorry to say that another lad I have chased around the school's Morton bay fig trees years ago, died in my arms at our clearing station.[29]

17

Early Reactions in New Zealand

New Zealand's regular army was listed as having around 66,000 men in 1914, about half of them aged 15 to 18 years, being trained under the existing compulsory 'Territorial' system. By Christmas 1914, an additional 11,800 volunteers had been mobilised around the country, and sent to Wellington and Featherston in the North Island for training, with the first batch of 8000 heading to Egypt for further training in February 1915. The Territorials were expected to supply 8000 to 10,000 men each year of the war to the New Zealand Military Forces, 'which was in turn supplied by the graduating Senior Cadets (about 8000 a year)', the remainder coming from volunteers of all ages, until late 1916 when adult conscription came into being.[1]

> The strain placed upon the Territorial and cadet forces was considerable. Not only were these forces unexpectedly called upon to supply large numbers of officers and other ranks for immediate service abroad, but they were continually drained throughout the war of a large number of trained officers and non-commissioned officers for instructional and administrative duties in the Expeditionary Force training camps.[2]

One of the first to enlist from Maryborough High School was Captain J. H. Goulding, the school's much loved commanding officer of the cadet corps. Many of the teachers and a large number of past and present pupils were at the station to see him off, as later recounted in the school magazine *Marlburnian*: 'With cheers from the pupils and yet three more from the "old pupils", the train moved off, our Captain, a worthy soldier and an honoured man, standing at the salute. We wish him Godspeed and a safe return.'[3]

Barely six months later, Captain Goulding was killed in action at Gallipoli, with the school principal calling a special assembly to announce the sad news, and to convey their sympathy to his widow and her three children. No doubt inspired by this loss, a further 181 Old Boys from this school went on to serve in the New Zealand armed forces in World War I.[4]

At Hastings High School 'the outbreak of World War I was met with excitement, some trepidation and great confidence'. Barely ten years old, the school had just 176 Old Boys, but by the end of the war, 92 (52 percent) had served overseas, and 16 of them had been killed.[5]

The *Collegian* (a publication of Wanganui Collegiate School) of April 1915 reported that about one hundred Old Boys of the college had already enlisted, with most of them engaged in advanced military training in Egypt. They were no doubt preparing for the coming Anzac landing in the Dardanelles. The magazine also produced a photograph of 48 of them and a master at a dinner in Cairo. Of this group, 41 were to land on the Gallipoli Peninsula, with 13 of them killed, including the master; 'over the whole Gallipoli campaign, 33 Old Boys are known to have died'.[6]

Wanganui Collegiate School, New Zealand, 'old boys' dinner at the Continental Hotel, Cairo, 9 January 1915. Bruce Hamilton, *Never a Footstep Back: A History of Wanganui Collegiate School 1854–2003*, 2003, p. 175

18

Military Propaganda in the Schools

School texts

In Victoria, the revised Course of Study in 1902 had expanded the curriculum from the traditional three R's to include the new subjects of history, geography, nature study, health, physical education and music. While most of the topics for history were centred around events and people in Great Britain, an Australian supplement was gradually included several years later.[1] Texts introduced for the teaching of history in Australian schools in the early twentieth century included the *Highroads of History* series, published in London by Thomas Nelson and Sons. The sixth book of this series told of the British Army putting down republican rebellions in Ireland, for example 'The Siege of Londonderry', with 'one thousand five hundred Irish being killed, and five hundred drowned in Lough Erne, into which they were driven'.[2] Also in a similar vein was the brutal account of 'The Battle of the Boyne and Afterwards',[3] the 'Crimean War Parts I & II', and 'The Indian Mutiny':

> sacred to the perpetual memory of a great company of Christian People, chiefly women and children who were cruelly massacred by the followers of Nana Dhoomdopunt of Bithwoor, and cast into the well below, the dying with the dead, on July 15th, 1857.[4]

Much of the morality, health and hygiene, history, civics and geography that was taught in schools came from the graded reading texts in common use. *The Royal Readers* publication by Nelson in the late 1890s is one such example. There is a gruesome poem called 'Heroism' in the fifth book, which leaves little to the imagination:

> They never fail who die
> In a great cause: the block may soak their gore;
> Their heads may sodden in the sun; their limbs
> Be strung to city gates and castle walls —
> But still their spirit walks abroad.[5]

The 'Battle of Trafalgar, and Death of Nelson' covered four pages, followed by Thomas Campbell's poem 'Ye Mariners of England'. Then there was Tennyson's rousing 'The Charge of the Light Brigade', with:

> Half a league, half a league,
> Half a league onward,
> All in the valley of Death
> Rode the Six Hundred

***The School Paper* (pre-war)**

Undoubtedly the most effective means of indoctrinating children in military matters was through the monthly school journals, published by the respective state education departments, also used in independent and some Catholic schools.[6] These contained material for oral reading, discussion and comprehension purposes. In addition, *The School Paper* was commonly read by parents and other family members in the home.[7]

Usually the journals were grouped according to age and reading ability, and available in grades 3 and 4 (ages 9 and 10 approx.), grades 5 and 6 (ages 11 and 12 approx.) and grades 7 and 8 (ages 13 and 14 approx.). Jointly published in Victoria, Tasmania and Western Australia, they were known as *The School Paper*, in New South Wales they were

The School Magazine, in South Australia *The Children's Hour*, and in New Zealand *The School Journal*. In most cases, they were usually sold at local newsagents for the cost of around one penny. In some states, Catholic Schools published their own material, such as in New South Wales which had *The Catholic School Paper*, for a time edited by His Grace The Archbishop of Sydney.

Most children waited eagerly to purchase their copies, which usually were available on or near the first day of each month, because they enjoyed reading stories, poems and songs about nature study, history, special events like Empire Day and Christmas, and well-known children's stories and fables. Some teachers also used these printed materials for teaching spelling, dictation and grammar, along with other texts.

One of the earliest of the school journals, Victoria's *The School Paper*, was first published in February 1896, with an initial print run of 40,000 copies per month. Ten years later, the circulation was between 145,000 and 150,000 per month.[8]

Examples of patriotic themes in some of the early editions of *The School Paper* prior to the 1910 compulsory legislation include 'Cadet Encampment of the Public and Private Schools of Geelong and Melbourne', which reported on a four-day camp for the 2nd Battalion Cadets from eight schools. This ran from Thursday October 18 to Monday October 22 in 1900, where a total of '24 officers and 380 rank and file' were in attendance under the command of Major-General Downes. Photographs of cadets in tents and on parade grounds were included.[9] A similar feature was included a year later, under the banner of 'Secondary School Cadets at Langwarrin', where units from Wesley College, Geelong College and Carlton College were engaged in a 'sham fight' with Melbourne, Hawthorn and Brighton Grammar Schools.[10]

The article 'Discipline' appeared in August 1902, telling of the sinking of the barque *Birkenhead* that was carrying British soldiers and their families to Cape Colony in South Africa, in 1852. As there were only enough lifeboats for the women and children, the soldiers and crew 'stood together on deck in their ranks, shoulder to shoulder, and waited for an almost certain death'. Later Queen Victoria had a monument erected in their memory, which lauded their 'heroic constancy and unbroken discipline'.[11]

The 'British Empire' featured in 1904, with a world map 'showing the British Possessions', from Canada across the Atlantic, Indian and Pacific Oceans to New Zealand and Fiji.[12]

A glaring example of British elitist and racial superiority towards many of its European neighbours appeared in the August 1904 edition of *The School Paper* for grades 5 and 6, reprinted for 'the boys in elementary schools in Great Britain and good reading for the young subjects of King Edward VII the world over':

> Now, the people who live in France, and Russia and in Germany, and in Italy and Austria do not differ from us *only* because they speak other languages, but in many ways besides. To begin with, they are not really so free as we are. They cannot even say what they like, as we can. The mass of the people in those countries are very much worse off than most of the people here … they work for longer hours and for less wages than we do, and besides this they are much worse fed, and they live in much worse houses.[13]

'Young subjects of King Edward VII', in the same article, are next enlightened about the military differences between Britain and the aforementioned nations, a prejudice that would need to be abandoned in 1916 with the introduction of military conscription in Britain:

> Then there is another great evil from which they have to suffer, and that is that nearly all the men in Europe have to serve two or three years in the army, whether they like it or not … But you see all English soldiers enter the army of their own accord, because they wish to do so … and that makes an enormous difference.[14]

A three-stanza poem 'The Call to Serve' appeared on the front cover of the August 1910 *School Paper*, complemented by a picture of 'a young knight', complete with armour and lance. The closing lines of the poem are a clear call for all young men to be ready to fight for their country, at any time:

> Rise for the day is passing,
> The sound that you scarcely hear,
> Is the enemy marching to battle —
> Rise, for the foe is here.[15]

Other examples printed around that time include 'How the Castle was Taken' (the recapture of Edinburgh Castle by the highlanders under Sir Thomas Randolph),[16] a poem, 'Retreat of the French Army from Moscow' (the winter defeat of Napoleon by the Russian army)[17] and 'An Empire Catechism', listing sixteen questions and answers about the British Empire, the answers of which pupils in grades 5 and 6 were expected to memorise as one of their normal 'wrote learning' exercises.

No doubt as inspiration for boys in grades 5 and 6 to join a cadet rifle squad, the May edition for 1912 featured a photographic portrait of the victorious Melbourne High School, with the coveted *Herald and Weekly Times* shield under the banner of 'A Successful Rifle Team'.[18] Melbourne High got another mention in February of that year, when J Company of the 64th Battalion came in second to Newington College (NSW) in the interstate rifle shooting competition held in Sydney. The article is accompanied by a photograph of J Company under the caption 'Cadets from the Melbourne High School Marching in Sydney'.[19]

Several months into 1913, a photograph of the arrival of a new Australian warship from Britain featured on the cover of the May *School Paper* for grades 7 and 8. Headlined 'The Coming of H.M.A.S. Melbourne', it is followed by an article on the Royal Australian Navy, which 'now boasts 8 battle cruisers, 10 protected cruisers, 18 destroyers (carrying torpedoes), 12 submarines, 3 depot ships and one repair ship.'[20]

A search through the pre-World War I Victorian *School Papers* shows that the levels of patriotic/militaristic articles per issue would be around 15 to 20 percent, except for the month of May (80 to 90 percent) after 1905, when the annual Empire Day celebrations were inaugurated.

The war-time Victorian *School Paper* and the South Australian *Children's Hour*

The first issue of *The School Paper* for grades 7 and 8, after war was declared in August 1914, was released on September 1, less than three weeks after the declaration. The entire issue of fifteen pages was devoted to 'war' material, from the front cover portraying a photograph of King George V with an extract of his 'Britain at War' speech, to the last page where the usual song appeared, this time the rousing 'Ye Mariners of England' prefaced by 'The King's Speech to the Fleet'. The remaining pages included the poem 'The Call', alongside a photo of the Australian Mounted Cadets parading in London.

Other features covered 'The Immediate Causes of the War', which said that 'the neutrality of Belgium was violated by the entry of German troops into her territory'; the William Wordsworth poem 'British Freedom'; five pages of 'What Are We Fighting For?', set among photos of British generals like Earl Kitchener, Sir John French and Brigadier-General Bridges, Commander of the Australian Expeditionary Force; and a full page map showing 'The Theatre of War in Western Europe'.[21]

Unlike its Victorian counterpart, South Australia's *Children's Hour* took a more low-key approach to reporting war articles within its pages, particularly early in the war. The December 1914 issue did contain a poem, 'The Sentry', accompanied by a photograph of an Australian soldier in full battle kit, challenging 'Halt! Who goes there?'[22] By June 1914, a map of Turkey and surrounding countries appeared, to indicate the beginning of the Allies Gallipoli Campaign, along with a posed photograph of a detachment of 'Turkish Infantry who are Opposing the Australians at the Dardanelles'.[23]

The October copy of *The School Paper* was more blatantly patriotic, the front cover leading with the poem 'To the Helpers at Home' and a picture of 'state school children making garments for the troops', then 'Victoria's Contingent at Langwarrin Camp', set among photographs of troops drilling on the parade ground, and a Light Horse Regiment preparing to charge in line. The double page 'A Send Off to Teachers', together with an image of said teachers and their families dining at the Melbourne Athenaeum, applauded the forty-seven Victorian State School staff 'among those who have been chosen to go to the war'. This included farewell speeches given by no less than the Premier of Victoria Sir Alexander Peacock, the Minister of Public Instruction Thomas Livingstone, and the Director of Education Mr Frank Tate. The song to be learnt in this issue was, understandably, 'Red, White and Blue'.[24]

With the war continuing into 1915, there were signs of strengthening the military propaganda, the call to active service for youths (there were to be many lads under the age of eighteen who volunteered illegally) and teachers of military age, in the pages of *The School Papers* and their equivalents, in both Victoria and the other states of Australia, and in New Zealand. This was particularly noticeable in Victoria during the months of April to September of that year. For instance, in April grades 7 and 8 pupils could read about the trench warfare, beginning on the Western Front. 'In the Trenches' showed a detailed sketch of the zig-zaging lines of dugouts, showing the opposing enemy and Allied Forces, with 'no-man's-land' in between: 'In the last two months the Germans have lost 40,000 men along that stretch of front on which you are looking.'[25] Not surprisingly, there was no mention of Allied casualties during this period.

Under 'A Night Attack', the pupils could read about British troops advancing and clearing the enemy from their line of trenches. There is even a sketch of an Allied soldier throwing a hand grenade into a

German dugout, with the caption 'Trench Warfare: Throwing Hand Grenades. (The hand grenade is a small shell with a rope tail. It can be thrown from 40 to 50 yards.)' Also in this issue, under the banner 'Volunteers', there is a photo of a crowd of men outside a recruiting office, jostling each other in an attempt to enlist, with the caption 'Volunteers Enlisting, Victoria'.[26]

However, the increasing militancy found in the pages of *The School Paper* did not go unchallenged, for on 31 August 1915 its Editor, Charles Long, faced a deputation of twelve concerned citizens pleading that its content should be 'less warlike'. The members of the deputation included Mr W. Ross of the Socialist Party; Miss Story of the Australian Church; Miss Moore and Miss Baker of the sisterhood of peace; Mr Dillon and Mr Colville of the Peace Society; and Mrs Allen, a Quaker. Citing remarks like 'the young people are apt to be carried away by the glamour and seeming glory of war', and 'certain articles gave children the impression they should side with their country whether it was fighting in a just cause or not', each group representative stated his or her objection.[27] Although Long may have listened patiently to their criticism, there is little evidence to suggest it made any impact on the flow of propaganda.

By November 1915, for instance, there were stories appearing of Australian troops fighting at Gallipoli. An eye-catching headline 'The Good Samaritan of the Dardanelles' (with a photo of Private John Simpson and another of a wounded Australian soldier astride Simpson's donkey) is followed by a two-page description of the pair, and their lifesaving efforts:

> They were a quaint couple. The man was a six-foot Australian, hard-bitten and active. His gaunt profile spoke of wide experience, of hard struggle in rough places. The donkey was a little mouse-coloured animal, no taller than a Newfoundland dog. His master called him Abdul … There was a hush through the Australian

> trenches that night, when the news went round that the man with the Donkey had 'got it'. There was a reverent silence, too, when they buried him next day.[28]

The last edition of *The School Paper* for 1915 showed a map of the Dardanelles, with Australian positions at places like Anzac Cove, Lone Pine and Suvla Bay. Under the headline 'The Lone Pine Charge' it mentioned 'the many incidents of splendid bravery and gallant effort in which Australian troops have had a part since the memorable landing at Gaba Tepe on the 25th of April'.[29]

Occasionally, there were references to patriotism and the Great War in the pages of even the grades 3 and 4 *School Papers*. In May 1916 (the Empire Day edition), children were alerted to the bravery of Lord Nelson fighting Napoleon's navy at Waterloo, in an article titled 'Admiral Nelson and Duty' and a picture of his ship, HMS *Victory*. As with the two more senior levels of *The School Paper*, these younger pupils were encouraged to help in 'The War Effort' by making or raising money for certain comforts for the soldiers, such as gloves, scarves, balaclavas, or contributing to provide bandages or medicines for wounded Australian soldiers. Hence a section appears towards the back of each issue headed 'Aid in Wartime'.[30]

With the weary conflict dragging on into 1917, a regular feature in the grades 7 and 8 *School Paper* was 'Progress in the War', which gave a monthly update of the progress of the fighting on the Western and Eastern Fronts, usually with accounts of the Allied advances being made, and (like the Australian press in general) little mention of their retreats or the horrific casualties inflicted:

> The West Front — Several successful offences have been launched by Sir Douglas Haig in the neighbourhood of Ypres. Passchendaele, an important point on a ridge, was taken by assault, the Canadians showing special gallantry. The French have forced back the invaders from the Chemin des Dames.[31]

Sometimes in the *Children's Hour*, photographs of the war would suddenly appear in the midst of an unrelated article. For example, there appears the exquisite medieval 'The Cloth Hall of Ypres' and two pages later 'The Ruined Cloth Hall of Ypres', with a caption '... the Germans savagely bombarded Ypres and made the noble Cloth Hall a heap of smoldering ruins.'[32] Then, in December 1918, a photograph of a child, Mary Hefferman from Hilltown, New Zealand, appears with the caption 'She has knitted 15 pairs of socks and 10 facewashers for the soldiers' in the middle of a narrative, 'The Duck-billed Platypus'. [33]

A slightly more militant approach was evident around this time in the *Children's Hour*, in the grades 7 and 8 edition in February 1917, with an attempt to describe 'The Tanks on the Western Front': 'The Tank is a land Dreadnought; it is a land submarine; it is a caterpillar; it is a moving fort; it is a great prehistoric toad come to life in armour to spit fire; it is the ancient Jabberwock.'[34]

Then in May 1917, 'The Empire Number' of *Children's Hour*, again for grades 7 and 8, the front page article 'Some Heroes of Anzac' described the landing at Anzac Cove, and indicated that the term 'Anzac' was coined by the then British commander of the Australian and New Zealand forces, General Birdwood, 'from the initial letters of the phrase Australian and New Zealand Army Corps'.[35]

'The Motherland in Relation to the War in Australia' was the lead article in the May 1917 issue of *The School Paper* for grades 7 and 8, much of which related to a 'British Empire' theme. It showed how dependent Australia and other Empire countries were on British armaments. An accompanying photo showed a British sailor amidst two naval shells, one of which was 'a 16 in. capped armour piercing shell — cost £100.12.00' above the caption 'Shells for Some of Britain's Big Guns'.[36] On a lighter note, the December (Christmas) edition for grades 5 and 6 in 1917 carried 'A Fairy Story for Little Children whose Daddies are at the War'.[37]

The final year of the Great War, 1918, saw an increase in war propaganda in the schools, with a notable increase in exploits of the AIF; the April, May and June *School Papers* gave a virtual 100 percent coverage. This was not surprising, given the failure of the second referendum on 'compulsory military service' the year before, and the extreme shortage of new volunteers for the savage fighting and huge casualties on the Western Front. With the recent German advances, the conflict seemed to show no sign of ending, so the Australian Government's efforts to 'rally the flag' in the community only intensified.

A poem of four verses by British author Lawrence Binyon, the opening lines of which would become legendry thereafter, entitled 'For the Fallen', appeared on the first page of the grades 5 and 6 *School Paper* for the month of April:

> They shall not grow old, as we that are left grow old;
> Age shall not weary them, nor the years condemn.
> At the going down of the sun and in the morning,
> We will remember them.[38]

April, being the 'Anzac' edition, featured the four-page 'The Landing at Anzac: Sunday 25th April, 1915', with the text 'all that day and all through the night the awful din continued. Water was scarce; wounded and dying men were all around us ...'[39] Then followed another four-page account of 'After the Landing'. Leisure time at Gallipoli was depicted in an image of our soldiers 'Bathing at Anzac Cove' under the banner 'The Light Side of the Life at Anzac':

> And we went swimming down at the beach, just as if it had been Manly or Coogee, only it was more exciting. Shells took the place of sharks. Instead of the sudden cry one would sometimes hear at manly or Coogee of 'ware shark' it was 'ware shell'. The Turks are not the surfers that the Australians are.[40]

The cover of the May issue that year showed a photograph of King George V, in Hyde Park, London, presenting a Victoria Cross to an invalid Australian soldier, Private Thomas Hughes. The accompanying poem 'The Order of Valour' was written by Sir Edwin Arnold, not long after Queen Victoria commissioned the medal for casting. The following lines are from the second stanza:

> Let there be made a cross of bronze;
> And grave thereon my queenly crest,
> Write VALOUR on its haughty scroll,
> And hang it on his breast.[41]

A second poem, 'Faithful Unto Death', commemorated another VC winner, this time a sixteen-year-old British naval rating, John Travers Cornwell, who was killed on board HMS *Chester* in the Battle of Jutland in 1916:

> There was his duty to be done —
> And he did it.
> No thought of glory to be won;
> There was his duty to be done —
> And he did it.[42]

Special features appeared in *The School Paper* celebrating the end of the war in the December 1918 issues. Under 'The Path to Victory', it was plain to see the relief shown after four years of writing about such long, devastating and wearisome warfare: 'The signing of the Armistice marks the most sanguine struggle that modern history records ... the war has taught us what courage, devotion, discipline and above all, a sense of comradeship can do for men.'

In the midst of the above text was a photograph of the jubilant crowds in the city streets, with the caption 'Crowds outside the Melbourne Town Hall on November 12th, 1918'.[43]

BRAVE DEEDS AT GALLIPOLI.

Con'voy, train of wagons, or the like, employed in the transportation of munitions of war, clothing, &c.

Des-ti-na'tion, place set for the end of a journey.

Con-spic'u-ous, distinguished; readily seen.

Pos-ter'i-ty, one's descendants.

Vol-un-teered', entered into any service of one's own free will.

I'so-lat-ed (the "i" as in *ice*) or **is'o-lat-ed** (the "i" as in *miss*; the "a" as in *mate*), placed in a lonely position; separated from others.

Sig'nal-ling, making known by means of signals.

Lions of war, our noblest and our best,
Who won the desperate beach and death lashed crest,
And looked on Fate's most awful face unhid;
Poorly our praise may match the thing you did,
Who, from those ultimate isles and warless seas,
Bade Hellespont[1] *and Golden Chersonese*[2]
Wake from their dream and perished glory, and thrill
To know the heart of valor flaming still.

—Chris. Brennan.

[During the eight months the Australasians were on the Gallipoli Peninsula, deeds of heroism, almost innumerable, were performed, but, of very many of them, there is, unfortunately, no record. The following are four that have been rescued from oblivion:—]

1. The important duty that falls to the lot of the Army Service Corps is to keep up a constant stream of supplies for the men in the firing-line. This duty at Gallipoli was a very dangerous one, for the supplies were landed on the beach under a constant fire from the enemy's guns.

From The Times History and Encyclopedia of the War.]

Throwing a Bomb.

2. On the 4th of August, 1915, Driver Farlow, of the 4th Infantry Brigade Train of the A.I.F., was placed in charge of a convoy of twenty-five mules to carry supplies to the trenches. The convoy came under very heavy shrapnel fire; several of the native drivers were hit, and the rest were soon in a state of panic.

3. To make matters worse, the soldier in charge of another convoy had been wounded, and the mules scattered. Driver Farlow collected the scattered mules, took charge of both convoys, and drove them safely to

The School Paper, Victoria, April 1916, p. 34

A KIND-HEARTED TURK.

1. People used to tell us that the Turks were cruel, and that they tortured the wounded; but no Australian who was at Anzac believes that now.

2. I might tell you of an experience we had with one. He was in the trenches opposite us at Russell's Top, and we named him Fatty Burns. He was always popping up his head and getting fired at. Then, he would signal a miss, and burst into a fit of laughter. We could hear him quite plainly, for the trenches were only twenty-five yards apart.

3. At last, the fellows gave up shooting at him. "It is only Fatty Burns," they used to say. We got to look for his cheerful grin; and, sometimes, we used to fire just to hear him laugh.

4. Early one morning, we made a bit of a demonstration, and left two of our men wounded out on an open place between the trenches. No one could go to them; and there they lay in the burning sun. Presently, some one said, "Here comes Fatty Burns." The old fellow put his head and shoulders out of the trench, and salaamed like a Cairo shopkeeper. We were all struck dumb. Next, he climbed out of the trench (a bold thing to do), and walked over to our wounded comrades. A dozen rifles were covering him, as, no doubt, he was aware; but he took his time.

5. We watched him go over to the two men, lift up their heads, and give them a drink of water each. He tried to make them comfortable, with us looking on, hardly able to believe our eyes. Then, he strolled back to his trench, quite unconcerned. We gave him a cheer. That's not all. Just before dusk, he came out again, and dragged both men over to a spot near a bit of cover, so that we could get them in when darkness came. Here was one Turk, at any rate, who wasn't cruel.

[From "*The Times History and Encyclopædia of the War*.]

AN AUSTRALIAN GIVING A TURK A DRINK.

(The story tells of the sympathy of a Turk for one who is suffering: the picture shows a similar feeling on the part of an Australian.)

6. We always had too much bully beef; and, before leaving the firing line, we used to dispose of the surplus, and leave the trench in good order for those who were to relieve us. This time, we made up our minds to throw the beef—there were three four-pound tins of it—across to Fatty Burns. We did, and there was a terrible hullabaloo when the tins landed. I suppose the Turks thought they were a new kind of bomb. But, an hour or so later, a package of fine dates was thrown into our trench. We credited the gift to Fatty. Some one said the dates might be poisoned, but we risked that and enjoyed them.

—From *Glorious Deeds of Australasians*, by E. C. Buley.

The School Paper, Victoria, grades 5 and 6, April 1916

* HOW A VICTORIAN WON THE VICTORIA CROSS.

1. Captain Robert Cuthbert Grieve,[1] of the 37th Battalion, A.I.F., won his Victoria Cross during an attack on the German third-line system, on the 7th of June, 1917, at Messines.[2] He led his company forward under very heavy machine-gun fire and shell fire, which inflicted many casualties. During the whole of the advance, he moved constantly up and down the leading line, reassuring and cheering the men.

2. After passing the enemy's second system of trenches, the company came under an even more intense fire from two machine-guns situated in a concrete building on the right front of the advancing line. All the officers, with the exception of Captain Grieve, had fallen or been wounded, a considerable portion of the company was put out of action, and the whole attack was temporarily checked.

By permission, from the original picture by Mr. H. M. Rolland.]
Captain Grieve bombing the "Pill-box."

3. Captain Grieve gave orders for the company to push on, and dashed off himself towards the spot from which the machine-gun fire was coming. He had to cover about fifty yards of open ground under the direct observation of the enemy, who fired on him continuously, but without success.

4. Going from shell-hole to shell-hole, he worked up till he was within thirty yards of the "pill-box," and then aimed four grenades at the small openings through which the machine-guns were firing. He was successful in getting two of the grenades through, and then rushed up to a doorway at the side, from which he silenced the two machine-guns. Searching round the building to see if any German was in hiding, he suddenly came under severe fire from a neighboring hedge, where he located two additional machine-guns. From behind the building, he bombed these guns, silenced them, and then rejoined his company.

5. "With characteristic coolness and ability," as stated by the Official Chronicler, "he reorganized his men and entered the German trenches at

The School Paper, Victoria, grades 7 and 8, November 1917

waited under cover, while the man crawled through the thick scrub until he got to within the desired distance. Then, a lightning dash, and he had the wounded man on his back, and was making for cover again. In those fierce seconds, he always seemed to bear a charmed life. Once in cover, he tended his charge with quick, skilful movements. (" He had hands like a woman's," said one who thinks he owes his

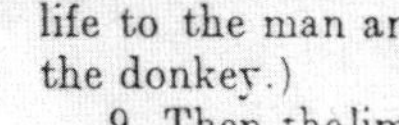

life to the man and the donkey.)

9. Then, the limp form was balanced across the back of the patient animal, and, with a slap on its back and the Arab donkey-boy's cry of "Gee;" the man started off for the beach, the donkey trotting unruffled by his side.

From an enlargement of a kodak photo. kindly lent by the Kodak Ld., Melbourne.]

BRINGING IN THE WOUNDED.

A snapshot of Private Simpson taken on the battle-field.

10. For a month and more, they continued their work. No one kept count of the number of wounded men they brought back from the firing line. One morning, the dressers at the station near the dangerous turn in the valley called "The Pump" saw them go past, and shouted a warning to the man.

11. The Turks up on Dead Man's Ridge were very busy that day; moreover, a machine gun was turned on a dangerous part of the valley path. The man replied to the warning with a wave of his hand.

12. Later, he was seen returning, he himself carrying one wounded man, and the donkey laden with another. As they reached the dangerous turn, the machine gun rattled out, and the man fell with a bullet through his heart. The donkey walked unscathed into safety.

13. There was a hush through the Australian trenches that night, when the news went round that the Man with the Donkey had "got it." There was a reverent silence, too, when they buried him next day.

14. His grave bears the brief inscription :—

"Sacred to the memory of Private W. Simpson, of the Third Field Ambulance, Queensland."

But, if you wish an Australian to tell you his story, you must ask for the Man with the Donkey. —From *The Herald*, Melbourne.

Simpson and his Donkey at Gallipoli, *The School Paper*, Victoria, November 1915, p. 148

Children's Hour

FOR READING AND RECREATION

[REGISTERED AT THE GENERAL POST OFFICE, ADELAIDE, FOR TRANSMISSION BY POST AS A NEWSPAPER.]

VOL. XV., No. 166.] GRADES III. & IV. [FEBRUARY, 1916.

FAIR SOLDIERS OF THE EMPIRE. [Photo. A. C

Girls at Paskeville School. Teacher—Mr. A. Canning.

Price ½d.]

The Children's Hour, South Australia, grades 3 and 4, February 1916, p. 1

The New Zealand *School Journal*

Like its counterparts for students in Australia, the New Zealand *School Journal*, established in 1907, was subjected to 'a heavy barrage of Imperialist propaganda'. Initially, the Journal was distributed free to public schools wishing to use it, and at low cost to other school systems. Made compulsory in public schools in 1914, the Journal was used as a teaching tool for at least a half hour each day for reading comprehension, spoken English and spelling, and 'on average about thirty percent of its space was devoted to Imperial, military and other "patriotic" topics'. Because it was often used for homework purposes, the Journal had a wider exposure.[44] It expounded on the nature of New Zealand's place in the world within the 'family of Empire', particularly in the Empire Day editions in May each year: 'The little mother and all her big children we call the Empire, and we keep up Empire Day just as we might keep up our mother's birthday in the family, to show that we are still her loving children.'[45]

With the approach of 1914, there was no inkling of the impending war until the September issue of the Journal. But there was mention of the Balkan Wars of 1912 to 1913 in the February 1914 publication, which it described as 'one of the most wicked wars in history — wicked because it was unnecessary'.[46]

Soon after the outbreak of the war in September 1914, New Zealand's Major-General Alexander Godley reminded the first batch of departing troops that 'much of what they had learned in school cricket and football applied equally well to soldiering'.[47]

The April 1915 edition of the *School Journal* for grades 5 and 6 opened with the rallying poem 'Admirals All', and produced a five-page article 'Our First Sea Fight' on the battle between HMAS *Sydney* and the German cruiser *Emden*.[48] Not to be outdone, the accompanying grades 3 and 4 edition of that date led with the poem 'The Union Jack' by Edward Shirley, followed by an intense five-page prose on 'The Story of the Union Jack', then 'Crossing the Line', a letter from a New Zealand soldier on board a troopship:

> My Dear Mavis,
>
> I just want to tell you something good. Last night the man who was on the look-out blew his whistle, and then called to the captain that Father Neptune was coming aboard in the morning ...[49]

July that year featured an eight-page account of how wounded New Zealand soldiers were cared for on the battlefield, entitled 'The Care of the Sick and Wounded', complete with photographs and sketches of stretcher-bearers, an ambulance dog, motor ambulance and a Red Cross hospital ship.[50]

During the Gallipoli campaign in 1915, the Journal was reporting the events much like those to be found in the popular press, loudly praising the feats and heroism of the Anzacs, who, in the words of Sir Ian Hamilton, 'gloriously upheld the finest traditions of our race during this struggle'.[51] In 'The Dardanelles' in April 1915, grades 5 and 6 students were subject to optimistic reports of the landing at Anzac Cove, along with a local map of the area: 'Although the Allied fleet is large, its task is no easy one, yet at the time of writing it has met with wonderful success.'[52]

'Christmas and the War' featured in the November 1915 issue for grades 5 and 6, which outlined in graphic detail the incredible story of the Christmas truce on the battlefield in France on Christmas Day in 1914, between the Allies and the German troops. Strangely, there was to be no corresponding article on this topic in the wartime Australian school journals and papers. The concluding paragraph bemoaned the fact that there would be no end in sight for the war at Christmas 1915 (and as we now know there were to be no repeat Christmas truces for the duration of the war):

> Unhappily, there is no likelihood that the war will be over this year (1915), but it is to be hoped that there will be peace and goodwill in the trenches for at least one day in the year, and that greetings less deadly than shrapnel will be exchanged between the contending armies.[53]

Also featured in this Journal was a front page portrait of the French Marshall Foch, commander of the Allied Forces in Europe. The concluding article, 'A Brave Indian Soldier', told the story of how Lieutenant Gobind Singh won the Victoria Cross by single-handedly charging on his horse and demolishing a German machine-gun post:

> Mounted on his charge, he galloped at full speed into 'No Man's Land', and made straight for his objective. The German machine guns riddled his horse's body, and it fell under him, but he escaped unhurt, and completed on foot the remaining 600 yards of his journey.[54]

174 THE SCHOOL JOURNAL. [PART III.

all sides, a wounded man must needs attend to his injuries as best he can.

Many people think that because members of the field ambulance corps are regarded as neutrals, and may not be deliberately fired upon, they run no risk in carrying out their work, but this is by no means the case. The stretcher-bearers and field doctors must lose no time in bringing aid to the fallen. To find the

The "Graphic."]
COLLECTING THE WOUNDED UNDER FIRE.

JULY, 1915.] THE SCHOOL JOURNAL. 175

In carrying out their work the field ambulance is greatly assisted by ambulance dogs. Our armies are now provided with packs of trained dogs, which rush hither and thither about the battlefield searching for the wounded. At night the dogs are especially useful. At a signal from his master a dog will rush off into the darkness, the little bell tied round his neck faintly tinkling as he runs this way and that in his search. Then the tinkling suddenly ceases, and a low whine is heard. The stretcher-bearer, knowing that a fallen soldier has been found, hastens to his assistance.

"London" Magazine.]
AN AMBULANCE DOG.

'The Care of the Sick and Wounded', *The School Journal*, New Zealand, grades 5 and 6, July 1915, p. 174–175

Nov., 1915.] THE SCHOOL JOURNAL. 293

singing "God Save the King," to which our men replied by singing "The Watch on the Rhine." Here is an account of last Christmas in the trenches, written by a soldier to his mother in Auckland:

The "Illustrated London News."]

The Light of Truce.

"I suppose that I have spent the most unique Christmas that I ever shall spend or want to spend. On marching up to relieve the Dublins on Christmas Eve we noticed that there was little, if any, firing going on. When we got there they said the Germans wanted to have a 'local peace.'

'Christmas and the War', *The School Journal,* New Zealand, grades 5 and 6, November 1915, p. 293

Popular leisure reading about the war

Besides the daily newspaper articles about the progress of the war, there were a number of annuals and books published in Britain and Australia for young readers. For example, *The War 1915–16, For Boys & Girls* by British author Elizabeth O'Neill was updated with a new edition each year. Chapters like 'The Great Offensive in the West' and 'War by Air and Sea' made the fighting sound like a great adventure. This was particularly evident in 'The Romance of the Dardanelles', which described in some detail the Gallipoli campaign by the Allies, whose heroic efforts were not to be considered a failure: 'The expedition was not altogether a loss, for great numbers of Turks, who might have been fighting elsewhere, had been kept occupied on this front.'[55]

The following year, the 1916 edition, gave an account of 'The Battle of the Somme' and, in reference to the Canadian contingent, adds some revealing propaganda: 'The Germans lost very heavily. Afterwards they said that they had taken very few prisoners because the Canadians fled. This is one of the worst of the many lies the Germans have told during the war.'[56]

The same author published *Battles for Peace: The Story of the Great War Told for Children in 1918*, several months before the war ended. In the last chapter, 'The War for Peace', the war had not been going well for the Allies. O'Neill confesses:

> … this war is a war to end war. If Germany should win it would appear that wrong had triumphed, that might is right. It must not be. And so the Allies will fight on until the Germans are ready to make what reparation they can for the wrong they have done.[57]

War-mongering material for children written by Australian authors include writers such as Reverend W. H. Fitchett, headmaster of the Methodist Ladies College in Melbourne. Fitchett, once dubbed

'England's Bugler',[58] an avowed monarchist and Anglophile, wrote *Deeds That Won the Empire* in 1899 and followed up with *Fights For The Flag* the following year. In Australia, the books were 'a common piece of luggage for earnest men leaving for the First World War'. They also became 'a standard prize for schoolboys ... so readable was it that Harrow and Winchester made their boys cram it over school holidays'.[59] Even John Monash later confessed to Fitchett that he carried the book throughout the war, and 'used it to considerable advantage on several occasions in stimulating the interests of the men in our military traditions at Gallipoli ... during the Messines and Passchendaele fighting in 1917, and during the victorious advance in 1918'.[60]

Fitchett's writings included chapters titled 'The Light Cavalry Brigade in the Crimea', in the thick of which 'some officer put his hand to his mouth, and delivered a shrill Tally-ho!'[61] and in 'The Men in the Ranks' he admits, 'I should say that the British are amongst the most splendid soldiers in the world,'[62] and, 'What thrill of passion kindles in him as, through the smoke-filled air, he sees the bent heads and sparkling bayonet-points of the hostile line coming on in fiercest charge.'[63]

The horror, pain, suffering and violent death of warfare were completely ignored here, and although Fitchett claimed his purpose was not to glorify war but to nurture patriotism, he 'managed to present his impressionable young audience with a sanitised and romanticised representation of the battlefield experience.'[64]

A popular gift for boys for birthdays and at Christmastime was *The Boy's Own Annual* (there was also a *Girl's Own Annual*). They were designed for boys 12 to 15 years old and were full of public school escapades, adventure stories, poems, engineering feats and lots of British Empire and general patriotic material. Not surprisingly, during the Great War they were full of wartime heroics, mainly concerning the British forces, and the instruments of modern warfare. Even before the war, there were military articles like 'In Camp with the Cadets', with some 'useful hints for those beginning their military training'.[65]

The front cover of the 1914–15 edition of the Annual set the tone for much of the contents inside, with a British mounted lancer charging the enemy on horseback. 'Big Guns in the Field' featured a 'British 60 pounder in action, the heavy arm that inflicted such terrible havoc in the German entrenched positions.'[66] In 'Young French Heroes', there was a photo of a French boy lying in a hospital bed: 'A youth of about 15 lies in the hospital at Lyon. He was so anxious to fight the Germans that he threw a soldier's cloak over his school clothes and went to the battlefield. It shows what stuff some French schoolboys are made of.'[67]

'The Romance of the Red Cross' told of how well the British soldiers were cared for on the battlefield: 'never have the British wounded been so well looked after as in the present campaign.'[68] The poem 'To the Old Boys at the Front', by Frank Ellis, depicted a class of schoolboys from a private school pondering over the perceived exploits of some of the school's ex-pupils:

> With books before us, on our forms and benches,
> Learning our lessons still from day to day,
> We think of you in battlefields and trenches,
> Fighting your country's battles far away.[69]

There was the action-packed 'Bombing a German Troop Train' sketch with the caption 'An incident on the Western Front' in the 1917–18 Annual, and four pages of technical descriptions in 'All About Machine-guns': 'Have you seen the wonderful Maxim Gun that loads itself and fires over 600 times a minute from a single barrel?'[70]

For some years, boys of fifteen years were able to be recruited for the Royal Navy and the Royal Australian Navy, mainly as apprentices on land and at sea, so it would have been no surprise to see advertisements and other articles pressuring lads (with their parents' permission) to join the Navy. This was the case in the 1915–16 issue of *The Boy's Own Annual*, which ran 'From Ship's Boy to Lieutenant — Chances for the Lads of England in the Royal Navy', with the words, 'The Navy wants boys. It wants them today not only for the war, but for the days after the war.'[71]

TOP
The cover of a popular wartime children's annual. Elizabeth O'Neill, *The War 1915–16, For Boys & Girls*, 1916

BOTTOM
Elizabeth O'Neill, *The War 1915–16, For Boys & Girls*, 1916, p. 63

CHAPTER V

THE ROMANCE OF THE DARDANELLES

The story of how the Allies tried by sea and land to win the Dardanelles in the spring of 1915 has already been told. Perhaps the bravest deeds of the war were done there, then and later. The most splendid results were hoped for if only the Straits could be won. Russia would then have been able to send out and sell great quantities of wheat and other things which she grows, and which cannot be used up by her own population, and the Allies would have been able to send in to Russia the munitions she so much needed.

One great mistake was made at the beginning, when it was thought that the warships alone might break down the forts and win the Straits. Afterwards, of course, soldiers were sent to fight by land; but the Turks had been warned, and great numbers of Turkish soldiers had been sent to defend the Straits. This made the landing of the French and British troops very difficult, and it was only because they were splendid men that they were able to land at all.

Every inch of ground won in Gallipoli was won by the hardest fighting and the loss of many lives. The Australian and New Zealand troops, and some of the Irish regiments, especially fought like heroes; but the land was of the most difficult kind to win. They were always fighting uphill against an enemy splendidly concealed among the "scrub," the low prickly bushes which covered the ground. By the end of May the Turks had lost 55,000 men in Gallipoli; but they threw more men in, and as the summer drew near it looked as though

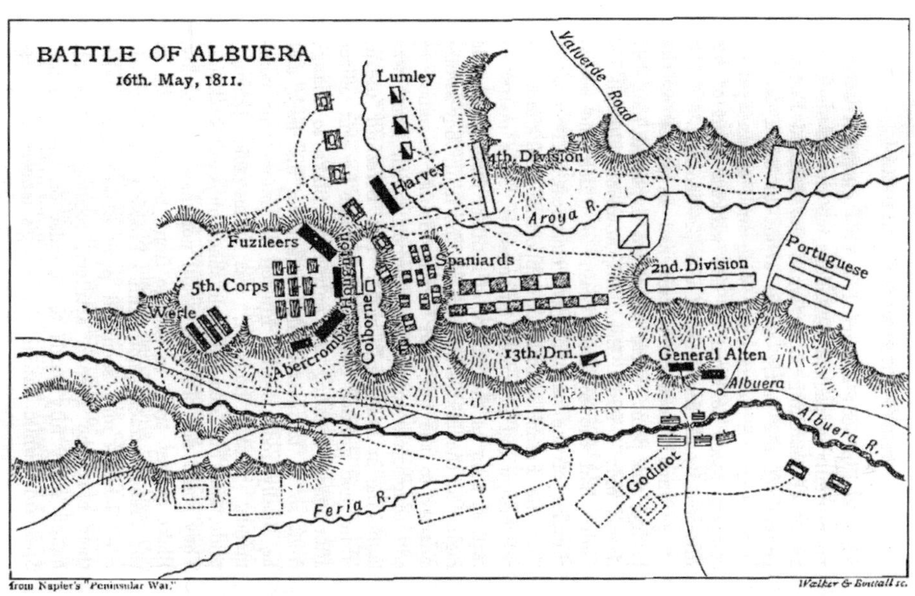

TOP
Battle plan. Reverend W. H. Fitchett, *Deeds That Won the Empire*, 1879

BOTTOM
A popular annual for boys in the WWI era, 1914–15 edition

A finished 12-inch British Naval Gun.

How Big Guns are Made.

Facts about the Nation's Naval Armament. The 12-inch and 15-inch Guns of the Wonder-craft, "Queen Elizabeth."

By RAYMOND RAIFE.

"THE 15-inch guns of the 'Queen Lizzie' shelled Forts Hamidieh I. and III., across the Gallipoli Peninsula, firing one-ton projectiles at a range of fully twelve miles, and the vibrating boom of the explosions was heard ninety-seven miles away."

That is a brief extract from an account of the doings of the British Fleet in the Dardanelles. "Queen Lizzie" is, of course, our sailors' pet name for H.M.S. "Queen Elizabeth," which is the fastest and most powerful battleship afloat, and is universally acknowledged to be the wonder-warship of the world. Naturally enough, such a premier fighting-craft is armed with the world's best naval gun. Our 13·5 weapons have proved formidable indeed, but the high explosive charge which our 15-inch gun can carry through and get inside the thickest armour ever put upon a battleship is very nearly half as large again in the 15-inch gun as in the 13·5-inch. The "Queen Elizabeth" and her sister ship, the "Warspite," have eight of these 15-inch guns, with turrets upon the centre line of the ship, two forward and two aft, and these splendid units of the British Navy provide the first instance in which a gun of such large calibre has been mounted upon a warship.

The making of these big guns is one of the most remarkable processes known to engineering, and those who are responsible for their production, either as designers or machinists, embody the acme of inventive genius and of trained skill that is available amongst the professional and artisan classes of our community. By official direction the writer is prohibited from publishing certain particulars concerning the 15-inch guns, such details being calculated to prove acceptable to this country's enemies. But the actual process of manufacture of big guns is no such secret to be closely guarded: it applies alike to the 12-inch, 13·5-inch, and 15-inch guns with which our British warships are armed; accordingly, we find ourselves permitted, and will take advantage of the opportunity, to describe how these big guns are made for war. The photographs that we reproduce were taken in the world-famous Elswick Works of Messrs. Sir W. G. Armstrong, Whitworth & Co., Limited, at Newcastle-upon-Tyne, and they present an exceedingly clear and instructive delineation of the method of making mammoth ordnance, giving pictures of the beginning and the completing of the wonderful weapons that have been aptly termed "Britain's peace-persuaders."

Nickel-chrome gun-steel of special quality is the material of which the gun is made. It is melted in huge furnaces, run into monster ladles, and thence emptied into an octagonal mould, from which, when the molten metal has cooled, is taken the eight-sided, huge mass of steel that is to form the inner tube of the great gun. This mass of metal weighs many tons, and it is called the ingot. It is found that the impurities in steel collect mostly in the part of the ingot that cools last, which part is the centre; therefore, in order to remove the weak portion, the centre of the ingot is cut right out by a boring machine which drives a hole clean through the ingot from end to end. In similar fashion is prepared an outer tube of steel which is to be fitted over the inner tube; each tube is reheated and placed in a gigantic press for the operation of forging, which

A page from the popular *Boy's Own Annual*, 1914–15, p. 674

19

Pressures on Teachers in WWI

For military training and indoctrination of cadets

In Victoria, the Education Department communicated with teachers through its monthly publication to schools, the *Education Gazette and Teachers' Aid*. The Gazettes notified teachers of any changes to departmental regulations and procedures, in-service training opportunities, teacher vacancies, general curriculum guidelines and suggestions for classroom activities with students. An early example of a patriotic curriculum discussion with students appeared under the headline of 'Patriotism' in the April 1910 edition:

> (a) *Definition*
> Patriotism is love of one's country — an attribute of both civilised and uncivilised countries. It elevates the mind — acts as an antidote of selfishness.
>
> (b) *Forms of Patriotism*
> I. Love of native land shown by great distress on leaving it.
> II. Patriotism of the soldier (ready to die in order to defend or maintain the honour of the flag). Examples: Nelson, Wellington, Gordon, Garibaldi and Kosciuszko.[1]

Following the 1910 Universal Training Act, there were frequent instructions given through the Gazettes in relation to 'compulsory cadet training'. Under 'Universal Training: Information for Head Teachers', instructions were given on the 'proper keeping of the *Junior Cadet Record Book* by the head-teacher, who is responsible for the proper keeping of the roll book', on 30 June each year.[2] Advertisements for rifle-shooting events, like the Junior Cadets Sargood Trophy were also publicised.[3] Notices of the entry examination for the Naval College were periodically published under 'Royal Australian Naval College: Cadets Wanted'.[4]

Not unexpectedly, even the school syllabus was modified for the duration of the war. Teachers were urged to use a 'thematic' approach in their lessons across the curriculum. In Written English, children were encouraged to correspond with their friends and relatives in the trenches, and to give short 'daily talks' on the war. For Mathematics, students studied practical calculations, with graphs showing the relative sizes of armies and navies, and money sums of the expenditure on the war. The relevance of Geography could be shown in deciding the fate of military campaigns, and for Art students studied sectional drawings of 'modern engines of warfare such as the submarine and the aeroplane'.[5] The syllabus was:

> In addition to the few minutes daily talk in all grades after roll call, one period weekly should be set aside in the fifth and higher grades for the discussion of 'current events'. During this period the teacher may deal with the progress of the war as reported in the cable news, with particular incidents in the war … how the security of Australia depends wholly on British naval supremacy … or the story of Gallipoli, of the *Emden* … the martyrdom of Belgium, etc, may be told.[6]

As a class composition exercise, older children were encouraged to write letters to soldiers at the Front, and much excitement occurred when return letters were received by the schools and read out in class or at assemblies. Examples were often featured in the *School Papers* and in the *Education Gazettes*. Predictably, most of the soldiers tended to play down or ignore the horrors they were experiencing, undoubtedly for the sake of their young audiences:

> Dear George,
>
> It was nice of you to write me a letter, and you cannot guess how pleased I am to hear from one of my little friends so far away … We are all living like rabbits, and, at present, I am in a dugout, sitting on a box with another box to serve as a table, and the place is lighted up with a candle stuck in a tobacco tin.[7]

Children were also urged to write to their serving relatives and friends, and even their former teachers. From Lieutenant H. J. Sparrow, formerly head-teacher of Tongio State School, Victoria:

> Imbros, Greece, 12.12.1915 — I'm on an island 'somewhere in the Mediterranean'. Have been here for eleven days, and it has been somewhat in the nature of a holiday … I saw an old chap in Greek costume ploughing with a wooden plough and a pair of oxen.[8]

Similar means of indoctrinating young and impressionable children was used in government schools in all Australian states, and in most of the private schools as well, for the duration of the war.

For their enlistment in the AIF

> Teacher's Going to the Front
>
> Our teacher's gone away —
> He'll soon be at the front
> To keep the foe at bay,
> And help to bear the brunt.
> He always loved to tell
> Of men, brave, pure, and true;
> And, now, I feel full well
> He lived the life he drew.[9]

There was a huge demand for teachers to enlist in the AIF right from the outset of war being declared. As so many of them had previously served as military drill instructors in the voluntary, and later compulsory, school cadet corps, this was not surprising. War correspondent and later official WWI historian C. E. W. Bean commented on the large number of Australian teachers engaged in the war, in his *Official History of Australia in the War of 1914–18.* Citing the important contribution made by former teacher, Captain Carl Jess, then Colonel John Monash's Staff Captain at Gallipoli, he claimed, 'Jess, like an extraordinary proportion of Australian regular soldiers, was an ex-schoolmaster.'[10]

In Victoria during the war years, out of an estimated 1500 male teachers between the ages of 18 and 45, the qualifying years for military service, no fewer than 873 volunteered. Of these, 751 men, as well as two women (one of whom, a nurse, Sister Margaret Waterstrom, received an OBE) were accepted.[11] This constitutes just over 50 percent of eligible teachers accepted, the highest percentage in the Australian states. Only Germany had a higher ratio, where by January 1918, over 98,000 had volunteered or been conscripted, being some two-thirds of the predominantly male teaching force.[12]

Victorian Director of Education, Frank Tate, keen to encourage teachers to enlist, promised volunteers that they would not forgo any sub-divisional promotions and increments while they were on active service.[13] Tate claimed that of the teachers who were accepted into the AIF, 'the greater number were married men with responsibilities … who volunteered cheerfully for the front'.[14]

The New South Wales ratio, with 755 males enlisted, was much lower at around 10 percent of the total teaching force, largely due to the Minister of Education, Peter Board, declaring early on that teaching was a 'reserved occupation'.[15] In South Australia, of 645 eligible teachers, some 181 were away at the war,[16] and 396 teachers and departmental officers enlisted in Queensland between the outbreak of the war in 1914 and 31 December 1917, of whom 104 were reported killed, wounded or missing.[17]

It is quite probable that the high incidence of Victorian teacher recruitment in the war was a direct result of the pressure applied by the 52-year-old Director of Education, Frank Tate. A child of British immigrants, Tate had a rapid rise through the ranks as an educator, from teenaged pupil teacher, head-teacher, school inspector, Principal of the Teachers' Training College, and finally as Director from 1901 onwards. A staunch Anglophile, and with both of his sons serving as medical officers in the AIF, he 'had no respect for pacifists'.[18] Unlike Peter Board, his NSW counterpart, Tate placed no restrictions on his male teaching force to enlist. In fact, he actively encouraged them to do so. As early as 10 September 1914, he proudly addressed a 'send off' to forty-five Victorian state school teachers and their relatives at a lavish dinner in the Athenaeum Theatre in Melbourne.[19]

When the number of Australian casualties began to mount early in 1916, Tate did his part to send replacements (especially from the teaching service) by writing a series of three lengthy articles in the *Education Gazettes* (reprinted by the Melbourne *Herald*) in April and May of that year, under 'Some Soul of Goodness in Things Evil', with the subtitle 'No. 1 — Public Duty':

> Each new morn widows grieve, new orphans cry, new sorrows strike heaven on the face …
>
> But the war is not by any means wholly evil. It is a great testing and trying out of the real character of individuals and nations …
>
> And does there not come, at times, to every thoughtful Australian, a feeling of shame when he reads of the great efforts being made to persuade and cajole men to do what should be their plain duty …
>
> … I should not like to be a home-keeping youth, or the father of a home-keeping youth, when our soldiers come home again. In the years to come, a man who can say he fought at Anzac 'will stand a-tip-toe when that day is named', and the man who failed to go,

when it was his plain duty to go, 'shall think himself accursed, and hold his manhood cheap'.[20]

Reading such a diatribe, in particular the last of the above quotes, from the Director of Education, which occupies two full pages in the *Teachers' Gazette*, it is no wonder that Victorian male teachers had the highest participation rate in the country.

So when the number of new recruits really started to wane in 1916, and Australian Prime Minister W. M. Hughes floated the idea of a referendum for military conscription for those aged 18 to 35 to make up the shortfall, it was not surprising that Tate would join the chorus: 'I do hope that Australia may not be disguised in the eyes of the world by an adverse decision.'[21] Frank Tate, among many others, must have been bitterly disappointed when the referenda failed in 1916 and again in 1917.

It was only natural that many of the teacher recruits soon found themselves among the NCOs and junior commissioned officers in the AIF, not only because of their previous service in the school cadet corps, but also because so many of them had received a better education than the majority of other recruits. But the downside of this was that these men, particularly the junior officers, had very high casualty rates in the trenches on the Western Front, as they were expected to lead the charges into 'no man's land'. By the Armistice, an estimated 22 percent of the AIF reached the rank of Commissioned Officer or NCO, but in the case of teachers it was 30 percent. Not surprisingly, of the 752 male teachers enlisted, a staggering 163 (21 percent) were killed in action or died of wounds soon afterwards.[22]

Teachers who persevered after being rejected for service on medical or age grounds were praised by the Education Department, like Private John Edmondson from Bengworden, who had unsuccessfully applied eight times until June 1918, when he was finally accepted. Multiple attempts were also made by Private William Anderson, who made five tries, and Private Charles Chester-Ryton, successful on his fourth attempt.[23]

Victorian teacher casualties also featured regularly in the *Teachers' Gazettes*, where photographs and names of the dead from all ranks were shown, and a short outline of service with the Education Department:

> Herewith appears a portrait of Private Charles Allen. The Mirboo paper says that 'Charlie' was a great favourite with everybody — the best cricketer in the district and one of the best footballers, beloved by the pupils of his school, and highly respected by the parents.[24]

> Lieutenant Frank L. Cousins was killed in action [Fromelles] on 19th July, 1916. He entered the service in 1904, being appointed junior teacher at Long Gully, Bendigo. After a transfer to Waanyarra, he took charge of schools at Corack East, Gunbower Island West, and Teal Point.[25]

> Killed in action, 4th June, 1918, Flight Lieutenant Leslie J. Primrose, formerly science master at the Bendigo Technical School. In February 1918 he went to France with the 2nd Squadron, A.F.C. — 'after completing a patrol, he was returning to the squadron when something went wrong with his machine, and he was forced to land … after seeing the state of the machine, death was instantaneous and painless'.[26]

At the end of the war, the Education Department of Victoria produced a *Record of War Service 1914–1919* book containing the names, last school appointment and detailed war record of all the 606 teachers who returned and the 146 who died, as a tribute to those who served in the Great War. A copy was sent to every school in the state. This substantial book of over 300 pages also contained a record of the 'war relief' activities carried out in the state schools during the war years, with the amounts raised by each school.[27]

Teacher trainee enlistments

In those days, the vast majority of teachers were trained by the respective state education departments, at teachers colleges located in the capital cities. In Victoria this occurred at the Melbourne Teachers' College, Carlton, a division of the Education Department of Victoria.

Dr John Smyth, Principal of the college, 'shared the Education Department's desire to serve' and was known to 'infect' his students with 'his own patriotic fervour'. Referring to both past and present students who had enlisted as 'our soldiers', there was no questioning of the rightness of Australia's response to the 'call', even in times of heated debate over the conscription issue in 1916 and 1917. When the first contingent of troops left for training in Egypt in November 1914, there were twelve trainees on board the ship, each carrying with them 'a letter of encouragement from Smyth and a College badge as a talisman, given to them at a farewell assembly'.[28]

In April 1916, Smyth proudly announced that 51 percent of the men who had been through the college since 1900 had enlisted. By war's end he had claimed that 190 of the 555 men who had entered the college between 1900 and 1918 had served their country, including 24 of the 33 students (73 percent) who enrolled in 1913. Two staff members enlisted together in March 1915. Both Smyth and his wife, Emma, sent and received an endless supply of letters from ex-students at the Front, extracts of which appeared regularly in the college publication *Trainee*. Some of the men who returned spoke at college assemblies, one of whom was Lieutenant-Colonel Walter McNichol, the first Australian to receive the DSO. But no doubt the most popular 'old collegian' to return was Captain Frank McNamara, who addressed a gathering of past and present students in September 1916. The guest speaker, a pilot in the Australian Flying Corps, had been awarded the Victoria Cross for 'landing his plane behind enemy lines in Palestine, while wounded and under fire, to rescue a fellow airman who had been forced down'.[29]

Such gatherings could only further enhance the college motto, 'Non Omnis Moriar' — 'all is not mortal', or 'we shall not wholly die' — and the college anthem, named after the same Latin motto, gained another verse:

> Hail to our fallen, their spirits triumphant,
> Faithful to duty, not fearing to die,
> They give to our College a glory unfading,
> A new note of triumph resounds in our cry.[30]

An article in the *Education Gazette and Teachers' Aid* under the banner 'How the Teachers' College Treats its Men at the Front' revealed that women students at the college had been preparing Christmas parcels for male ex-collegians containing their own hand-knitted socks, soap, toothbrush, bootlaces, a writing pad, a copy of the latest *Trainee* and 'a musical instrument'. It appeared that some of the musical instruments contained in the parcels proved quite a sensation, as one of the recipients, Corporal Eggington, later revealed:

> With several other 'trainees' on a bleak cold night I sounded my 'toot-toot' outside a dugout. The men were out of their dugouts in half a second, and cheered and laughed until the tears nearly started, so the 'musical' instrument did its share towards making things brighter here.[31]

After the war, Lieutenant George Browne, a distinguished ex-collegian who had won a Military Cross in France, was awarded a scholarship to Oxford, and on his return at the age of thirty-two was appointed to the college as Vice Principal. Browne later became a Professor of Education at the University of Melbourne, and in later life was renowned as the presenter of the weekly documentary series *Professor Brown's Study* on Channel Nine, in the pioneering days of television in Australia.[32]

In the hallway of the former Melbourne Teachers' College in

Rathdown Street, Carlton, are three ornate stained-glass windows and two tiled tablets, the latter containing 183 hand-painted busts in military uniform, of ex-collegians who served in the Great War. An asterisk marks the names of the thirty-six students from the college who did not return. At the unveiling of the memorial the mother of one of the deceased was heard to say, 'Now I feel comforted. I have left my son with the students he loved so well.'[33]

TEACHER'S GOING TO THE FRONT.

Our teacher's gone away—
He'll soon be at the front
To keep the foe at bay,
And help to bear the brunt.

He always loved to tell
Of men, brave, pure, and true;
And, now, I feel full well
He lived the life he drew.

He told us, 'fore he went,
The reasons why we fight—
That England's word was meant,
And God would prove us right.

Our need, he said, was great,
Still greater Belgium's need,
That men should not now wait,
But help with utmost speed.

So he was going away
With friends, old, tried, and true,
And would we sometimes pray
That they'd their duty do?

Yes, duty! that's the word
That seemed to thrill him through,
Whose call he clear had heard,
And to it he'll prove true.

So teacher's gone away—
He'll soon be at the front
To keep the foe at bay,
And help to bear the brunt.

—J.H.P., in *The Teacher's World*.

Education Gazette, 18 March 1915, p. 75

Pressure on Victorian teachers to enlist in the Great War. *Education Gazette and Teachers' Aid*, Victoria, 18 March 1915

32 EDUCATION GAZETTE AND TEACHERS' AID. [20TH FEBRUARY, 1917.

OUR DEPARTMENT AND THE WAR.

CASUALTIES AMONG TEACHERS AND OTHER DEPARTMENTAL OFFICERS.

THE DEAD.

Private Robert Campbell.

Robert William Campbell was killed in action in France on the 23rd of November, 1916. He was nineteen years of age, a

PRIVATE ROBERT WILLIAM CAMPBELL.
Ob. 23.11.16.

fresh, active, conscientious young teacher, who had relinquished charge of his first school (No. 2244, Mologa Central) for the "famine, toil, and fray" of military service in a far land. He has a brother, Mr. A. G. Campbell, head teacher of No. 2159, Knowsley. R. W. Campbell is well known in Bendigo, where he spent some five or six years as junior teacher at School No. 1976—the old school at Camp Hill. His official reports are consistently favorable with regard to his diligence and capacity as a teacher, and his maintenance of order and discipline.

Private Bourchier.

Herewith appears a protrait of Private Arthur P. Bourchier, whose death was announced in the January number. His father, Mr Patrick Bourchier, of Warrenheip, writes thus: —"He was an only son, born at Warrenheip in 1896. He attended the local State school and the one at Humffray-street, Ballarat East, then, in 1912 and 1913, was a student of the Ballarat Agricultural High School. He was appointed a junior teacher at the Humffray-street school in 1914, and from there enlisted in July, 1915. Attached to the machine-gun section of the 58th Battalion, he had been in France since the end of last June." The parents have as yet received no particulars beyond the bare statement that he was killed in action on the 22nd of last November.

Private Chester.

The death is announced of Private Charles Chester at Tidworth Hospital, England, of meningitis. He was head teacher at School No. 3586, Ryton, from May to August of last year. He died four weeks after his landing in England. His parents are Mr. and Mrs. W. Chester, of Collins-st., Traralgon. A longer notice is deferred.

THE WOUNDED.

Private Norval Birrell, son of Mr. B. W. Birrell, head teacher at No. 2831, Serviceton, was wounded in France, and is in hospital in England.

CASUALTIES AMONG RELATIVES OF TEACHERS AND OF OTHER DEPARTMENTAL OFFICERS.

THE DEAD.

Sergeant Houston.

In last month's number, mention was made of the death of Sergeant F. Gerald Houston, son of Mr. James Houston,

PRIVATE ARTHUR P. BOURCHIER.
Ob. 22.11.16.

SERGEANT FRANCIS GERALD HOUSTON.
Ob. 8.12.16.

Notification of teacher casualties in the Great War. *Education Gazette and Teachers' Aid*, Victoria, 20 February 1917, p. 22

EDUCATION GAZETTE AND TEACHERS' AID.

[13TH APRIL, 1916.

THE WAR: CORRELATION WITH SCHOOL SUBJECTS.

1. A school roll of honor, showing the names of ex-pupils who have gone on active service, is a stimulating record.

2. An intelligent interest in the newspaper demands a better knowledge of the somewhat neglected subject of notation. Graphs, showing the relative sizes of armies and navies, daily expenditure on the war, &c., are interesting.

3. Newspaper cuttings, soldiers' letters from the front, should be preserved. For many reasons, children should be encouraged to write to their friends and relatives at the Front.

4. Short daily "talks" on the war are instructive.

5. A school diary of the war has its advantages. Children who are writing present-day history are likely to feel the reality of the past.

6. The plan of selling the products of the school-garden for the patriotic funds is worthy of consideration.

7. Geometrical problems, dealing with map-reading, heights and distances of inaccessible points, are all of practical interest.

8. In history, the opportunities for the use of the principles of comparison and contrast are almost unlimited. We may use the known present to explain and illustrate the unknown past.

9. Geography is intimately connected with the war. Physical configuration and climatic conditions have decided the fate of campaigns. Physical features, climate, people, products, routes, and distances may be made interesting.

10. It would be hard to imagine a more favorable opportunity for the inculcation of a love for our national patriotic literature in the form of prose, poetry, and song.

11. Sectional drawings of the modern engines of warfare, such as the submarine and aeroplane, are interesting.

F. PUTLAND, Grafton School, N.S.W.

The Education Gazette and Teachers' Aid, Victoria, 13 April 1916

Listing of the 752 (51 percent) of the approximately 1500 eligible male teachers in Victoria aged 18 to 45 who volunteered in WWI, and the obituaries of the 146 (19 percent) who were killed in action or died of wounds. *The Education Department's Record of War Service, Victoria 1914–1919*

WWI Memorial Windows at Melbourne Teachers' Training College, listing the names of 190 students, staff and ex-students who served in the AIF, and the 39 (including one staff member) who died. Courtesy Education Department, Victoria

20

War Casualties Among the Ex-cadets

<u>Anthem for Doomed Youth</u>

What passing bells for these who die as cattle?
Only the monstrous anger of the guns.
Only the stuttering rifles' rapid rattle
Can patter out their hasty orisons.
No mockeries for them from prayers or bells,
Nor any voice of mourning save the choirs —
The shrill, demented choirs of wailing shells;
And bugles calling for them from sad shires.[1]

By war's end, in November 1918, the casualties among the Australian AIF were immense. The initial rush of 52,561 volunteers to the recruiting centres around the country by the end of 1914 had increased to 416,809, of whom some 331,781 had seen action overseas. Given that the male population was around 2,500,000 in 1914, nearly one-third of males of eligible age enlisted. Of these, 59,342 were killed in action or had died of wounds, and 152,171 were wounded. The casualty rate for Australian servicemen was a staggering 64.8 percent, while New Zealanders were 58.6 percent, Canadians 49.7 percent and Britons 47.1 percent.[2]

While no records have been kept concerning the number of casualties who were either voluntary or compulsory cadets before enlistment, it can be said with some confidence that a substantial quantity were ex-cadets. There are many examples of statistics given of Old Boy numbers of the dead and the wounded, in the various school histories of both government and private schools around the country.

Government schools

At Melbourne High School, for example, 515 ex-pupils (the vast majority of them ex-MHS cadets), fought in the war, with 86 of them killed (17 percent), among their number some 21 officers, from lieutenant to major.[3] As wartime Principal, Joseph Hocking, reflected:

> During the years of war, a marked change came over the spirit of the school. Into the fabric of its soul was woven a new element. Fellowship in suffering and common effort in the great cause bound students, staff and parents, with a subtle tie.[4]

In addition, there were 58 of their number seriously wounded, who together with their fallen comrades were listed on the school's Great War Roll of Honour.[5]

Another government school in Victoria, Ballarat High School, 'looked back on its war effort with pride', boasting that of 275 ex-students and staff who enlisted, 52 obtained commissions, 75 reached non-commission rank and 36 won military decorations, and some 43 (17 percent) lost their lives. A further 10 percent of those who volunteered were rejected on medical grounds.[6] They were celebrated: 'During school assemblies, wounded "heroes" addressed the school, and school magazines presented detailed accounts of the deeds of the school's sons.'[7]

When the 'military conscription' issue was before the Australian public in 1916, a female school captain at Ballarat High claimed in the school magazine that 'the students would vote 20 to 1 for conscription, if given the vote'.[8]

Sydney's Fort Street High School estimates that 1343 Old Boys enlisted for active service, 'of whom 129 made the supreme sacrifice' and that 'many honours had been gained by fighting Fortonians, including 21 M.C.s, 8 M.M.s, 4 D.S.O.s, a White Eagle of Serbia, and a Croix de Guerre'.[9]

Photographs of the 190 students, staff and ex- students of Melbourne Teachers' College who served in the Great War 1914–18. Courtesy University of Melbourne

Private schools

The largest contingent of Old Boys from the Associated Public Schools of Victoria sector comprised Scotch College, Melbourne Grammar, Geelong Grammar, Geelong College, Xavier College and Wesley College. Together these schools supplied about 4700 recruits (the vast majority ex-cadets of their respective schools), with 756 killed in action or dying of wounds (12.5 percent).[10] These schools were also proud of the proportion of their group who obtained 'officer' status, with

Geelong Grammar at 52 percent, Melbourne Grammar at 52 percent, Xavier College at 34 percent, Wesley at 29 percent and Scotch College at 22 percent.[11]

Geelong Grammar claims that among the 417 ex-collegians who enlisted, 216 became officers, including one brigadier-general, 10 colonels, 24 majors, 53 captains and 110 lieutenants. The school also revealed that 'one in five was killed, and 10% of those who served won military crosses'.[12]

The Roll of Honour at Geelong College names the 522 'Old Boys who served' and a cross indicates the 86 (16.5 percent) who never returned. *Pegasus*, the college magazine, 'became an outlet for expressions of hope and grief and news of Old Collegians on active service around the world'.[13] In it, 'letters were included from Gallipoli survivors, and later, from those fighting in the Somme. The Anzac legend became the only positive to be drawn from all the death and destruction'.[14]

With over 1200 Old Scotch Collegians enlisted, there were 'more than enough to make up a battalion'. Although the bulk of them joined the AIF, there were some who served in the Royal Australian Navy and the newly established Australian Flying Corps. Old school camaraderie was common throughout the army: 'Many of these young soldiers thought of themselves as "Scotch Collegians" as much as "Australians", and fought and died to defend the ideals and moral standards imparted to them by the "mother school"'.[15]

Camberwell Grammar, a much smaller school, supplied around 250 ex-collegians, with 'forty of them dying for their country, a match with the death-rate of Australia's enlisted men as a whole.'[16] The school was often in mourning of battlefield casualties of ex-collegians, perhaps none more solemn than when its most decorated serviceman, 'Capt. R. A. Little, D. S. O, D. S. C., Croix de Guerre' was killed in France. Another famous Old Boy, Captain Keith Murdoch, distinguished himself as a war correspondent. So strongly did Murdoch criticise Sir

Ian Hamilton's leadership failures at Gallipoli to Prime Minister Billy Hughes and the British War Office that his report led to the removal of Hamilton from the Dardanelles Campaign, and his relocation to another theatre of the war.[17]

L. A. Adamson, the long-serving headmaster of Wesley College, had a habit of quoting the progress of the war, directly from the newspaper, to the boys at morning assembly. Sometimes he would also read out the name of a 'fallen Old Boy', and in his daily after-school association with the boarders 'would drink a silent toast in water with them'.[18]

Adamson also suggested that each boy 'adopt in his mind an Old Boy who had been killed', and by his daily tasks attempt to complete the work that had been started by 'those who did not return'.[19] Wesley College took much pride in their '1910 cricket team', all of whom served together in the AIF, of which 'six gained commissions, four were killed'. A photograph of that team hangs in the Adamson Hall.[20] In one of the 1918 editions of the school magazine *The Lion*, a senior pupil concluded his patriotic article with, 'many of us who are here now will soon pass out to take the places of those who have fallen; so the tradition goes on.'[21]

By May 1918, the death toll from amongst the 914 Wesley old collegians enlisted had risen to 117 (13 percent). The names, deeds and death details of each ex-pupil was published in *The Lion*, among them Signaller Angus Mackay, 'killed in action on the night of 17th of August this year (1916). He was only nineteen-and-a-half years old, but had already shown much promise in the literary career he had chosen'.[22] There was also much celebration over the award of the Victoria Cross to Old Boy Captain Robert Cuthbert Grieve in 1917. A photograph of King George V presenting the medal to him at Buckingham Palace is given prominence in the official school history, and a college scholarship has since been awarded in his honour.[23]

For Xavier, the only Catholic College in the Melbourne group, of a 'probable 400 men under 35 years of age in 1914 who had been at the school, about 75% enlisted'. Of these at least 69 received commissions, 'a slightly higher rate than the national average for Catholics in the forces at the time', 53 were killed and a further 44 wounded. Six priests of the Xaverian Order became military chaplains, and three of the Old Boys, Jacques Playoust, Rene Chaleyer and Andre Prenant, continued Xavier's French connection and joined the French Army.[24]

St Patrick's College, Ballarat, also well-known in Catholic circles, lists 249 ex-students who served in the war, of whom 38 (15 percent) were killed. Throughout the four years of the war, 'there was an abiding interest and concern for those at the front'.[25] Regular snippets appeared in the *College Annual*, from or about 'old collegians' who had been killed or were still serving at the Front:

> Private W. Butler enlisted in Queensland in December, 1914. He was in the trenches at Gallipoli seventeen weeks until the evacuation. He was engaged in fighting against the Turks on the Suez Canal. At present he is in some part of France.
>
> Lieutenant J. Franklyn died of wounds. We insert the substance of a letter written by (Catholic Chaplain) Fr. J. Fahey, of Western Australia … How I wish I could do justice to his memory in this letter! Never have I met such a brave and saintly lad. His character can be summed up in two words: a hero and a saint. I used to meet him often in the trenches, and he was always the same, happy and cheerful … His men, many of whom were twice his age, loved him and would do anything for him.[26]

A Sydney priest, Father Forrest, quoted Catholic school AIF enlistment statistics in answer to charges of Catholic disloyalty in WW I. Producing figures in July 1918, he showed that St Patrick's College in Hunter's Hill 'led the way with over 400 recruits', then St Ignatius in Riverview with 274, then Marist Brothers' Waverley with 155, 'including a Victoria Cross winner who enlisted straight from school'.[27]

At Prince Alfred College in Adelaide, 'the war left the school badly shaken', for of the 870 old scholars who had enlisted, 117 had been killed. Boys attending the college in the war years were made 'fully conscious of the role of old scholars in the fighting',[28] including periodic visits to school assemblies by repatriated former student and Victoria Cross winner, Hugo Throssell. Among the names of deceased former scholars, recorded in red ink in the school register, often referred to at these assemblies was Bertie Collins, who left school to enlist in the AIF at the end of 1914, and subsequently died in camp from meningitis. Other revered 'old reds' included Major Alfred Cook, 'dead from wounds received at Gallipoli', and Sergeant Douglas Adams, 'fatally wounded in the trenches'.[29] Adelaide's Anglican Pulteney Grammar School 'contributed notably to the fighting services', with 251 Old Boys enlisted, of whom 33 were killed.[30]

Wesley College Head of the River crew, Melbourne, 1911. All nine crew members enlisted in the AIF, and four were subsequently killed: Captain Dickinson, Lieutenant Abernathy, Captain Holmes and Lieutenant Edmonstone. G. Blainey, J. Morrisey and S. E. K. Hulme, *Wesley College: The First Hundred Years*, 1967, p. 112

TOP
The 1910 Cricket Champions, Wesley College, Melbourne. All subsequently enlisted in WWI, and four of them were killed. Courtesy Ms M. Vaughan, Archivist, Wesley College

BOTTOM
The 1909 cricket team from Sydney Grammar School. All but one, plus the scorer, enlisted in WWI. Courtesy Mr G. Cooper, Archivist, Sydney Grammar School

New Zealand's casualties

Noted for its cadet artillery unit, Hamilton Boys High was to lose 41 former pupils and one teacher, and of the 115 who returned some 34 had been wounded in some way. Several years later one of the returned men wrote an article of his wartime experiences for the school's memorial booklet, concluding:

> Time deals softly with the horrors of the line … If that danger should arise again, which God forbid, let us hope that the present generation will have the will and the power to avert it by other means than war.[31]

Kings College in Auckland, 'not immune from the hysteria of war', suffered 109 deaths, including two masters, among several hundred ex-pupils, or one in ten of eligible age. Like the vast majority of New Zealand's secondary schools, all their names are inscribed in the Roll of Honour in the chapel, some are further honoured by memorial stain-glass windows, and all are remembered each Anzac Day. Two of them, former School Prefects, killed by the same shell on the battlefield in France, have their memorial windows placed side by side, with the shared inscription 'In Death they were not divided'.[32]

By December 1916, before NZ conscripts were included, over 500 Old Boys of Wanganui Collegiate School had volunteered for overseas service, including ten former masters. The School's Honour Board shows that 67 of them perished.[33]

Some V.C.s of New Zealand.

1. Lieut. L. W. Andrew, V.C., Wanganui.
2. Lieut. C. R. G. Bassett, V.C., Auckland.
3. The late Sergt. D. F. Brown, V.C., Oamaru.
4. Private James Crichton, V.C., Auckland.
5. Brig.-General B. C. Freyberg, V.C., Wellington.
6. Sergt. R. S. Judson, V.C., Oamaru.
7. Sergt. H. J. Laurent, V.C., Hawera.
8. The late Sergt. H. J. Nicholas, V.C., Christchurch.
9. The late Capt. A. J. Shout, V.C., Wellington.

New Zealand's WWI Victoria Cross Winners. *The School Journal*, New Zealand, grades 5 and 6, March 1919, p. 20

21

Discrimination of German-Australians and their Schools in WWI

With Australia's population around 4.5 million by 1914, overwhelmingly of British — English, Scottish, Irish and Welsh — stock, those of German origin, an estimated 180,000, were the fifth-largest ethnic grouping in the country. A 1912 national census showed that six percent of first generation Australians had German parentage.[1] South Australia, where most of original German settlers arrived in 1840s to pioneer the wine industry there, had by far the largest proportion, followed by Queensland and Victoria, with smaller numbers dispersed throughout the remaining states.

There was some suspicion of the German community at the time of the Boer War (1898–1901) because Germany tended to side with the Boers against the British. Concern had also been raised before Federation, when Britain and her colonies eyed suspiciously the build-up of the German Navy, leading to fortifications being built into the cliffs of The Heads in Sydney and at Queenscliff and Portsea, the entrance either side of 'The Rip' that leads into Port Phillip Bay in Victoria.

Anti-German sentiment intensified once the war began, 'when {Lutheran} became synonymous with {German}, and therefore the enemy'.[2] Around mid-1915, allegations of German atrocities against civilians in Belgium and France began to circulate in earnest. Police raids on mainly innocent Germans accused of being enemy spies and potential saboteurs by their suspicious neighbours became commonplace, notably in South Australia. Around 4500 Australians of

German origin were interned in camps around Australia, about 700 of whom were naturalised British subjects and another 70 being born in Australia,[3] and 'thousands more lived under suspicion in the wider community'. John Wenke and Herrman Paesch were arrested at Walla Walla in South Australia and interned for being outspoken in the anti-conscription debate. Wenke was later released when it was discovered that his son David had been wounded in France fighting with the AIF.[4]

While it is not known how many AIF volunteers were of German origin, one reason being that many of them anglicised their names in order to enlist, it can be assumed that according to their proportion, some 18,000 fought for the British cause.[5] Volunteers of German descent were readily accepted early in the war before the 'atrocities' hysteria, but those already in the ranks found it difficult to be trusted with a commission. A notable exception was the then-Colonel John Monash, a former cadet at Scotch College, colour-sergeant in the Melbourne University Regiment in 1886 and, just prior to 1914, in command of the 13th Infantry Brigade.[6] But with the dwindling number of volunteers in 1917 and 1918, especially after the public rejection of the second conscription referendum in 1917, many who had been refused previously on racial or physical grounds were reluctantly accepted.[7]

The Australian War Precautions Act of 1914

The passing of the War Precautions Act of 1914 by the Federal Parliament placed restrictions on Australian-born persons of 'enemy origin'. Among them were restrictions on the right to vote (notably in the second referendum on conscription), denial of the right of action for slander and libel, the right of employers to dismiss employees of enemy origin, and the right of employees to refuse to work with such people. Care was to be taken 'that men of enemy nationality, even if naturalised, are not enlisted', and even men born in Australia of enemy parentage 'must be specially approved by the district commander' before being accepted.[8]

Under the Act, the publication of all German language newspapers and magazines was prohibited in Australia, including those of church (largely Lutheran) origin. John Verran MP and former Premier of South Australia, an active Methodist, announced in the House that 'German pastors were the most disloyal of all'.[9] Even John Monash felt under pressure, instructing his relatives not to write letters to each other through the post, and advising his Aunt Ulrike not to speak German in public.[10] In Melbourne, there were rumours in 1915, circulated from returning soldiers, that the then-Colonel Monash (at the time serving at Gallipoli) had been executed as a German spy.[11] Slandered for anglicising his surname by dropping the 'c', a decision taken much earlier by his father,[12] continually underrated by C. E. W. Bean the AIF Historian, by Keith Murdoch the noted Australian War Correspondent, and the Australian Prime Minister Billy Hughes,[13] Monash went on to be lauded as one of the best generals for the Allies by the end of WWI.

John Monash, aged sixteen, in 1881. A school cadet and dux of Scotch College, Melbourne (LEFT). Colour-sergeant John Monash in 1886, 4th Battalion, Melbourne University Company (RIGHT). R. Perry, *Monash: The Outsider Who Won a War*, 2004

TOP
AIF Commander General John Monash with Australian Prime Minister Billy Hughes, prior to the battle of Hamel in France, early July 1918 (note the abundance of German names). R. Perry, *Monash: The Outsider Who Won a War*, 2004

BOTTOM
War Memorial at Tanunda, South Australia. I. Harmstorf and M. Cigler, *The Germans in Australia*, 1985, p. 124

Alleged German atrocities against civilians in the war

US Senator Hiram Johnson's dictum, 'The first casualty when war comes is truth', was certainly the case in the early years of World War I, when anti-German sentiment accelerated around the world in mid-1915, with reports of alleged German atrocities of civilians in occupied Belgium. A number of Belgian soldiers reportedly witnessed blatant instances of savagery, murder and rape by the invaders:

> … four children, three girls and a boy, each with their hands cut and hanging to their arms by the skin. They were dying but not quite dead.
>
> … the dead body of a child about two years of age. A German lance was in the child's body and it was stuck into the ground through the body.[14]

Such hysteria was soon spurred on by the release of the 'Report of the British Committee on Alleged German Atrocities', presented to both Houses of Parliament in Britain. Known as the 'Bryce Report', after the Chairman Viscount Bryce, it appears that the Committee relied mainly on Belgian refugees for the 1200 pieces of evidence it collected. None of the witnesses were named or placed under oath, and after the war the files of evidence 'mysteriously disappeared from the Home Office', never to be seen again. Further, a Belgian commission of enquiry in 1922 'failed markedly to corroborate a single major allegation in the Bryce report'.[15] Strange also that there were little or no photographs taken of these allegations, but there were ample cartoons and sketches printed in newspapers and magazines in England and Australia. The renowned Australian artist Norman Lindsay regularly had grotesque cartoons published in *The Bulletin*, one of which was on the front page of the 1 July 1915 edition, with a sketch of a vicious German soldier advancing with a dead baby skewered on the end of his bayonet.[16]

Examples of alleged outrages given in the Bryce Report include eyewitness accounts, such as:

> … a soldier stepped aside of the road and drove his bayonet with both hands into the child's stomach … carried it away on his bayonet, he and his comrades still singing.
>
> … one was the body of a woman 40–50 years old … Her bodice was undone and torn at the sides. Her breasts were cut off.[17]

It appears that the German public also heard tales of Belgian atrocities committed against their own soldiers:

> Belgian girls gouged out the eyes of German wounded … and cut the throats of sleeping German soldiers whom they had quartered in their homes.
>
> Belgians under the protection of civilian clothes beat the German wounded to death in cruel ways, and shot down doctors fulfilling their professional duties.[18]

After the war, Phillip Gibbs, the renowned British war correspondent wrote on this issue:

> Doubtless there had been many atrocities, but I could never get evidence of any of them. … No living babies had their hands cut off, or women their breasts. No Canadians were crucified, though it will be believed in Canada for all time.[19]

Example of supposed German 'atrocities' in Belgium, drawn by Australian war artist Lindsay Norman. *The Bulletin*, 1 July 1915

Effects of anti-German propaganda in Australia

John Pender, a member of the South Australian Legislative Assembly, condemned such atrocities in the House, adding that 'the Germans have not been fighting in a Christian manner'. Supported by the racist War Precautions Act, Pender successfully moved in the Legislative Assembly, 'That in the opinion of this House the time has now arrived when the names of all the towns and districts of South Australia, which indicate a foreign enemy origin should be altered.'[20]

What followed involved the name change (or anglicisation) of sixty-nine mainly rural towns in that state with German spelling, some of which were even switched to the names of current British generals. From 1917, for example, 'Blumberg' became 'Birdwood', 'Petersburg' became 'Peterborough', 'Kaiserstuhl' became 'Mount Kitchener', 'Harndorf' became 'Ambleside', and 'Lohethal' became 'Tweedville'. Most of them remain unchanged to this day, though Hahndorf and Loethal reverted back to the original German in 1936, and Kaiserstuhl and Hoffnungsthal as late as 1975.[21] A list of placename changes in the *Adelaide Advertiser* in 1916 prompted one cynical correspondent to write:

> One important name change is missing. That of 'Adelaide', a German name if ever there was one, and called after Adelaide, a German lady, the daughter of Herzog Sax-Coburg … the Queen Consort of William IV.[22]

It is interesting to note the WWI (and WWII) memorial stones and honour rolls in towns with names of German origin. At Hahndorf in South Australia, for example, of 32 names listed as serving in the AIF in WWI, no less than 17 (53 percent) had German surnames, of whom 9 were killed. The ratio in WWII is even higher, with 40 out of 71 volunteers (56 percent) of German origin.[23] Meyer indicates similar statistics in his research on Victorian Lutheran communities following the Great War:

> The memorial at Murtoa shows twenty German Australian names out of 119 soldiers. The Jeparit monument in the heart of the Mallee shows twenty-one German Australian names out of 116. So there should be absolutely no misunderstanding about the loyalty of German Australians.[24]

Besides mandatory placename changes, there were some Germans who changed or altered their own names to avoid the 'enemy' stigma. Erik Klienschmidt became Eric Gowell (his mother's maiden name), and Heinrich Otto Zinc became Frank Raynor, when he unlawfully enlisted as a fifteen-year-old in 1914.[25] Even 'Monasch' was anglicised to 'Monash' soon after Louis and Bertha, John Monash's parents, arrived from Prussia in 1864, a slur delivered against Monash by a jealous fellow officer, Major McInerney, in 1915.[26] But it was more common to change a Christian name. 'Otto' became 'Oscar', 'Friedrich' became 'Frederick' or simply 'Fred', and 'Henrich' became 'Henry'. Although 90 percent of those of German origin were Lutherans by religion, on their enlistment papers some chose the disguise of Church of England, Presbyterian or Methodist.[27]

Rage against German-Australians intensified, particularly in South Australia, where their numbers were strong. Angry mobs smashed windows of Lutheran churches, and several were burnt down. Lutherans were not allowed to assemble in their annual Church Synod conventions, and many joined the churches of other denominations to escape the prejudice. At Blumberg, like many other towns, the hours of attendance at the Lutheran school were varied with the local state school, 'so that anti-German emotions would not erupt'. Persons of 'enemy descent' in the State Public Service were forced to resign, including Justices of the Peace, and those elected to civic positions were not re-elected. There were even objections to the playing of German-composed music in public places.[28]

Speaking again in the House, John Verran MP railed against

the German community for 'trying to monopolise the land in South Australia': 'the whole of the Murray frontage is in their hands. It is possible to travel 150 miles there and not find more than two Englishmen.'[29]

Among the anti-German propaganda in the newspapers in 1916 was a hand-drawn map that appeared under the banner 'Is This a Map of Germany or South Australia?' It showed the location of over thirty towns in South Australia with German-sounding names.[30]

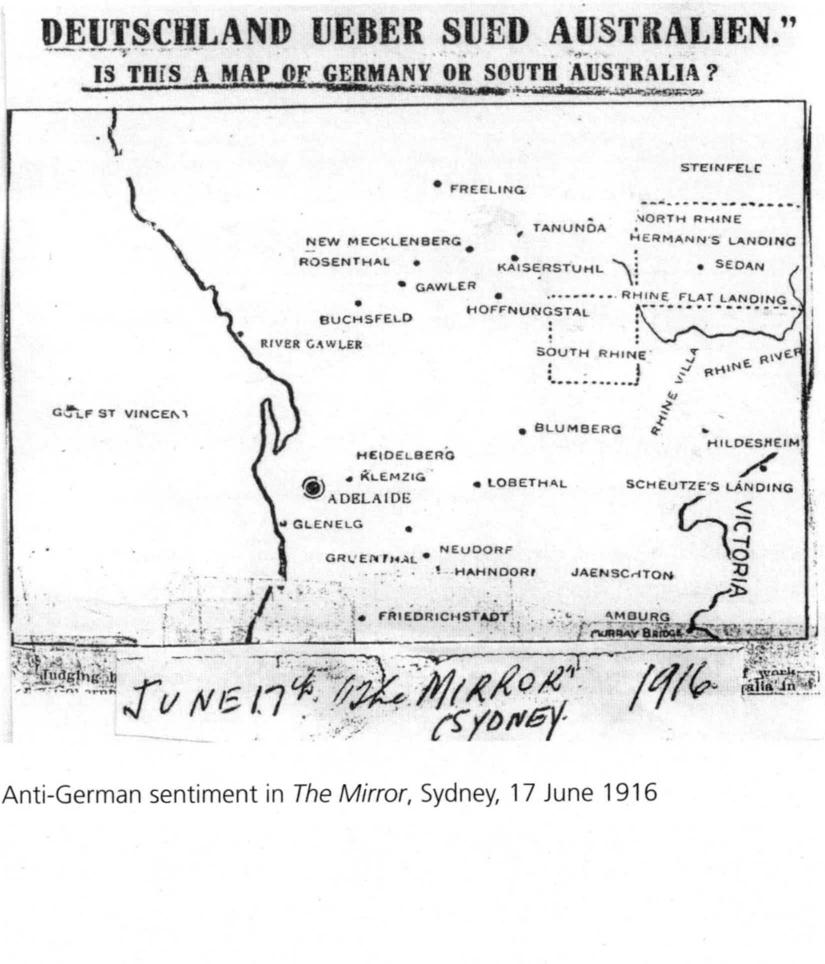

DEUTSCHLAND UEBER SUED AUSTRALIEN."

IS THIS A MAP OF GERMANY OR SOUTH AUSTRALIA?

Anti-German sentiment in *The Mirror*, Sydney, 17 June 1916

COMMONWEALTH MILITARY FORCES.
2ND MILITARY DISTRICT.

Regiment Australian Light Horse
Liverpool.
8th October 1915.

D.P.M.
2nd Military District.

The Bearer Trooper Eberle, Geo.
has been discharged from Training Squadron,
(a) Reason for discharge German parentage.
(b) Length of time in camp 7 days.
(c) Date of last pay 30th Sept. 1915
(d) Amount of pay due 14 days @ 5/- £3 . 10 . 0
(e) Stoppage to deduct. Fine —
" " " Kit —

Approved [signature] Colonel.
Commandant A.I.F. Camp.
Date, 1915.

George Eberle's discharge notice from the Light Horse, 1915.

Trooper George Eberle's discharge notification from the Australian Light Horse in 1915 for having German parentage. Courtesy Lutheran Church Archives, South Australia

Suspension of voting rights for German-born Australians

With recruitment for the AIF plummeting in 1916, Australian Prime Minister Billy Hughes pushed for a referendum on the issue of 'conscription', hoping to boost the numbers. The result was 1,087,557 'Yes' and 1,160,033 'No', giving the 'No' vote a winning majority of 72,476. This was a tremendous blow for Hughes and his government. Besides blaming the Catholic Archbishop of Melbourne, Daniel Mannix, and the 'Irish vote' for the loss, Hughes also accused many of those of German extraction for voting against the legislation. So when Hughes was framing the legislation for the second referendum on conscription in 1917, he inserted a clause disqualifying from voting those 'naturalised British subjects born in an enemy country', excepting anyone whose son was serving in the AIF. Consequentially, the second referendum was defeated by a greater margin than the first, proving the lie that German-Australians were unpatriotic.[31]

Understandably, the German community were incensed that their voting rights had been quashed, but felt vindicated by the outcome. Thomas Heinrich, 'a German-Australian of enemy origin' from Williamstown, South Australia, had been permitted to vote because his four sons had enlisted, 'one of whom was already killed, and another maimed for life in a mustard gas attack'. Much to his disappointment, Heinrich, on presenting himself to vote at his local polling booth, was ordered, 'Get out of here you bloody German, you don't get a vote!'[32] One wonders how many others 'of alien descent' suffered a similar embarrassment on that day.

Last Day South Kilkerran Lutheran School 1917.

One of the forty-eight German Lutheran schools closed in South Australia in June 1917 by the South Australian Government. Courtesy Lutheran Church Archives, South Australia

Restrictions on Lutheran schools and the teaching of German

With South Australia having the highest number and percentage of ethnic Germans, it was not surprising that with all the hysteria against 'enemy aliens', South Australian schools and their communities suffered the most:

> The government was determined to destroy 'the German schools'. It was feared that school buildings were being used to store arms and munitions. In a number of schools the teacher's dais was dismantled in the search for weapons; in one school floorboards were closely inspected for evidence of recent removal. Nothing, of course, was ever found.[33]

As an indication of this hostility, an 'Act to Amend the Education Act of 1915' was given assent on 16 November 1916 in the South Australian Legislative Assembly. While cleverly not naming the offending nationality, the relevant clauses were:

> Section 53/3 (1) All instruction given in any school shall be through the English language.
>
> Section 53/5 (1) After the expiry of six months from the passing of this Act … all schools referred to in the Schedule hereto shall be closed.[34]

Angered by the severity of the school closures, the presidents of four Lutheran Synods presented a petition of protest to the South Australian Parliament:

> We affirm that Lutheran schools are not 'German' schools, but church schools in the fullest sense … We protest against the accusations that we are 'a stain of Prussianism' and that we are 'the enemy within the gates'. The present inspection of our schools under the existing Education Act is sufficient guarantee that our schools impart an efficient English education, and cultivate true

> British sentiments … We Lutherans are not Germans, but British subjects, practically all born under the British flag, and should not be deprived of our democratic rights.[35]

The protest, of course, was in vain, and the closure of the primary schools proceeded as per schedule. In effect, all headmasters and teachers in these schools were dismissed. They virtually found it impossible to find another teaching position until well after the war ended. Many of the closed schools were soon reopened and staffed by 'English' teachers, while others were amalgamated into existing schools, causing overcrowding in some cases.

At Friedensberg the dismissed headmaster, Edward Duldig, was forced to move to Gawler with his young family, where he started up a wood yard. On learning of his 'Lutheran teacher' background, a group of patriotic youths 'gathered outside his house and threw stones on his roof. When Duldig emerged they demanded that he sing "God Save the Queen" to show his loyalty'.[36]

Like their South Australian counterparts, the Queensland Government decided to close all twelve of its Lutheran schools for most of the war. Propagandists had accused the schools of 'expressly training their pupils intellectually, if not physically, for service in the German Army'.[37] At a 'Children's Day' exhibition in Brisbane in 1915, the Queensland Governor, Hamilton Gould Adams, showed little sensitivity on the occasion when mentioning the progress of the war in his address: '… the skewering of babies on bayonets amidst the songs of German soldiers, the crucifying of children, the violation with every attribute of horror, girls of tender years.'[38]

Such comments at public functions, and invariably featured in the local press, simply intensified the situation of those of German origin. At Darling Downs State School, Rudi Haenke, the son of the local German baker, was so often beaten and humiliated by schoolmates chanting 'Rudi the Hun' that the family had to move away and attempt to make a fresh start. In November 1915, the *Brisbane Courier Mail* reported the suicide of the German headmaster of a state school in Mackay, following 'continued sneers against his nationality'.[39]

Aware of the extreme retribution being taken against German schools in South Australia and Queensland, the Council of Education in Victoria was given the task of making recommendations on this issue to the Director of Education, Frank Tate. In addition, the Minister for Public Instruction, H. S. Lawson, appointed a senior Inspector of Secondary Schools, Lesley J. Wrigley (who was also an examiner in German at the University of Melbourne) to visit all eleven Lutheran schools in Victoria. Wrigley was asked to investigate the degree of loyalty evident in each school, the proportion of German to English language being used by the teachers, the names and origins of text books being used, and the nationality of the teachers. His arrival at each school was to be unannounced. After inspecting the syllabuses, he observed the instruction being given, quizzed the children, and where possible interviewed local non-German residents. In his subsequent report to the Minister, Wrigley found no evidence of disloyalty, 'on the contrary, there were many signs of a loyal and patriotic disposition'. The curriculum and associated texts were inoffensive and 'the teachers are endeavouring to make loyal Imperial and Australian citizens of their pupils'.[40]

After considering Wrigley's favourable Ministerial report, and being given assurances and documentation from leading Lutheran Pastor, Reverend J. Darsow, 'proving their loyalty as subjects of the British Empire', the Council recommended a more lenient approach than their South Australian counterparts: '... there is not sufficient evidence to warrant the closing of schools ... but at the most, it would advise that the authorities of these schools should substitute English for German in all their teaching.'[41]

But keeping Lutheran schools open did not lessen the discrimination against those of German origin in Victoria. Within the hallowed walls of the Methodist Ladies College in Melbourne, the recently appointed headmaster Otto Krome suffered frequent prejudice from members of the public jealous of his standing within the school. Even with the support of the patriotic Reverend W. H. Fitchett, and the Methodist Conference, the undermining continued, with one anonymous writer (possibly a parent) warning that some of the girls, 'the future mothers of Australia … reflect a certain anti-British sentiment' because of their association with the new headmaster. Such rumours prompted a police investigation of both Krome and Fitchett, with the former acknowledging his 'sympathies were all pro-British', and Fitchett stating he 'had not received one complaint from any pupils or persons at the College'.[42]

A Melbourne magazine, *Graphic*, took up the cause with the headline 'Otto Krome at Methodist Seminary: To be "Kultured" or Cultured — Which?':

> is it patriotic … that our young ladies, who are to be the future cultured mothers of Anzacs, should be trained by Germans, and have instilled into their impressionable minds that 'Kultur' which is not the culture Britain approves of …[43]

Fortunately, with Fitchett's continued backing, the murmurings against Krome eventually subsided.

Even at university level, anti-German prejudice continued, with Dr Alexander Leeper, Warden of Trinity College in Melbourne, attacking colleagues Walter von Dechend, Lecturer in German, and Eduard Scharf, pianoforte teacher at the Conservatorium of Music, for their alleged lack of loyalty. Although both men had married Australian citizens, their homes and offices were subsequently searched by officers of the Defence Department, after tipoffs by 'the ruthless Anti-German' Leeper. Although the cases against the two were 'built on shaky ground', their respective appointments were terminated at the end of 1915.[44]

In the state system Franz Stielow, head-teacher at Mandurang, was suspended by the Education Department in October 1914, while charges of disloyalty put forth by parents were investigated. Stielow was accused of refusing to fly the flag at the school, hold a weekly patriotic ceremony, or to speak about the Royal family, Britain and the war. In his defence, Stielow claimed there was no flag to fly or salute, and that no head-teacher had conducted a patriotic ceremony at the school for three years.[45] Although the Public Commissioner who was investigating ruled that the charges could not be sustained, he was transferred to Lockwood State School, just four miles away, where fresh allegations surfaced soon afterwards. Transferred again to Bacchus Marsh in 1918, his reputation preceded him, and a deputation of parents accused Stielow of refusing to answer the question, 'Are you a loyal British subject?' Fortunately for him, a counter deputation of parents defended Stielow and no further enquiry was necessary.[46]

Cadets in Lutheran schools

Like all other government and non-government schools, compulsory cadet training was also the norm in the Lutheran schools of Australia. There appears to be an exception in South Australia, where there was 'physical training' without the use of arms, in keeping with the Lutheran belief in 'the separation of church and state'.[47] At Tanunda in South Australia, for example, a staff photograph at the Lutheran school portrays a Lieutenant Wooley in military uniform, posed among other staff, all with German-sounding names like Eckerman, Schwartz, Dohler and Brauer. Other photographs at the school show 'Lutheran teachers of all Synods taking part in physical drill conducted by Lieutenant Wooley'.[48] Wooley's task was to train Lutheran teachers to conduct a military-style physical drill among the cadet units of their respective schools, in the same way that hundreds of other teachers were instructed across the country at this time, only in his case without the use of weapons.

Concordia College and Immanuel College, two South Australian Lutheran secondary schools in Adelaide that were allowed to re-open during the war, with the added restrictions on the teaching of German and the expulsion of German teachers, had a cadet corps imposed on them after 1916 by the Education Department.

There are numerous examples of ex-cadets from Lutheran schools who served in the AIF in many theatres of the war. Lawrence Jeurs 'had previous experience with the cadets' in South Australia and was 'not afraid to admit to his Lutheran faith'. Arriving with the 32nd battalion in France in 1916, Jeurs was captured by the Germans in the fighting at Mouquet Farm in France, and spent the remainder of the war in a prison camp.[49] Leslie Gosewinckel enlisted in Melbourne in July 1915, stating his experience with the 'South Yarra Senior Cadets', before being assigned as a reinforcement for the 5th Battalion.[50]

A more notable example was Walter Leslie Schwartz, who had the distinction of being named 'Patriot, Deserter, War Hero'. Born in Toowoomba, Queensland in 1896, his parents were both born in Australian and of German descent. At the age of fourteen, Schwartz was 'happily involved in compulsory training':

> … it was with great joy that I became a cadet of Training Area IIa. I took every advantage of the opportunity offered and after passing through the Non Commissioned ranks, I studied for and passed the examination for Second Lieutenant.[51]

At eighteen, Schwartz joined the army just prior to the outbreak of the war, and expected to be among the first volunteers when war was declared. At the interview, an officer looked at his surname and gruffly asked, 'When are you going to be naturalised?' This was just one of many insults he received, such as 'people with German names should not be allowed to serve as they would probably turn traitor'.

Admitted as a Private, Gunner Schwartz was furious that his previous experience as a cadet officer could not gain him a non-commissioned or commissioned rank, and that he had been made to be a 'mess orderly' when the rest of his unit was on military manoeuvres. Frustrated with his situation, Schwartz went AWOL (absent without leave), bought a passage on a ship to England, and soon after arrival joined the 23rd Royal Fusiliers. There he was quickly promoted to Lance Corporal and thence to 2nd Lieutenant, before accompanying his unit to the Western Front in June 1917. Schwartz was wounded at Passchendaele, but not before being awarded the Military Cross for 'keeping the line with his men under extremely heavy fire and at close range'. Severely wounded in the leg, Schwartz was repatriated back to England, where an amputation was performed.[52]

Meanwhile in Toowoomba, Schwartz's mother, unaware of his whereabouts, was notified by the Australian authorities that her son was listed as a deserter. Schwartz returned to Australia in 1920 to have his desertion expunged, which of course took much explaining, and after much administrative red tape he was finally pardoned the following year.[53]

TOP
A platoon of cadets from Concordia Lutheran College, South Australia, c. 1917. Courtesy Concordia Lutheran College Archives, South Australia

BOTTOM
Lutheran teachers receiving drill instruction from AIF Lieutenant Woolley at Tanunda, South Australia, 1913. Courtesy Lutheran Church Archives, South Australia

Treatment of German immigrants in New Zealand

Between 1843 and 1914, about 10,000 (mainly Lutheran) German immigrants from Northern and Central Germany, and some from South Australia, arrived in New Zealand. Germans were the largest non-British race in the country from 1890 to 1900. Besides joining the gold rushes in Otaga and Westland in the 1860s, they were pioneers of dairy farming in the Rangitikei-Manawatu regions.

Soon after World War I began, the New Zealand Government drafted a raft of legislation aimed at 'aliens', including the War Regulation Act of 1914, the Alien Enemy Teachers Act of 1915, and the Registration of Aliens Act of 1917, which forbade the employment of any teacher who had been a citizen of an enemy state. The main internment camps for suspect German sympathisers were located on Somes Island in Wellington Harbour and Motuihe Island in the Hauraki Gulf. When New Zealand forces commandeered German West Samoa in late 1914, its German leaders were interned on these islands.

Like in Australia, there was a 'wave of anti-German hysteria', and Lutheran churches and schools were closed. The main Lutheran church in Christchurch was demolished and the bells melted down for war materials.[54]

As early as January 1915, the Board of the prestigious Kings College in Auckland decided to place limits on enrolling boys of German origin, resolving that 'it is inadvisable to accept boys of German name (without special investigation)'. With such an atmosphere prevailing, it was not surprising that a music tutor, Herr Kreutzner, was dismissed from the school in April 1916.[55]

22

Boy Soldiers in the AIF

> One result of the 'Boy Conscription Act of 1910' we can be certain. By August 1914 the country had a substantial army of trained men, and thousands volunteered for service overseas. That many thousands who volunteered and went were underage, is unquestionable.[1]

With the recruiting age for the AIF set at a minimum of eighteen years, one hesitates to consider how many lads of that age, or even older, were mature enough to realise what they were in for when volunteering for the WWI conflict. No doubt many of their parents had reservations, as their permission had to be given if a son was under the legal age of twenty-one years. And how many such parents or guardians lived with the guilt of their decision for the remainder of their lives, when the death or serious injury of their loved one ensued?

But what of the cases of mere boys of 14 to 17, known to have enlisted by falsifying their ages? Some even had the blessing of their parents, no matter how reluctant their parents may have been, and in a spirit of adventure sailed proudly away to do their country's bidding. This, of course, was not only the case for hundreds of Australian lads, but also with their counterparts in Great Britain and the other Empire counties engaged in the conflict.

There were also many examples of 'boy soldiers' among the enemy troops, as Private E. P. F. Lynch mentions in his reminiscences in *Somme Mud: The Experiences of an Infantryman in France 1916–1919*, when referring to some of the German youths he encountered in the trenches:

> We've seen that scared, nervously apprehensive look before on Fritz faces and our own … somehow we can't keep our eyes off these poor devils, for they aren't men, but mere boys of no more than fifteen. Tear stains are on many of their boyish faces. Tears of fear. Boys thrown into what even hardened men can barely stand.[2]

With the enormous pressure put on the boys in the Junior and Senior Cadets in Australia, largely through the schools and their patriotic ceremonies, and through military training and the many forms of political indoctrination they encountered, it was not surprising to find large numbers of underage recruits in the ranks of the AIF.

Such was the case with Private Harold Katte, a sixteen-year-old Senior Cadet who was inspired to enlist after reading in the newspaper about the Anzacs and their daring exploits at Gallipoli. With his father's written consent, young Harold falsely claimed he had served with the Senior Cadets for four years, changed his name to Marcel Caux to conceal his proper identity, and was accepted without question.[3]

Private R. E. G. Cunningham, a Sydney Grammar Old Boy, enlisted at age fifteen and served the next two-and-a-half years on the battlefields of Gallipoli and France. Wounded and gassed at Passchendaele, he was repatriated back to Australia and in 1918 resumed his studies at Sydney Grammar 'to make up some of the work he had missed', giving valuable help to the school's cadet corps in the process.[4]

Private Alec Campbell

Then there was the celebrated Anzac veteran Alec Campbell, literally the 'last man standing' as he was the last of the Anzacs still alive in

2002, who died in Hobart at the age of 103. Young Alec had just started working as an insurance clerk in Launceston when the war started, and he promptly enlisted because 'most of my mates were joining up for a bit of fun'. Alec's father took a lot of convincing before giving written permission and vouching he was eighteen, when he was actually sixteen years and four months old, because 'like most other people he thought the war would be over in a few months, well before young Alec got to the front'. Barely five feet and five inches tall and weighing 135 pounds, he was lucky he was accepted.[5] After training in Egypt, he was sent to Gallipoli with the 15th Battalion. While digging a trench, a German sniper shot and killed the New Zealander standing alongside him 'and the top of his head was blown off'. Alec spent his seventeenth birthday fighting on the Western Front in France, where he was badly wounded and repatriated to Australia in June 1916.[6]

A 8759

AUSTRALIAN MILITARY FORCES.

AUSTRALIAN IMPERIAL FORCE.

Attestation Paper of Persons Enlisted for Service Abroad.

No. 2731 Name CAMPBELL Alex William

Unit 15th Battalion A.I.F.

15th Battalion Joined on 2/7/15

Questions to be put to the Person Enlisting before Attestation.

1. What is your Name? ... 1. Alex William Campbell
2. In or near what Parish or Town were you born? ... 2. In the Parish of ... in or near the Town of Launceston in the County of Tas
3. Are you a natural born British Subject or a Naturalized British Subject? (N.B.—If the latter, papers to be shown.) ... 3. Yes
4. What is your age? ... 4. 18 3/12
5. What is your trade or calling? ... 5. Clerk
6. Are you, or have you been, an Apprentice? If so, where, to whom, and for what period? ... 6. No
7. Are you married? ... 7. No
8. Who is your next of kin? (Address to be stated) ... Mother Mrs Maria J. Campbell Mayne St Invermay Lnss
9. Have you ever been convicted by the Civil Power? ... 9. Yes Riding without a light
10. Have you ever been discharged from any part of His Majesty's Forces, with Ignominy, or as Incorrigible and Worthless, or on account of Conviction of Felony, or of a Sentence of Penal Servitude, or have you been dismissed with Disgrace from the Navy? ... 10. No
11. Do you now belong to, or have you ever served in, His Majesty's Army, the Marines, the Militia, the Militia Reserve, the Territorial Force, Royal Navy, or Colonial Forces? If so, state which, and if not now serving, state cause of discharge ... 11. Yes Cadets 92 B 3 years
12. Have you stated the whole, if any, of your previous service? 12. Yes
13. Have you ever been rejected as unfit for His Majesty's Service? If so, on what grounds? ... 13. No
14. (*For married men, widowers with children, and soldiers who are the sole support of widowed mother*)—Do you understand that no Separation Allowance will be issued to you after embarkation during your term of service? ... 14. ✓
15. Are you prepared to undergo inoculation against small pox and enteric fever? ... 15. Yes

I, Alex William Campbell do solemnly declare that the above answers made by me to the above questions are true, and I am willing and hereby voluntarily agree to serve in the Military Forces of the Commonwealth of Australia within or beyond the limits of the Commonwealth.

~~And I further agree to allot not less than two-fifths three-fifths of the pay payable to me from time to time during my service for the support of my wife* wife and children.~~ A.W. Campbell A.W. Campbell

Date 2/7/15 A.W. Campbell A.W. Campbell

Signature of person enlisted.

**This clause should be struck out in the case of unmarried men or widowers without children under 18 years of age.*
† *Two-fifths must be allotted to the wife, and if there are children three-fifths must be allotted.*

D.377/1.15.—C.968.

Alec's enlistment form, signed on 2 July 1915 (Australian Archives)

The kid soldier photographed in August 1915 at Claremont Camp, Hobart

Jonathan King "Gallipoli Our Last Man Standing"

Enlistment papers for ex-cadet Alec William Campbell of Hobart, Tasmania, aged sixteen years. He later served in Gallipoli with the AIF. Jonathan King, *Gallipoli: Our last Man Standing*, 2003

Private Jim Martin

The most publicised 'boy soldier' was James Martin, accepted into the ranks of the AIF as a fourteen-year-old ex-pupil of Manningtree Road State School in Glenferrie, Melbourne. As a small child, Jim could hardly wait until he reached the age of twelve, when he could join the Junior Cadets at school. Much to his delight, he became a drummer in the cadets, and was also a crack shot with a .22 rifle at the miniature rifle range attached to the school. The headmaster was James McClaren, a Lieutenant Colonel in the reserves, who was also the drill instructor for the cadets, as well as a fountain of information for the boys on patriotic and military matters.[7] Jim left school at the age of fourteen. When the war started, Jim's father Charlie was eager to join the first batch of the AIF, but was rejected for service because he was deemed too old. Young Jim pleaded with his parents to allow him to fake his age so that he could go in place of his father, and when they naturally forbade it he threatened to run away and enlist himself under a different name. Realising that James was serious, his parents reluctantly signed their approval, stating his age was eighteen. This was much to their lasting regret, for their boy died of dysentery after a month fighting at Gallipoli.[8] The Melbourne *Herald* newspaper of 18 December 1915 reported his death 'of enteric' (the intestines) in a brief article under the subtitle 'Youngest Soldier Dies'.[9] He was fourteen years and nine months old.

Sixteen-year-old Private Cecil Hogan befriended Jim Martin when they arrived together at Gallipoli. Sensing they had something in common, the boys confided in each other that they were both underage recruits. Cecil also had badgered his parents, and even the headmaster of his school, with similar threats and succeeded in joining the AIF in 1914. Unlike his friend, Cecil saw the war out, becoming a sergeant in the process.[10]

TOP
The 'Youngest Anzac', Melbourne cadet James Martin, enlisted illegally in the AIF aged fourteen years. He died at Gallipoli in 1915. Anthony Hill, *Soldier Boy: The True Story of Jim Martin the Youngest Anzac*, 2001, book cover

BOTTOM
James Martin photographed with his five sisters before leaving for Gallipoli in 1915. Anthony Hill, *Soldier boy: The True Story of Jim Martin the Youngest Anzac*, 2001, p. 33

Boy stowaways — John Smith and Frank Day

In the same issue of *The Herald* that reported the death of Jim Martin, a much larger article under the banner of 'Boys Stow Away with Troops' told the story of two boys, with accompanying photographs of the boys in uniform. They were John Smith, aged fourteen, and Frank Day, aged eleven, who were sent back to Melbourne on board a troopship from Egypt. Both boys arrived in Egypt separately after stowing away on departing troopships from Melbourne and Fremantle respectively. Being found out shortly after arrival, young Frank was given the job of 'mess orderly' for several weeks while awaiting transport back to Western Australia. Asked his opinion of the adventure by a reporter, he replied:

> That was great. The lieutenant had given me my rank and I had my instructions. I served out meals and waited on the tables in the mess shed for three weeks, and then I was taken by a guard to headquarters and they told me they were going to send me home. I would rather be in Egypt.[11]

The other stowaway, John Smith, had been working at the Union Can Company in Port Melbourne. He commented, 'I thought I would like a trip to the Front with the boys, as a lot of my cobbers had gone there.' John gave himself up to the first mate 'when the vessel was well out of the Heads' and was put to work in the bakehouse. Once in Egypt he stowed away again, this time under the bags on a troop train, saying, 'it was the hottest time I ever had in my life, and I was six hours without food and thought I was going to die.'[12]

THE HERALD, SAT

"RATHER BE IN EGYPT"

BOYS STOW AWAY WITH TROOP

"YOUR JOB IS MESS ORDERLY"

"I only hope the war will last until I am 18—then I can enlist and nobody will be able to send me home," said John Smith, the 11-year-old lad, who stowed away in a troopship at Port Melbourne some months ago, inspired with the thought of seeing active service in Gallipoli. Much against his will he was returned from Egypt after leading the glorious life of a soldier in camp. He arrived here by the troopship on Monday.

"After we had landed at Egypt," he added, "I went in the train with the troops to Zeitun and marched with the Field Artillery to Base Details. I went up to the commanding officer and a lieutenant asked me my name, and where I lived. I told him I lived with my auntie at Station street, Port Melbourne.

"'All right,' said the lieutenant, 'you will sleep with the boys. Your job is mess orderly.'"

In the same troopship Frank Day was returned to Fremantle. He is only 11 years of age, and, like Smith, stowed away in a vessel bound for Egypt, where he hoped to join the Expeditionary Force.

"That was great. The lieutenant had given me my rank, and I had my instructions. I served out meals, and waited on the tables in the mess shed for three weeks, and then I was taken to headquarters with a guard, and they told me they were going to send me home. But instead of that they took me to the camp military police, and told me they were going to give me a job in the army shop. I worked there cleaning gun parts and rifles and greasing them.

"And then I'm blowed if I did not get sick, and I was sent to Heliopolis, and when I came out of the hospital after ten days I returned to Zeitun, and had a good look round, and then I was put on the ship, and returned home.

"When I was in camp the military police gave me a uniform, and I gave my old duds to the niggers.

"I would rather be in Egypt, and I do not know why they wanted to shove me back here. The military police took me to Flinders street on Monday, and gave me a new suit of clothes. They were very pretty, but I would rather have my old uniform.

"When I left school I worked for Messrs. Harvey, Drake and Shaw, tinsmiths, for six months, after which I took on a job at the Union Can Company, Port Melbourne. Then I went to the front. I thought I would like to have a trip with the boys as a lot of my cobbers had gone. I knew I was too young to enlist, for I was not a turnip, but when the troops were being sent I made up my mind I would go as far as I could with them. I went down to the town pier, climbed up a life line of the troopship, and went well for'ard, where I waited for the send-off. When the ropes were let go I scrambled to the top of the boilers, where I found it was pretty hot on the firebricks. But when a friendly fireman gave me some stew I felt all right. There was a lot of coal dust in the stew, but I stuck it.

"I went to sleep, and after two or three hours, when the vessel was well out of the Heads, I gave myself up to the first mate, who took me to see the captain, who wanted to have me taken back in the pilot boat. I thought it was all up, and I thought it was awfully hard luck, too, because the next troopship would not be going away for a long while. You see I knew all the movements of the ships. I went down on the pier more often than my auntie knew. Well, I ups and I told the captain I wanted work. He gave me work in the bakehouse and let me sleep in the glory hole.

"And when I got to Egypt I stowed myself under the kit bags in the troop train. It was the hottest time I ever had in my life, and I was for six hours

CHILDREN OF EMPIRE SHOW METTLE

JOHN SMITH FRANK DAY

TOP

Stowaways John Smith, eleven, and Frank Day, ten, bound for Egypt. *The Herald*, Melbourne, 19 December 1915, p. 12

OPPOSITE

Private Ernie Lee (alias Private Ernest John Jeffries) from Mossiface, Victoria, enlisted in the 5th battalion AIF as a fifteen-year-old. He fought at Ypres and Pozieres in France, 1916. *The Age*, 28 March 2011, News, p. 7

Private Ernest Victor Lee of Mossiface, Victoria — the author's great-uncle — enlisted at 14 under the alias Ernest John Jefferies. After the war, newspaper articles glowingly referred to Lee as a splendid specimen of Australian manhood, but made no mention of his troubled past.
(Author's collection)

German-Australian underage recruits

Not surprisingly, there were underage recruits among the German-Australian community as well. Private Herbert Coppleman (anglicised from Koppelman) joined the AIF's 40th Battalion late in 1916, and while serving at Messines in France he was shot in the left hand. After resuming duty six months later he was wounded in the right knee and shell-shocked, and sent to hospital in England. In January 1918, he was repatriated back to Australia, not for medical reasons, but for being underage, as a Defence Department memorandum of 21 September 1917 indicated:

> Application has been made for No.1837 Herbert Cylus John Coppleman to be retained from the firing line on the grounds that he is not yet sixteen years of age and has been wounded twice. The birth certificate of this soldier shows that his correct age is 15 years 9 months.[13]

It is not known how the authorities uncovered this information on Herbert, which shows he was actually fourteen years old on enlistment, nor how he was not intercepted during his medical examination considering his record states he was under five feet and three inches tall and weighed under 115 pounds.[14]

Examples in the Royal Australian Navy

It must be remembered that in those days the majority of boys (and girls) left school for the workforce as soon as they reached the minimum age of fourteen years. At fourteen, boys could join the emerging Royal Australian Navy, or the merchant navy as sailors, stokers or signallers, and many did so. Advertisements such as 'Royal Australian Naval

College: Cadets Wanted', which appeared in the *Education Gazette and Teachers' Aid* in May 1914, asked teachers to remind their pupils and their parents that boys soon to reach the age of fourteen years needed to apply:

> … for boys born in 1901. The applications should be made before the 30th June, 1914, to the Naval Secretary, Navy Office, Melbourne, who will supply application forms, conditions of entry, the syllabus of the qualifying examination …[15]

After several months of basic training, most of the lads went to sea to gain some real experience. In wartime, if their ship was engaged with the enemy they were not spared from gun battles, torpedoes and the like, and many were listed in the casualties that befell their older and more mature comrades. One such example was the renowned Evan Allan, the 'last warrior' (the last Australian serviceman of WWI) who died in a Melbourne nursing home in 2005 at the age of 106. Evan had joined the RAN as a fourteen-year-old in March 1914. Assigned to the light cruiser HMAS *Encounter* in 1915 as 'ship's boy', he spent the next two years on active service in the Pacific and Far East waters, at the end of which he was promoted to the rank of 'able bodied seaman'. Evan also served during WWII, retiring in 1948 after thirty-four years in the navy.[16]

Boy soldiers in the German army

There were also, of course, many 'under-age' youths fighting with the German army against the Russians on the Eastern Front and the Allies on the Western Front, with volunteers as young as sixteen legally allowed to enlist, with their parents' permission.[17] Many of them belonged to the previously mentioned German youth groups

Wandervogel, who had embraced the conflict almost 'to the man'. They were among the decimated 26th Reserve Corps ordered to take the village of Langemarck in Belgium, heavily defended by the British, on 10 November 1914. Singing their trademark song 'Deutschlandlied', the volunteers faced the British machine guns time and time again, until the Langemarck landscape had been 'transformed into an arena of death, littered with corpses and wounded … among the moans and groans and the shouts of "Kamerad!"'[18] Less than half of the 12,000 *Wandervogel* who had gone into that battle returned.[19] The Germans, like the British, resorted to military conscription once the supply of volunteers diminished, reducing the minimum age from 18 to 17 as the conflict dragged on.

23

The War Effort in Australian Schools

Activities for children at school and at home

One of the few positive outcomes of the militarisation of schools during the Great War was the way the respective state governments engaged them as funding sources for the 'war effort'. Hundreds of thousands of pounds were raised by school children throughout the duration of the war, and in the years immediately after it, to supply a few comforts for the men in the trenches and for the wounded convalescing in the hospitals.

A week after the Declaration of War in August 1914, some 200 female teachers from metropolitan Melbourne met at the State Public Offices to form the Women Teachers' Patriotic League to 'assist the Empire in its contest for justice and liberty'. Four weeks later, a mass meeting of Melbourne teachers was convened by the Minister for Education, the Honourable Thomas Livingstone, and the Director of Education, Frank Tate, in the Melbourne Town Hall. This meeting was to raise awareness of the needs of the soldiers heading off to war, and how the schools could be of assistance. One of the outcomes of this gathering was the formation of the Education Department's War Relief Organisation, which also amalgamated with the aforementioned Women Teachers' League, with the stated aims:

1. To organise and carry out classes of instruction for teachers and senior pupils in first aid and in nursing.
2. To provide comforts, such as extra clothing, food, tobacco, and other things, for our men abroad.

3. To alleviate distress among our Allies by donations of money to special funds established for the purpose.
4. To provide comforts, such as extra clothing, food, tobacco and other things, for our sick and wounded men under treatment in Victoria.
5. To assist returned soldiers and their dependents if in need.[1]

It seems that the first aim was designed more for female teachers and senior girls. With the popular catch cry 'It'll all be over by Christmas', one wonders if the War Relief Organisation had a more realistic outlook on the conflict than what the general public was led to believe. Once the Returned Sailors and Soldiers' Imperial League (the forerunner of the RSL) was formed in 1916, the fifth aim on the list was largely made redundant. In effect, the main focus of the Organisation became the second, third and fourth aims.

The Montague Street State School in South Melbourne was set up as the 'central depot' for receiving goods designated for the soldiers, and soon 'the click of knitting needles and the clink of pennies in the collection box' could be heard around the state. Knitted garments such as socks, scarves, gloves and balaclava hats were made largely by the girls and other women in their families, while wooden splints, crutches and empty canvas sandbags were created by the boys in their sloyd (woodwork) classes. Here, the goods were packed into wooden crates and shipped off.[2]

Besides the school headmasters, headmistresses and staff, and the parent-operated State School Committees which instigated fundraising activities, the school children themselves organised cake stalls, knitting activities and concert items at home, bringing the proceeds along to school to boost the fundraising coffers:

> Instances were recorded of school children making brooms, selling rabbit skins, collecting firewood, selling eggs ... they trapped foxes, caught fish and frogs and leeches, dug gardens,

> cleaned chimneys ... caught horses, did odd jobs before their home duties commenced, and handed in all of their pocket money.[3]

The fundraising in state schools gathered momentum as the war dragged on, and even after the Armistice, as there were many thousands of wounded in the hospitals abroad and at home who still depended on their efforts. Until 1921, the money raised from tiny one-teacher rural schools, to large regional and metropolitan primary and high schools, and technical colleges totalled £438,044. 3s. 6d.[4] Most of the money raised was forwarded to the Australian Red Cross, the British Red Cross, the Belgian Relief Fund, the Salvation Army, the Returned Soldiers' Association, and various repatriation hospitals.[5]

In Tasmania, school children were urged to buy 'war savings certificates' for the Children's Twenty Thousand (pounds) Appeal, but the response far exceeded the anticipation, with a grand total of £73,050 being raised by the end of the war. A further £79,824 was raised by the children to provide comforts for the military base hospitals in Hobart and Launceston.[6]

About £100,000 was paid into the Western Australian Education Department's State Schools' Patriotic Fund by students after the fund was declared open in May 1916. News that the soldiers in Gallipoli were short of sandbags fired up Perth schoolboys, who reportedly made 10,000 of them. School children in South Australia made 50,000 fly nets for cavalry horses in the Palestine campaign, while their counterparts in New South Wales raised £83,416 for the Belgian Orphans' Fund.[7]

When the efforts of the thousands of non-government school children around the country are included as well, it can be seen that the schools around Australia played a vital part in the many war effort ventures conducted on the 'home front'. This sentiment is reflected in the final paragraph of the 'Report of the Victorian Education Department's War Relief Fund' of 1920:

No other patriotic organisation in Victoria has inspired the same personal sacrifice, cheerful direct giving and patriotic fervour. The influence of the Fund has spread to every corner of the State, however remote … The record of patriotic effort by school-children is one of the brightest chapters in the story of the Great War.[8]

LEFT
Working for the war effort. *The Children's Hour*, Education Department of South Australia, grade 4, December 1918, p. 175

OPPOSITE
Fundraising activities for sick and wounded soldiers by Victorian school children during WWI. *Education Gazette and Teachers' Aid*, Victoria, 21 January 1915, p. 16

AIDS FOR THE WOUNDED.

The picture reproduced on this page explains itself, even without the terse description that accompanied it:—"Two hundred and forty crutches made by boys attending Sloyd Center, California Gully. Funds to purchase material provided by Mayor of Eaglehawk's Patriotic Fund. Sticks for

YOUNG HELPERS AT CALIFORNIA GULLY.

handles furnished by Messrs. F. and E. Stilwell, of Bendigo, at a nominal cost. Rubber tips furnished by the Dunlop Rubber Company at a nominal cost. In order to complete the work, a number of boys attended on four days of the vacation voluntarily."

WILLING MESSENGERS.

The illustration herewith shows four swift-footed lads from the Montague-street School (the Central Depot), preparing to run to the railway station with a hand-cart bearing parcels of material addressed to various schools, where it will be made

WILLING MESSENGERS.

up into garments for the troops. The expression of each of the lads indicates that he is seized of the importance of his mission.

Restoration of the war-damaged school of Villers-Bretonneux

The French town of Villers-Bretonneux on the Western Front came under intense enemy attack early in April 1915, when over 20,000 German shells, some containing mustard gas, hit the township. As war correspondent C. E. W. Bean remarked, 'It was a shocking site. Every house seemed to have been hit.'[9] A successful counterattack on Anzac Day by the Australian 13th and 15th Brigades was able to retake the town, but suffered the loss of 1200 diggers in action.[10]

After the war, at the suggestion of Lieutenant-Colonel C. F. Watson, Frank Tate gave the approval to set aside £10,000 from war relief funds for the rebuilding of the damaged boys' school at Villers-Bretonneux, as a memorial to the Australian soldiers who had died there. An inscribed four-faced memorial pillar was erected on the site, and the boys' school was re-opened on 16 June 1923. The inscription on the front wall of the school reads, in part: '… the gift of the school children of Victoria, in memory of the liberation of the territory of Villers-Bretonneux by the Australian troops on the 25th of April, 1918.'[11]

Opened by the Agent General, Sir George Fairbairn, representing the people of Victoria, the town was 'decked out in triumphal arches, flags, banners and placards', and a public holiday was declared for the occasion. The Official Luncheon, attended by 300 guests, was held in the school hall, which was panelled with Australian hardwoods. The new school was also renamed *L'Ecole Victoria* (Victoria School) and the outdoor covered area displays a large banner that reads, 'Don't Forget Australia'.[12]

Since then, Victoria has 'adopted' not only the school, but the town of Villers-Bretonneux. Thousands of tourists and WWI pilgrims journey through the township that bears street signs such as 'Rue de Melbourne' and 'Rue du Victoria'. A French-Australian war memorial museum has been incorporated into the building, and the boys' school has since become a co-ed primary school, with around 130 students.

THIS SCHOOL BUILDING IS THE GIFT OF THE SCHOOL CHILDREN OF VICTORIA, AUSTRALIA, TO THE CHILDREN OF VILLERS-BRETONNEUX AS A PROOF OF THEIR LOVE AND GOOD-WILL TOWARDS FRANCE. TWELVE HUNDRED AUSTRALIAN SOLDIERS, THE FATHERS AND BROTHERS OF THESE CHILDREN, GAVE THEIR LIVES IN THE HEROIC RECAPTURE OF THIS TOWN FROM THE INVADER ON 24TH APRIL 1918, AND ARE BURIED NEAR THIS SPOT. MAY THE MEMORY OF GREAT SACRIFICES IN A COMMON CAUSE KEEP FRANCE AND AUSTRALIA TOGETHER FOREVER IN BONDS OF FRIENDSHIP AND MUTUAL ESTEEM.

TOP
Ruins of the Villers-Bretonneux Boys School (centre, left), July 1917. Courtesy Franco-Australian Museum

MIDDLE
French children of the Villers-Bretonneux School prepare to sing 'Australia Will Be There' at the opening of the new school in May 1917. Courtesy Franco-Australian Museum

BOTTOM
Foundation stone of the Villers-Bretonneux School. Photo by the author, July 2010

TOP
Primary classroom of the Villers-Bretonneux School. Photo by the author, July, 2010

BOTTOM
The author with daughter Alison Waugh at the Franco-Australian Museum, Villers-Bretonneux, July 2010. Photo courtesy the author

Villers-Bretonneux returns the favour in 2011

Hearing of the three Victorian schools destroyed in the Black Saturday bushfires of 2009, a group of citizens from Villers-Bretonneux decided to repay the favour by raising $21,000 towards the rebuilding of one of them — Strathewen Primary School. Over twenty of the Villers-Bretonneux citizens, including the town Mayor, Patrick Simon, visited the newly built school in November 2011. They were there to see the French courtyard and its outdoor chessboard which was their town's contribution to the refurbishment. A plaque outside the new school commemorates the occasion:

> This chess courtyard is a gift from the people of Villers-Bretonneux who generously supported Strathewen Primary School after the devastation of Black Saturday, 2009. We shall carry on this historic connection into the future.[13]

Bound by history, French children honour their debt

From Page 1

The 35 students from kindergarten to Year 6 have taken up home in two demountable classrooms in Wattle Glen primary school. It is only 20km away, but many of the students say they don't enjoy "the suburbs" and long for their school in the bush.

In the lead-up to today's Anzac Day commemorations, Strathewen principal Jane Hayward told her students about what another group of children, in a French village on the other side of the world, were doing to help.

As the Strathewen students made Anzac Day wreaths yesterday, they expressed surprise that children who lived so far away would care about their loss.

"They're thinking about us and they want to help us," said Siena Hyland of Year 6. "It's a bit weird they know what happened to us, when Strathewen was a little place nobody knew about.

"We learned today that all the Victorian kids sent over a penny to rebuild their school, and now they're doing the same for us."

Alanah and Lachie Chapman, who lost their home on February 7, said they would today be thinking about the Australian soldiers who fought at Villers-Bretonneux. "They would have been very brave," said Lachie, a Year 4 student.

When construction was finished on the new Villers-Bretonneux school in 1926, it was renamed Ecole Victoria. A part of

Remembering a debt: Alanah and Lachie Chapman, who lost their home on February 7, work on Anzac Day wreaths at Wattle Glen primary school yesterday. Picture: Stuart McEvoy

The Australian, 25 April 2011

after the firestorm

Strathewen Primary school principal Jane Hayward with some of her pupils at the rebuilt school; the grounds after Black Saturday.
PICTURES: RODGER CUMMINS, PENNY STEPHENS

TOP

The new Strathewen Primary School, Victoria, rebuilt after the 2010 bushfires. *The Age*, 3 October 2012

BOTTOM

Children's book telling of the special relationship between the school children of Villers-Bretonneux and Victoria

Summary

Military training in schools, and its accompanying indoctrination, began voluntarily in the nineteenth century in Australia, peaked in the World War I (compulsory) period, and continues by choice in some schools to this day. Our cadet units were originally modelled on the British public (private) schools, and although optional at first, they were an expected 'optional extra' in many cases.

Concern over Australia's isolation and vulnerability to foreign attack by sea was a major factor in the federation of Australian colonies in 1901, and national defence became a high priority for the emerging nation. A review of the fledgling Australian Military Forces, and those of New Zealand, by Lord Kitchener in 1909–10 confirmed that a form of compulsory military training in Junior and Senior Cadets, and a militia, was needed along lines that had previously been decided by a number of state and federal politicians of all persuasions.

While the majority of youths and their parents conformed to this form of conscription, there were thousands of prosecutions for non-compliance, resulting in heavy fines. In cases of repeat offences, some of the Senior Cadets were even jailed. Once the war began the non-compliance rate plummeted, and the system of military conscription of our youth continued until it was finally abolished in 1929.

There was little opposition to the Junior Cadets, who paraded after school once a week, drilled mainly by their teachers, who were happy to earn the extra money for their tuition. The schools were also used for political indoctrination, originally through the patriotic ceremonies associated with events such as British Empire Day or the King's Birthday. As war approached, monthly school magazines like *The School Paper* became a major source of war articles, stories, poems and patriotic songs, all designed to brainwash young minds and encourage recruitment into the armed forces.

Relentless pressure was placed on teachers through the *Education Gazette* and *The School Paper* to keep their young charges informed of the progress of the war. Teachers in the respective education departments were encouraged to enlist themselves in the AIF, and in the case of Victoria, around half of the eligible males did so.

In states with sizeable populations of German immigrants, like South Australia, Victoria and Queensland, there were many cases of internment. As the hysteria mounted against the alleged German atrocities committed in the occupied countries, public discrimination against them mounted. Most Lutheran schools were forced to close and their teachers made redundant, despite the fact that there were hundreds of men of German origin fighting in the AIF, many of them among the casualties that ensued.

As was the case in Britain and other British Empire countries, it was no surprise to find hundreds of 'under aged' Australian boys enlisting illegally in the AIF. Many of these boys would have been spurred on by the military training and patriotic indoctrination they received during their involvement in the compulsory school cadet system instigated in 1910.

As far as the schools were concerned, the only positive outcome from the conflict was the magnificent part they played in relieving the suffering of our troops in the 'war effort'. Throughout the country, public and private schools in cities and remote rural areas raised hundreds of thousands of pounds to supply soldiers in the trenches with a few basic comforts. Many thousands of hospitalised soldiers also benefited from the toiletries, splints, crutches and warm accessories made by the children. After the war, Victorian children raised money to rebuild the war-damaged school at Villers-Bretonneux, a favour returned in 2011 with refurbishment assistance to Strathewen Primary School, a casualty of the Victorian Black Saturday bushfires.

Conclusion

The Great War was a conflict brought about mainly by broken national alliances, and the two main protagonists, Britain and Germany, should never have allowed it to happen in the first place. Horrendous casualties ensued on both sides, with millions of men killed and wounded, along with thousands of civilian casualties. Many of those who survived remained traumatised for the rest of their lives, their misery shared by their close relatives.

By using the nation's schools as venues for military training, recruitment and propaganda, the Federal Government of Australia was able to supply sufficient troops for the front line without having to resort to military conscription, a fact that successive governments, along with many of the population, continue to boast (excluding, of course, the Vietnam War). But tragically, whether we recognise it or not, we did have military conscription before and during World War I — conscription in our schools and for youth in the workplace, who were well-trained, disciplined, politicised and ready to volunteer for the carnage.

Following the Treaty of Versailles in 1919, the reparations enforced by the Allies were so severe on the German population that they helped provide a breeding ground of such wretchedness and discontent, that an Austrian corporal, Adolf Hitler, was able to lead his people into yet another war in 1939, resulting in even greater casualties (particularly among innocent civilians). Through the Hitler Youth Movement of the 1930s and 1940s, aspects of which were modelled on their German predecessors in WWI, yet another generation of unsuspecting youth were used as cannon fodder, but this time also for the oppression of the 'enemy' (those groups of people targeted during the Holocaust) in their midst.

The Australian Government must have learnt a bitter lesson from its misuse of schools in WWI, because by the time Australia was involved in WWII, only a voluntary system of cadets was permitted, and the schools played a minor role (largely fundraising activities) this time. Then, most of the wartime propaganda was evident only in the patriotic ceremonies of Anzac Day, Remembrance Day and Empire Day, with very little focus on the conflict in the school curriculum, and even less in the wars that followed in Korea, Vietnam, Iraq and Afghanistan (both declared and undeclared). One would hope that never again Australian school children and their teachers be used so blatantly to promote warmongering as in the WWI period, and that we as a nation will continue to reflect on the terrible consequences that ensued. Lest we forget.

Endnotes

Introduction

1 Joseph Maxwell, *Hell's Bells and Mademoiselles*, Sydney: Angus & Robertson, 1939, pp. 1 and 11.

PART I

SCHOOL CADETS IN THE NINETEENTH CENTURY

1 Formation of Military Units in the Australian Colonies

1 Deborah E. Roberts, 'The Role of Victorian State Education in the Development of National Identity 1872–1918', PhD Thesis, Monash University, 1999, p. 58.

2 Ken S. Inglis, *The Australian Colonists: An Exploration of Social History 1788–1870*, p. 226.

3 ibid.

4 Thomas Tanner, *Compulsory Citizen Soldiers*, Sydney: Alternative Publishing Co-operative, 1980, p. 17.

2 School Cadets — Some European Precedents

1 William H. Dixon, *The Switzers*, London: Hurst & Blackett, 1872, p. 310.

2 ibid, p. 307.

3 ibid, p. 311.

4 *The New York Times*, 'Switzerland the Porcupine of Europe', 29 July 1915.

5 Dixon, *The Switzers*, p. 313.

6 ibid, pp. 315–316.

7 Craig Stockings, *The Torch and the Sword: A History of the Army Cadet Movement in Australia*, Sydney: University of New South Wales Press, 2007, p. 7.

8 Raymond Evans, 'The Lowest Common Denominator: Loyalism and School Children in War Torn Australia 1914–1918', *Queensland Review* (Special Edition), p. 103.

9 John MacKenzie, *Propaganda and Empire: The Manipulation of British Public Opinion 1880–1960*, Manchester University Press, p. 6.

10 ibid, p. 240.

11 ibid, p. 246.

12 James Retallack (ed.), *A Short History of Germany: Imperial Germany 1871–1918*, London: Oxford University Press, 2010, p. 200.

13 Michael Kater, *Hitler Youth*, London: Harvard University Press, 2004, p. 7.

14 Andrew Donson, *Youth in the Fearless Land: War Pedagogy, Nationalism and Authority in Germany 1914–1918*, Massachusetts, US: Harvard University Press, 2010, p. 4.

15 Hannsjoachim Wolfgang Koch, *The Hitler Youth: Origins and Development 1922–45*, London: Macdonald & James, 1975, p. 1.

3 School Cadets in the Australian Colonies

1 David Holloway, *The Inspectors: An Account of the Inspectorate of the State Schools of Victoria 1851–1983*, Melbourne: Institute of Senior Officers of the Victorian Education Services, 2000, p. 111.

2 James Alexander Allan, *The Old Model School: Its History and Romance 1852–1904*. Melbourne: Melbourne University Press, 1934, pp. 99–101.

3 Leslie Blake (ed.), *Vision And Realisation: A Centenary History of State Education in Victoria*, vol. 1, Education Department of Victoria, 1973, pp. 1281–1283.

4 G. Blainey, J. Morrissey and S. E. K. Hulme, *Wesley College: The First Hundred Years*, Melbourne: Robertson & Mullins, 1966, p. 189.

5 G. C. Notman and B. R. Keith, *The Geelong College 1861–1961*, Blackburn, Victoria: Specialty Press, 1961, pp. 86–87.

6 G. Denning and D. Kennedy, *Xavier Portraits*, South Melbourne: Graphic Print, 1993, pp. 85–86.

7 Major Charles Daley, 'The Story of the Victorian Junior Cadet Corps', in *The Victorian Historical Magazine*, vol. xx, no. 1, June 1943, p. 18.

8 Daley, 'The Story of the Victorian Junior Cadet Corps', p. 21.

9 John M. MacKenzie, *Propaganda and Empire: The Manipulation of British Public Opinion*, Manchester University Press, p. 6.

10 T. Brodribb, *Addresses 190: No. 2 — Military Training for Our Schoolboys*, Melbourne: Imperial Federation League, 1909, p. 4.

11 Deborah E. Roberts, 'The Role of Victorian State Education in the Development of National Identity 1872–1918', PhD Thesis, Monash University, 1999, p. 62.

12 Bob Bessant (ed.), *Mother State and Her Little Ones: Children and Youth in Australia 1860s–1930s*, Melbourne: Centre for Youth and Community Studies, 1987, p. 69.

13 Blake, *Vision and Realisation*, p. 1283.

14 David Jones, 'The Military Use of Australian Schools 1872–1914', PhD Thesis, Latrobe University, 1991, p. 151.

15 Holloway, *The Inspectors*, p. 111.

16 Bessant, *Mother State and Her Little Ones*, p. 63.

17 Candy, *Victorian Cadet Movement*, p. 24.

18 Daley, 'The Story of the Victorian Junior Cadet Corps', p. 20.

19 ibid, p. 29.

20 ibid.

21 Damian Powell, *Honour in the Field: Melbourne High School and the Military in the Century of Federation*, Melbourne: Melbourne University Press, 2003, p. 4.

22 J. Burnswood and J. Fletcher, *Sydney and the Bush: A Pictorial History of Education in New South Wales*, Sydney: Government Printer, 1980, p. 38.

23 Jones, 'The Military Use of Australian Schools', p. 189.

24 Craig Wilcox, *Red Coat Dreaming: How Colonial Australia Embraced the British Army*, Cambridge University Press, 2009, p. 84.

25 Jones, 'The Military Use of Australian Schools', p. 191.
26 ibid, p. 188.
27 *Parramatta Mercury*, 9 September 1877.
28 Bessant, *Mother State and Her Little Ones*, pp. 64–67.
29 ibid, p. 69.
30 Jones, 'The Military Use of Australian Schools', pp. 268–270.
31 Martin Crotty, *Making the Australian Male: Middle Class Masculinity 1870–1920*, Melbourne: Melbourne University Press, 2001, p. 26.
32 Bessant, *Mother State and Her Little Ones*, pp. 73–74.
33 Craig Stockings, *The Torch and the Sword: A History of the Army Cadet Movement in Australia*, Sydney: University of New South Wales Press, 2007, p. 9.
34 Jones, 'The Military Use of Australian Schools', pp. 342–343.
35 ibid.
36 ibid, p. 11.

4 New Zealand School Cadet Corps

1 James D. Milburn, 'New Zealand's First Experiment With Compulsory Military Training 1900–1914', MA Thesis, Wellington: Victoria University College, 1954, p. 31.
2 C. McGeorge, 'Military Training in New Zealand Primary Schools, 1900–1912', *ANZHES Journal*, vol. 3, no. 2, 1974, p. 2.
3 ibid.
4 ibid, p. 3.
5 C. Caughey (ed.), *Remuera Primary School 125 years 1873–1998*, pp. 16–17.
6 Karen McKinnon, *The Gold and Blue: Maryborough High School (NZ) 1900–2000*, p. 37.
7 Bruce Hamilton and Don Hamilton, *Never a Footstep Back: A History of Wanganui Collegiate School 1854–2003*, Wanganui, New Zealand: Wanganui Collegiate Board of Trustees, 2003, p. 130.
8 A. W. Beasley, *The Light Accepted: 125 Years of Wellington College*, Wellington, NZ: Wordset Enterprises, 1992, p. 54.

PART II

EARLY TWENTIETH CENTURY DEVELOPMENTS

5 The Relevance of Empire Day

1 Maurice French, 'One People One Destiny: A Question of Loyalty. The Origins of Empire Day in NSW 1900–1905', *Journal of the Royal Australian Historical Society*, vol. 61, part 4, December 1975, p. 237.
2 ibid, p. 239.
3 Raymond Evans, 'The Lowest Common Denominator: Loyalism and School Children in War Torn Australia 1914–1918', *Queensland Review* (Special Edition), p. 102.
4 S. G. Firth, *Schooling in New South Wales 1880–1914*, MA Thesis, ANU, p. 110.
5 ibid, p. 112.
6 ibid, p. 113.

7 *The School Paper*, grades 5 and 6, May 1910, p. 52.
8 Firth, *Schooling in New South Wales*, p. 130.
9 ibid.
10 Tim Jeal, *Baden-Powell*, London: Hutchinson, 1989, p. 410.

6 Early Calls for Military Conscription in Europe

1 Thomas Tanner, *Compulsory Citizen Soldiers*, Sydney: Alternative Publishing Co-operative, 1980, p. xx.
2 Leslie Jauncey, *The Story of Conscription in Australia*, Sydney: MacMillan, 1968, pp. 6–9.
3 Tanner, *Compulsory Citizen Soldiers*, p. xx.
4 William H. Dixon, *The Switzers*, London: Hurst & Blackett, 1872, p. 304.
5 ibid.
6 ibid, p. 313.
7 *London Economist*, 5 June 1915.
8 Jauncey, *The Story of Conscription in Australia*, pp. 9–10.

7 Calls for Military Conscription in Australia and New Zealand

1 Stated by W. M. Hughes in the House of Representatives, 31 July 1901.
2 Commonwealth Parliamentary Debates, vol. III, 31 July 1901, p. 3434.
3 ibid, p. 3305.
4 ibid, p. 3544.
5 ibid, 9 August 1901, p. 3597–8.
6 ibid, 7 August 1901, p. 3534.
7 T. Brodribb, *Addresses 190: No. 2 — Military Training for Our Schoolboys*, Melbourne: Imperial Federation League, 1909, p 7.
8 ibid, p. 6.
9 James Dalton Milburn, 'New Zealand's First Experiment With Compulsory Military Training 1900–1914', MA Thesis, Victoria University College, Wellington, New Zealand, 1954, pp. 37–38.
10 ibid, p. 39.
11 ibid, p. 47.
12 ibid, p. 48.

8 The Defence Act of 1903 and the Establishment of the Australian Commonwealth Cadet Corps

1 Ken S. Inglis, 'Conscription in Peace and War 1911–1945' in R. Forward and B. Reece (eds.), *Conscription in Australia*, p. 23.
2 Helen Penrose, *Red, Black and Khaki: Cadets at Xavier College*, Melbourne: Eldon Hogan Trust, 1995, p. 12.
3 Craig Stockings, *The Torch and the Sword: A History of the Army Cadet Movement in Australia*, Sydney: University of New South Wales Press, 2007, p. 37.
4 Leslie Blake (ed.), *Vision And Realisation: A Centenary History of State Education in Victoria,* vol. 1, Education Department of Victoria, 1973, p. 1284.

5 Bob Bessant (ed.), *Mother State and Her Little Ones: Children and Youth in Australia 1860s–1930s*, Melbourne: Centre for Youth and Community Studies, 1987, p. 77.
6 Stockings, *The Torch and the Sword*, p. 40.
7 *The Age*, 9 July 1906, p. 4.
8 Stockings, *The Torch and the Sword*, pp. 44–46.
9 J. Pash and J. Treloar, *Adelaide High School 75th Anniversary 1908–1983: Souvenir Book*, Adelaide: Adelaide High School Council Incorporated, 1983, p. 36.
10 'Report of the Minister for Public Instruction 1910–11', Victoria, p. 24.
11 Deborah E. Roberts, 'The Role of Victorian State Education in the Development of National Identity 1872–1918', PhD Thesis, Monash University, 1999, p. 59.
12 ibid, 1911–12, p. 102.
13 Bessant, *Mother State and Her Little Ones*, p. 78.
14 Stockings, *The Torch and the Sword*, p. 45.
15 ibid, p. 42.
16 John Hamilton, *The Price of Valour*, Sydney: Macmillan, 2012, p. 53.
17 ibid, p. 32.
18 ibid, p. 60.
19 *The Argus*, 25 April 1910, p. 21.
20 *The Argus*, 26 April 1910, p. 5.
21 Ronald S. Horan, *Fort Street: The School*. Sydney: Honeyset Publications, 1989, p. 155.
22 ibid, p. 165.

9 The 1909 Defence Act Incorporating Compulsory Military Training

1 Craig Stockings, 'Khaki in the Classroom: Compulsory Junior Cadet Training in Australian Schools, 1911– 1931', *History of Education Review*, vol. 37, no. 1, 2008, p. 16.
2 Ian Kuring, *Redcoats to Cams: A History of Australian Infantry 1788–2001*, Canberra: Army History Unit, Defence Department, 2004, pp. 35–36.
3 Agnes Hannan, *Victoria Barracks, Melbourne: A Social History*, Australian Defence Force Journal Publication, p. 63.
4 Major Charles Daley, 'The Story of the Victorian Junior Cadet Corps', in *The Victorian Historical Magazine*, vol. xx, no. 1, June 1943, p. 20.
5 Commonwealth of Australia, 'Regulations and Instructions for Universal Training', Section 141, Defence Act 1903–1910.
6 Ken S. Inglis, 'Conscription in Peace and War 1911–1945' in R. Forward and B. Reece (eds.), *Conscription in Australia*, p. 27.
7 Craig Stockings, *The Torch and the Sword: A History of the Army Cadet Movement in Australia*, Sydney: University of New South Wales Press, 2007, p. 62.

10 Compulsory School Cadets — Regulations

1 Commonwealth of Australia, 'Regulations and Instructions for Universal Training', Defence Act 1903–1910, p. 7.

2 ibid, p. 9.
3 'Report of the Minister for Defence on the Progress of Universal Training', 30 June 1912, p. 15.
4 Brian Lewis, *Our War: Australia During World War I*, Melbourne: Melbourne University Press, 1980, p. 116.
5 Commonwealth of Australia, Australian Junior Cadet Regulations 1917, p. 12.
6 ibid, p. 13.
7 ibid, p. 14.
8 Brian Lewis, *Our War*, p. 116.
9 Craig Stockings, 'Khaki in the Classroom: Compulsory Junior Cadet Training in Australian Schools, 1911- 1931', *History of Education Review*, vol. 37, no. 1, 2008, p. 22.
10 Commonwealth of Australia, Australian Junior Cadet Regulations 1917, p. 18–19.
11 David Jones, 'Cadets and Military Training 1872–1914', Melbourne: Centre for Youth and Community Studies, 1987, p. 412; Lynette Silver, *Marcel Caux: A Life Unravelled*, Melbourne: Wiley, 2006, p. 142.
12 Commonwealth of Australia, Australian Junior Cadet Regulations 1917, p. 22.
13 ibid, p. 30.
14 Bob Bessant (ed.), *Mother State and Her Little Ones: Children and Youth in Australia 1860s–1930s*, Melbourne: Centre for Youth and Community Studies, 1987, p. 78.
15 Stockings, 'Khaki in the Classroom', p. 21.
16 A. G. Austin and R. J. W. Selleck, *The Australian Government School 1830–1914*, Melbourne: Pitman, 1975, p. 327.
17 Commonwealth of Australia, 'Regulations and Instructions for Universal Training', pp. 13–14.
18 'Report of the Minister for Defence', June 1912, p. 15.
19 ibid, pp. 5–7.
20 Commonwealth of Australia, 'Regulations and Instructions for Universal Training', p. 16.
21 Silver, *Marcel Caux: A Life Unravelled*, p. 143.
22 Commonwealth of Australia, 'Regulations and Instructions for Universal Training', p. 30.
23 'Report of the Minister for Defence', June 1912, p. 17.
24 Commonwealth Defence Force, 'Military Regulations for the Universal Training of Senior Cadets', Section 135, 25 July 1913, p. 23.
25 'Report of the Minister for Defence', June 1912, p. 14.
26 Education Department of Victoria, *Education Gazette and Teachers' Aid*, 21 August 1912, p. 332.
27 ibid, 24 June, p. 162.
28 ibid, 27 May 1913, p. 243.
29 Department of Defence Australia, Defence Act 1903–1927, pp. 23–25.
30 Commonwealth of Australia, 'Regulations and Instructions for Universal Training', p. 18.
31 ibid.

32 ibid.
33 ibid, p. 21.
34 The Defence Act 1903–1927: Regulations and Orders for the Australian Military Forces and Senior Cadets, pp. 320–323.
35 ibid, p. 22.

11 Officer Training for Teachers

1 Bob Bessant (ed.), *Mother State and Her Little Ones: Children and Youth in Australia 1860s–1930s*, Melbourne: Centre for Youth and Community Studies, 1987, p. 82.
2 ibid, p. 28.
3 'Report of the Minister for Defence on the Progress of Universal Training', 30 June 1912, pp. 17–18.
4 Education Department of Victoria, *Education Gazette and Teachers' Aid*, July 23, 1912, p. 200
5 Lieutenant C. R. Collins, 'The Training of Junior Cadets', *The Lone Hand*, 1 March 1913.

12 New Zealand's Defence Act of 1909 and the Subsequent Defence Amendment Act of 1910

1 James Dalton Milburn, 'New Zealand's First Experiment With Compulsory Military Training 1900–1914', MA Thesis, Victoria University College, Wellington, New Zealand, 1954, pp. 52–53.
2 ibid, pp. 54–55.
3 ibid, p. 58.
4 Milburn, 'New Zealand's First Experiment With Compulsory Military Training', pp. 60–64.
5 R. L. Weitzel, 'Pacifists and Anti-Militants in New Zealand 1909–1914', *New Zealand Journal of History*, vol. 7, no. 2, p. 129.
6 K. A. Trembath, *Ad Augusta: A Centennial History of Auckland Grammar School 1869-1969*, Auckland: Wilson & Horton, 1969, p. 161.

13 Reactions to the Introduction of Compulsory Military Training

1 Bobbie Oliver, *Peacemongers: Conscientious Objectors to Military Service in Australia 1911–1945*, Western Australia: Freemantle Arts Centre Press, 2003, p. 9.
2 ibid, p. 10.
3 Michael McKernan, *The Australian People and the Great War*, Melbourne: Nelson, 1980, p. 14.
4 Craig Wilcox. *Red Coat Dreaming: How Colonial Australia Embraced the British Army*, Cambridge University Press, 2009, p. 108.
5 ibid, pp. 16–17.
6 Ailsa Zainuddin, 'Reverend William Henry Fitchett (1841–1928)', *Australian Dictionary of Biography*, National Centre of Biography, Australian National University, published in hardcopy 1981, p. 512.

7 Reverend William Henry Fitchett, *Deeds That Won the Empire*, London: Smith Elder & Co., 1897, p. 2.
8 N. Meany, *The Search for Security in the Pacific 1901–1914*, Sydney, 1976, p. 155.
9 J. M. Main, *Conscription: The Australian Debate 1901–1970*, Australia: Cassell, 1970, p. 3.
10 ibid, p. 11.
11 John Barrett, *Falling In: Australians and Boy Conscription 1911–1915*, Sydney: Hale & Ironmonger, 1979, p. 48.
12 ibid, p. 53.
13 *The Socialist*, 25 August 1911, p. 1.
14 Oliver, *Peacemongers*, pp. 19–20.
15 *Freedom*, 24 June 1912, p. 1.
16 Barrett, *Falling In*, pp. 91–92.
17 ibid, pp. 102–103.
18 Agnes Hannan, *Victoria Barracks Melbourne: A Social History*, Australian Defence Force Journal Publication, p. 63.
19 Thomas Tanner, *Compulsory Citizen Soldiers*, Sydney: Alternative Publishing Co-operative, 1980, p. 190.
20 Barrett, *Falling In*, p. 32.
21 Jeffrey Grey, *A Military History of Australia*, England: Cambridge University Press, 1990, p. 81.
22 Barrett, *Falling In*, pp. 72–73.
23 Grey, *A Military History of Australia*, p. 81.
24 *The Argus*, 16 March 1912, p. 18.
25 J. P. Fletcher and J. F. Hills, *Conscription Under Camouflage: An Account of Compulsory Military Training in Australasia Down to the Outbreak of the Great War*, Glenelg, South Australia, 1919, p. 61.
26 Commonwealth Defence Force, 'Military Regulations for the Universal Training of Senior Cadets', 25 July 1913, Section 135.
27 Fletcher and Hills, *Conscription Under Camouflage*, pp. 42–43.
28 *Adelaide Register*, 23 October 1912.
29 ibid.
30 ibid.
31 *Daily Telegraph*, 23 September 1913.
32 *Daily Telegraph*, 29 August 1912.
33 *The Herald*, 4 September 1912.
34 ibid.
35 *The Socialist*, 5 December 1913.
36 *The Socialist*, 25 August 1911, p. 1.
37 *The Socialist*, 3 January 1913, p. 4.
38 ibid, 18 July 1913, p. 3.
39 ibid.
40 ibid, 1 May 1914, p. 4.
41 Fletcher and Hills, *Conscription Under Camouflage*, pp. 81–82.
42 *Daily Telegraph*, 6 February 1913.

43 Barrett, *Falling In*, pp. 171–172.
44 Education Department of Victoria, *Education Gazette and Teachers' Aid*, 23 July 1912, p. 196.
45 ibid, 19 June 1914, p. 2.
46 Barrett, *Falling In*, p. 186–187.
47 ibid, pp. 189–190.
48 ibid, p. 181.
49 *The Argus*, 3 October 1911, p. 4.
50 ibid, 17 June 1912, p. 12.
51 ibid, 18 June 1912.
52 Barrett, *Falling In*, pp. 212–213.
53 *The Argus*, 6 July 1914, p. 9.
54 ibid, p. 215.

14 Reactions to Compulsory Training in New Zealand

1 E. M. Fraser, *New Zealand Military Policy from the Boer War to the Great War 1900–1914*, MA Thesis, University of Auckland, 1938, p. 137.
2 ibid, pp. 138–139.
3 James Dalton Milburn, 'New Zealand's First Experiment With Compulsory Military Training 1900–1914', MA Thesis, Victoria University College, Wellington, New Zealand, 1954, pp. 65–66.
4 Milburn, 'New Zealand's First Experiment With Compulsory Military Training', pp. 66–67.
5 Fraser, *New Zealand Military Policy from the Boer War to the Great War*, pp. 129–130.
6 Milburn, 'New Zealand's First Experiment With Compulsory Military Training', pp. 102–103.
7 ibid, pp. 103–104.
8 R. L. Weitzel, 'Pacifists and Anti-Militants in New Zealand 1909–1914', *New Zealand Journal of History*, vol. 7, no. 2, p. 131.
9 ibid, pp. 76–77.
10 Milburn, 'New Zealand's First Experiment With Compulsory Military Training', pp. 78–79.
11 ibid, pp. 87–88.
12 ibid, p. 90.
13 *Maoriland Worker*, 9 February 1912.
14 Milburn, 'New Zealand's First Experiment With Compulsory Military Training', p. 68.
15 Fraser, *New Zealand Military Policy from the Boer War to the Great War*, p. 131.
16 Milburn, 'New Zealand's First Experiment With Compulsory Military Training', p. 84.
17 ibid.
18 ibid, p. 144.
19 Milburn, 'New Zealand's First Experiment With Compulsory Military Training', p. 82.

20 William Hillcourt, *Baden-Powell: the Two Lives of a Hero*, London: Heinemann, 1964, p. 331.
21 *Christchurch Press*, 16 May 1912.
22 Fraser, *New Zealand Military Policy from the Boer War to the Great War*, pp. 128–129.
23 J. P. Fletcher and J. F. Hills, *Conscription Under Camouflage: An Account of Compulsory Military Training in Australasia Down to the Outbreak of the Great War*, Glenelg, South Australia, 1919, p. 110.
24 Weitzel, 'Pacifists and Anti-Militants in New Zealand', p. 141.
25 Milburn, 'New Zealand's First Experiment With Compulsory Military Training', pp. 128–129.
26 ibid.
27 ibid, p. 129.
28 ibid, pp. 131–132.

PART III
THE WORLD WAR I PERIOD

15 Initial Responses of the Schools to the Outbreak of WWI

1 Education Department of Victoria, *Education Gazette and Teachers' Aid*, 22 September 1914, p. 344.
2 ibid, 23 October 1914, p. 373.
3 ibid.
4 ibid, 10 December 1914, pp. 474–475.
5 *The School Paper*, grades 5 and 6, 1 September 1914.
6 *The School Paper*, grades 7 and 8, 1 September 1914, pp. 146–147.
7 ibid.
8 Michael McKernan, *The Australian People and the Great War*, Melbourne: Nelson, 1980, pp. 49–53.
9 Patsy Adam-Smith, *The Anzacs*, West Melbourne: Nelson, 1978, p. 7.
10 ibid, p. 50.
11 Clifford Reeves, *A History of Tasmanian Education*, Melbourne, 1935, p. 112.
12 Colin Thiele, *Grains of Mustard Seed: A Narrative Outline of State Education in South Australia*, Education Department of South Australia, 1975, p. 130.
13 Ernest Scott, *Official History of Australia in the War of 1914–1918*, vol. 11, Sydney: Angus & Robertson, 1936, p. 735.
14 ibid, p. 737.

16 Ex-Cadets and Trainees Among the AIF

1 Sir George Jones, *From Private to Air Marshall: The Autobiography of Air Marshall Sir George Jones*, Richmond: Greenhouse, 1988, p. 8.
2 C. E. W. Bean, *Here, My Son: An Account of the Independent and Other Corporate Boys' Schools of Australia*, Sydney: Angus & Robertson, 1950, p. 178.
3 Ross McMullin, *Pompey Elliott*, Melbourne: Scribe Publishing, 2008, p. 85.
4 L. L. Robson, *The First AIF: A Study of its Recruitment 1914–1918*, Melbourne: Melbourne University Press, 1970, p. 30.

5 D. T. Merrett, 'The School at War: Scotch College and the Great War', *Melbourne Studies in Education*, 1982, pp. 217–218.
6 Jonathan King, *Gallipoli: Our Last Man Standing – The Extraordinary Life of Alec Campbell*, Milton, Queensland: John Wiley & Sons, 2003, p. 29.
7 Reverend Edward Nye, *The History of Wesley College 1865–1919*, Melbourne: McCarron Bird, 1921, p. 60.
8 ibid.
9 G. Blainey, J. Morrissey and S. E. K. Hulme, *Wesley College: The First Hundred Years*, Melbourne: Robertson & Mullins, 1966, pp. 125–130.
10 ibid, pp. 139–140.
11 G. Denning and D. Kennedy, *Xavier Portraits*, South Melbourne: Graphic Print, 1993, p. 97.
12 ibid, p. 92.
13 Ivan Hansen, *By Their Deeds: A Centenary History of Camberwell Grammar School 1886–1986*, Melbourne: Globe Press, 1986, p. 75.
14 Weston Bate, *Light Blue Down Under: The History of Geelong Grammar School*, Melbourne: Oxford University Press, 1990, pp. 161–162.
15 ibid, p. 162.
16 Michael McKernan, *The Australian People and the Great War*, Melbourne: Nelson, 1980, p. 57.
17 *The Age*, 'Voice' Supplement, Melbourne University, 12 December 2011 – 8 January 2012.
18 McKernan, *The Australian People and the Great War*, p. 57.
19 ibid, pp. 57–58.
20 R. M. Gibbs, *A History of Prince Alfred College*, Second Edition, London: Bloomsbury, 1988, pp. 161–162.
21 Phillip Roberts, *Duty Always: The History of Ballarat High School 1907–1982*, Victoria: Dominion Press, 1982, pp. 42–43.
22 Damien Powell, *Honour in the Field: Melbourne High School and the Military in the Century of Federation*, Melbourne: Melbourne University Press, 2003, p. 7.
23 ibid.
24 Raymond Evans, 'The Lowest Common Denominator: Loyalism and School Children in War Torn Australia 1914–1918', *Queensland Review* (Special Edition), p. 104.
25 J. N. Dawes, and L. L. Robson, *Citizen to Soldier*, Melbourne: Melbourne University Press, 1977, pp. 93, 108, 111, 145.
26 Ronald S. Horan, *Fort Street: The School*. Sydney: Honeyset Publications, 1989, p. 163.
27 ibid, p. 165.
28 Horan, *Fort Street*, p. 170.
29 ibid, pp. 171–172.

17 Early Reactions in New Zealand

1 John Crawford and I. McGibbon (eds.), *New Zealand's Great War: New Zealand, the Allies and the First World War*, Auckland, NZ: Excile Press, 2007, pp. 427–428.

2 ibid, p. 428.
3 Karen McKinnon, *The Gold and Blue: Maryborough High School (NZ) 1900–2000*, p. 40.
4 ibid, pp. 40–41.
5 G. Thomas, *100 years from 1904 to 2004: the Hastings District High School, the Hastings Technical High School, the Hastings High School, the Hastings Boys' High School*, 2004, p. 4.
6 Bruce Hamilton and Don Hamilton, *Never a Footstep Back: A History of Wanganui Collegiate School 1854–2003*, Wanganui, New Zealand: Wanganui Collegiate Board of Trustees, 2003, p. 178.

18 Military Propaganda in the Schools

1. P. W. Musgrave, *To be an Australian?: Victorian School Textbooks and National Identity 1895–1965*, Colloquium on Textbooks, Schools and Society, Monash University, Melbourne, 1996, p. 4.
2 Thomas Nelson & Sons, *High Roads of History*, Sixth Book, 1911, p. 27.
3 ibid, pp. 27–33.
4 ibid, p. 271.
5 Thomas Nelson & Sons, *The Royal Readers*, Book 5, 1912, p. 388.
6 Musgrave, *To be an Australian?*, p. 5.
7 R. J. W. Selleck, *Frank Tate: A Biography*, Melbourne: Melbourne University Press, 1982, p. 216.
8 ibid, pp. 5–6.
9 *The School Paper*, grades 5 and 6, December 1900, pp. 60–65.
10 ibid, December 1901, pp. 56–59.
11 *The School Paper*, grade 4, August 1902, pp. 108–110.
12 *The School Paper*, grades 5 and 6, November 1904, pp. 150–151.
13 ibid, August 1904, p. 98.
14 ibid.
15 *The School Paper*, grade 4, August 1910, p. 37.
16 ibid, November 1910, pp. 149–151.
17 *The School Paper*, grades 5 and 6, February 1910.
18 *The School Paper*, grades 7 and 8, May 1912, p. 61.
19 ibid, November 1913.
20 ibid, May 1913.
21 ibid, pp. 147–158.
22 *Children's Hour*, grades 5 and 6, December 1914, p. 222.
23 ibid, grades 5 and 6, June 1915, p. 117.
24 *The School Paper*, 1 October 1914, pp. 161–176.
25 *The School Paper*, grades 7 and 8, 1 April 1915, pp. 38–39.
26 ibid, pp. 39–41.
27 Deborah E. Roberts, 'The Role of Victorian State Education in the Development of National Identity 1872–1918', PhD Thesis, Monash University, 1999, pp. 146–147.
28 *The School Paper*, grades 7 and 8, 1 November 1915, pp. 147–148.

29 *The School Paper*, grades 7 and 8, 1 December 1915, pp. 170–171.
30 *The School Paper*, grades 3 and 4, 1 March 1916, p. 31.
31 ibid, grades 7 and 8, October 1917.
32 *Children's Hour*, grades 5 and 6, January 1917, pp. 3–5.
33 ibid, grades 4 and 5, December 1918, p. 175.
34 *Children's Hour*, grades 7 and 8, February 1917, p. 18.
35 ibid, grades 7 and 8, May 1917, cover page.
36 *The School Paper*, 1 May 1917, p. 51.
37 *The School Paper*, grades 5 and 6, 1 December 1917, pp. 170–172.
38 ibid, April 1918, pp. 33–34.
39 ibid, p. 36.
40 ibid, p. 44.
41 ibid, 1 May 1918, pp. 49–50.
42 ibid, p. 57–58.
43 ibid, grades 7 and 8, 2 December 1918, pp. 168–169.
44 E. P. Malone, 'The New Zealand School Journal and the Imperial Ideology', in *New Zealand Journal of History*, vol. 7, no. 1, 1973, pp. 12–13.
45 *New Zealand School Journal*, Part 1, May 1909, p. 50.
46 Malone, p. 17.
47 Roger Openshaw, 'Patriotism in the Primary School Curriculum 1900–1930', in *Delta*, no. 24, June 1979, Massey University, Palmerston North, NZ, p. 44.
48 *New Zealand School Journal*, grades 5 and 6, April 1915, pp. 89–94.
49 ibid, grades 3 and 4, April 1915, pp. 90–94.
50 ibid, grades 5 and 6, July 1915, pp. 173–180.
51 *A Nest of Singing Birds: 100 years of the New Zealand School Journal*, p. 16.
52 ibid, grades 5 and 6, April 1915, pp. 67–69.
53 ibid, grades 5 and 6, November 1915, p. 295.
54 ibid, p. 307.
55 Elizabeth O'Neill, *The War 1915–16, For Boys & Girls*, p. 74.
56 ibid, p. 55.
57 Elizabeth O'Neill, *Battles For Peace: The Story of the Great War Told For Children*, pp. 215–216.
58 Craig Wilcox, *Red Coat Dreaming: How Colonial Australia Embraced the British Army*, Cambridge University Press, 2009, pp. 109–122.
59 ibid, p. 119.
60 ibid, p. 118.
61 Reverend William Henry Fitchett, *Deeds That Won The Empire*, London: Smith Elder & Co., 1897, p. 11.
62 Reverend William Henry Fitchett, *Fights For The Flag*, p. 145.
63 ibid, p. 135.
64 Roberts, 'The Role of Victorian State Education in the Development of National Identity', p. 65.
65 *The Boy's Own Annual*, 1913–14, p. 722.
66 ibid, 1914–15, pp. 357–358.
67 ibid, p. 89.

68 ibid, p. 491.
69 ibid, p. 445.
70 ibid, 1917–18, p. 242.
71 ibid, 1915–16, p. 366.

19 Pressures on Teachers in WWI

1 Education Department of Victoria, *Education Gazette and Teachers' Aid*, 20 April 1910, p. 91.
2 ibid, 27 June 1913, p. 284.
3 ibid, 18 November 1913, p. 438.
4 ibid, 25 May 1914, p. 191.
5 Education Department of Victoria, *Education Gazette and Teachers' Aid*, 13 April 1916, p. 94.
6 ibid, 20 June 1918, p. 134.
7 ibid, 13 April 1916, p. 97.
8 ibid.
9 ibid, 18 March 1915, p. 75.
10 C. E. W. Bean, *Official History of Australia in the Great War 1914–18*, vol. 1, Sydney: Angus & Robertson, 1937, p. 137.
11 Rosalie Triolo, 'Our Schools and the War: Victoria's Education Department and the Great War 1914–18', PhD Thesis, Monash University, 2008 p. 184.
12 Andrew Donson, *Youth in the Fearless Land: War Pedagogy, Nationalism and Authority in Germany 1914–1918*, Massachusetts, US: Harvard University Press, 2010, p. 129.
13 Leslie Blake (ed.), *Vision And Realisation: A Centenary History of State Education in Victoria*, vol. 1, Education Department of Victoria, 1973, p. 1287.
14 *The Education Department's Record of Service 1914–1918*, p. 6.
15 J. Burnswood and J. Fletcher, *Sydney and the Bush: A Pictorial History of Education in New South Wales*, Sydney: Government Printer, 1980, p. 176.
16 Colin Thiele, *Grains of Mustard Seed: A Narrative Outline of State Education in South Australia*, Education Department of South Australia, 1975, pp. 137–8.
17 'Report of the Minister for Education', Queensland, 1918, p. 46.
18 R. J. W. Selleck, *Frank Tate: A Biography*, Melbourne: Melbourne University Press, 1982, p. 212.
19 *The School Paper*, grades 7 and 8, 1 October 1914, pp. 170–171.
20 Education Department of Victoria, *Education Gazette and Teachers' Aid*, 13 April 1916, p. 95.
21 Selleck, *Frank Tate*, p. 213.
22 Triolo, 'Our Schools and the War', p. 185.
23 ibid, p. 180.
24 Education Department of Victoria, *Education Gazette and Teachers' Aid*, 14 September 1916, p. 226.
25 ibid.
26 ibid, 19 September 1918, p. 265.
27 *The Education Department's Record of War Service, Victoria 1914–1919*.

28 Don Garden, *The Melbourne Teacher Training Colleges*, Melbourne: Heinemann, 1982, pp. 105–106.
29 ibid, p. 106.
30 Garden, *The Melbourne Teacher Training Colleges*, pp. 106–107.
31 Education Department of Victoria, *Education Gazette and Teachers' Aid*, 16 March 1916, pp. 61–62.
32 Garden, *The Melbourne Teacher Training Colleges*, p. 109.
33 George Dancy, *The Teachers College War Memorial 1914–1918*, pp. 2–3.

20 War Casualties Among the Ex-cadets

1 Wilfred Owen, 'Anthem for Doomed Youth', *Selected Poetry of the First World War*, Wordsworth Editions, U.K., 1999, p. 65.
2 A. D. Bell (ed.), *An Anzac's War Diary*, Adelaide: Rigby, 1980, p. 57.
3 J. Hocking, *The Story of Melbourne High School*, Melbourne: Specialty Press, 1922, pp. 46–51.
4 ibid, p. 31.
5 Damien Powell, *Honour in the Field: Melbourne High School and the Military in the Century of Federation*, Melbourne: Melbourne University Press, 2003, p. 6.
6 Phillip Roberts, *Duty Always: The History of Ballarat High School 1907–1982*, Maryborough, Victoria: Dominion Press, 1982, p. 45.
7 ibid, p. 44.
8 ibid.
9 Ronald S. Horan, *Fort Street: The School*. Sydney: Honeyset Publications, 1989, p. 172.
10 D. T. Merrett, 'The School at War: Scotch College and the Great War', *Melbourne Studies in Education*, 1982, p. 209.
11 Weston Bate, *Light Blue Down Under: The History of Geelong Grammar School*, Melbourne: Oxford University Press, 1990, p. 162.
12 ibid.
13 Helen Penrose, *The Way to the Stars: 150 Years of the Geelong College*, Melbourne: Eldon Hogan Trust, 1995, p. 37.
14 ibid.
15 Merrett, 'The School at War', p. 210.
16 Ivan Hansen, *By Their Deeds: A Centenary History of Camberwell Grammar School 1886–1986*, Melbourne: Globe Press, 1986, p. 77.
17 ibid, pp.75–77.
18 Felix Meyer, *Adamson of Wesley*, Melbourne: Robertson & Mullens, 1932, p. 108.
19 ibid, p. 142.
20 ibid, p. 60.
21 ibid, p. 106.
22 Reverend Edward Nye, *The History of Wesley College 1865–1919*, Melbourne: McCarron Bird, 1921, p. 69.
23 G. Blainey, J. Morrissey and S. E. K. Hulme, *Wesley College: The First Hundred Years*, Melbourne: Robertson & Mullins, 1966, pp. 139–140.

24 G. Denning and D. Kennedy, *Xavier Portraits*, South Melbourne: Graphic Print, 1993, p. 100.
25 P. C. Naughtin, *History and Heritage: St Patrick's College Ballarat 1893–1993*, Richmond, Victoria: Spectrum, 1993, p. 81.
26 ibid, pp. 83–84.
27 Michael McKernan, *Australian Churches at War 1914–18*. Sydney/Canberra: Catholic Theological Faculty and Australian War Memorial, 1980, pp. 56–57.
28 R. M. Gibbs, *A History of Prince Alfred College*, Second Edition, London: Bloomsbury, 1988, p. 177.
29 ibid, p. 167.
30 W. R. Ray, *Pulteney Grammar School 1847–1972: A Record*, South Australia: Council of Governors of Pulteney Grammar School Incorporated, 1973, p. 56.
31 B. Buckland and P. Pollard (eds.), *One School Two Stories 100 Years On: Hamilton Boys High School, Hamilton Girls High School*, Auckland: Imprint Graphics, 2006, p. 83.
32 Bruce Hamilton, *The History of Kings College 1896–1995*, Auckland: AGM Publishing, 1995, pp. 65–66.
33 Bruce Hamilton and Don Hamilton, *Never a Footstep Back: A History of Wanganui Collegiate School 1854–2003*, Wanganui, New Zealand: Wanganui Collegiate Board of Trustees, 2003, p. 178.

21 Discrimination of German-Australians and their Schools in WWI

1 John Williams, *German Anzacs and the First World War*, Sydney: University of New South Wales Press, 2003, p. 15.
2 Charles Meyer, 'The Lutheran Congregational Schools of Victoria 1854–1930: A History', PhD Thesis, Monash University, 1995, p. 338.
3 Joan Beaumont (ed.), *Australia's War 1914–18*, Sydney: Allen & Unwin, 1995, p. 86.
4 Thomas Keneally, *Australians: Eureka to the Diggers*, vol. 2, Sydney: Allen & Unwin, 2011, pp. 288–291.
5 Williams, *German Anzacs and the First World War*, p. xiii.
6 Cecil Edwards, *John Monash*, Melbourne: State Electricity Commission, pp. 15–25.
7 Williams, *German Anzacs and the First World War*, p. 7.
8 Dr Michael Loh, *Lutherans and the War*, an address given at the Lutheran Teachers College, Adelaide, November 6, 1969, p. 4.
9 ibid, p. 6.
10 Perry, Roland. *Monash: The Outsider Who Won a War*. Sydney: Random House, 2004, p. 150.
11 Les Carlyon, *The Great War*, Sydney: Macmillan, 2006, p. 160.
12 Keneally, *Australians: Eureka to the Diggers*, p. 291.
13 Keneally, *Australians: Eureka to the Diggers*, pp. 349–340.
14 Williams, *German Anzacs and the First World War*, p. 54.
15 ibid, p. 48.

16 *The Bulletin*, 1 July 1915, p. 1.
17 ibid, p. 54.
18 ibid, pp. 44–45.
19 ibid, p. 46.
20 *Advertiser*, 2 August 1916.
21 ibid, 10 October 2004, p. 88.
22 ibid, 11 September 1916.
23 Author's own photo account when visiting Hahndorf in 2009.
24 Charles Meyer, 'Religion and Ethnic Background — A Study of Lutheran Schools in Victoria at the time of the Great War 1914–1918, in *Orthodoxies and Diversity: Conference Papers of the Australian and New Zealand History of Education Society*, Sydney, New South Wales, July 1995, p. 246.
25 Williams, *German Anzacs and the First World War*, p. 73.
26 Roland Perry, *Monash: The Outsider Who Won a War*, Melbourne: Eldon Hogan Trust, 1995, p. 152.
27 Williams, *German Anzacs and the First World War*, p. 96.
28 Beth Hentschke, 'The Compulsory Closure of South Australia's German Speaking Schools in World War I', *Pivot: Journal of the South Australian Education Department*, vol. 1, no. 2, 1973, p. 53.
29 Loh, *Lutherans and the War*, p. 6.
30 *The Mirror*, Sydney, 7 June 1916, p. 3.
31 Loh, *Lutherans and the War*, p. 7.
32 Williams, *German Anzacs and the First World War*, p. 106.
33 D. V. Hansen, and I. V. Hansen, *With Wings: A Centenary History of Immanuel College Adelaide 1895–1995*, Adelaide: Open Book Publications, 1995, p. 83.
34 Parliament of South Australia, *Act to Amend the Education Act of 1915*, 16 November 1916, pp. 24–25.
The attached schedule listed the names of forty-eight South Australian Lutheran primary schools
35 *Advertiser*, 15 December 1916.
36 D. Herbig, 'Schooldays at Friedensberg', Lutheran Archives, South Australia, 1995.
37 Lynette Finch, 'Young in a Warm Climate', in *Queensland Review* (Special Edition), p. 111.
38 ibid, p. 110.
39 ibid, pp. 111–112.
40 Meyer, pp. 357–358.
41 Education Department of Victoria, *Education Gazette and Teachers' Aid*, 18 May 1916.
42 Ailsa Zainuddin, *They Dreamt of a School: Centenary History of Methodist Ladies College, Kew*, Melbourne: Hyland House, 1982, pp. 147–149.
43 ibid, p. 150.
44 R. J. W. Selleck, *Frank Tate: A Biography*, Melbourne: Melbourne University Press, 1982, p. 220.

45 *The Argus*, 12 October 1914, p. 10.
46 ibid, 10 May 1918, p. 8.
47 Valerie Volk, 'The Closing of Lutheran Primary Schools in South Australia During the First World War', BEd Research Study, University of Melbourne, 1962, p. 11.
48 Lutheran Archives, Adelaide, Unit 14, photo nos. 2282–2286.
49 Williams, *German Anzacs and the First World War*, p. 78.
50 ibid, p. 79.
51 ibid, p. 34.
52 ibid, pp. 133–143.
53 ibid, p. 145.
54 Terry Hamilton, 'German Immigrants/Settlers and the Link to German Schools and World War I', notes prepared for the author, September 2012, pp. 1–4.
55 Bruce Hamilton, *The History of Kings College 1896–1995*, Auckland: AGM Publishing, 1995, p. 66.

22 Boy Soldiers in the AIF

1 A. W. Cockerill, *Sons of the Brave: The Story of Boy Soldiers*, London: Cooper, Secker & Warburg, 1984, p. 151.
2 E. P. F. Lynch, *Somme Mud: The Experiences of an Infantryman in France 1916–1919*, Random House, Sydney, 2006, p. 245.
3 Lynette Silver, *Marcel Caux: A Life Unravelled*, Melbourne: Wiley, 2006, pp. 144–145.
4 Michael McKernan, *Australian Churches at War 1914–18*. Sydney/Canberra: Catholic Theological Faculty and Australian War Memorial, 1980, pp. 58–59.
5 Jonathan King, *Gallipoli: Our Last Man Standing — The Extraordinary Life of Alec Campbell*, Milton, Queensland: John Wiley & Sons, 2003, p. 40.
6 *Weekend Australian Magazine*, 19–20 April 2003, p. 21.
7 Anthony Hill, *Soldier Boy: The True Story of Jim Martin the Youngest Anzac*, Melbourne: Penguin, 2001, pp. 19–27.
8 ibid, pp. 128–131.
9 *The Herald*, 18 December 1915, p. 14.
10 Hill, p. 60.
11 *The Herald*, 18 December 1915, p. 6.
12 ibid.
13 John Williams, *German Anzacs and the First World War*, Sydney: University of New South Wales Press, 2003, p. 119.
14 ibid, pp. 108–109.
15 Education Department of Victoria, *Education Gazette and Teachers' Aid*, 25 May 1914, p. 191.
16 *The Age*, 19 October 2005, p. 1.
17 Andrew Donson, *Youth in the Fearless Land: War Pedagogy, Nationalism and Authority in Germany 1914–1918*, Massachusetts, US: Harvard University Press, 2010, p. 157.

18 Hannsjoachim Wolfgang Koch, *The Hitler Youth: Origins and Development 1922–45*, London: Macdonald & James, 1975, pp. 1–2.

19 Michael Kater, *Hitler Youth*, London: Harvard University Press, 2004, p. 8.

23 The War Effort in Australian Schools

1 *The Education Department's Record of War Service, Victoria 1914–1918*, p. 207.

2 Gilbert Wallace, *How We Raised the First Hundred Thousand: an account of two years' work (1915–1916) for the Education Department's War Relief Fund, Education Department of Victoria War Relief Fund*, 1917, pp. 5–7.

3 Ernest Scott, *Official History of Australia in the War of 1914–1918*, vol. 11, Sydney: Angus & Robertson, 1936, pp. 734–735.

4 *The Education Department's Record of War Service, Victoria 1914–1918*, p. 304.

5 D. H. Rankin, *The History of the Development of Education in Victoria*, Melbourne: Arrow, 1939, p. 169.

6 Clifford Reeves, *A History of Tasmanian Education*, Melbourne, 1935, p. 112.

7 Scott, *Official History of Australia in the War of 1914–1918*, p. 735.

8 *The Education Department's Record of War Service, Victoria 1914–1918*, p. 267.

9 Les Carlyon, *The Great War*, Sydney: Macmillan, 2006, p. 588.

10 ibid, p. 610.

11 Leslie Blake (ed.), *Vision And Realisation: A Centenary History of State Education in Victoria*, vol. 1, Education Department of Victoria, 1973, p. 1294.

12 Allan Blankfield and Robin S. Corfield, *Never Forget Australia: Australia and Villers-Bretonneux 1918–1993*, Melbourne: The Villers-Bretonneux 75th Anniversary Pilgrimage Project Committee, 1994, p. 103.

13 *Weekly Times*, Victoria, 4 November 2011.

Bibliography

Archival Sources

Commonwealth of Australia. 'Regulations and Instructions for Universal Training'. Defence Act 1903–1910.

Commonwealth of Australia. Defence Act 1919.

Commonwealth Defence Force. 'Military Regulations for the Universal Training of Senior Cadets', Section 135, 25 July 1913.

Commonwealth Parliamentary Debates: J. M. Fowler, William Knox, 31 July 1901.

Concordia (Lutheran) College Archives. Adelaide, South Australia.

Education Department of Victoria. *The Department's Record of War Service, Victoria 1914–1919.*

Department of Defence Australia. Defence Act 1903–1927, Government Printer, Melbourne, 1927.

Department of Defence Australia. *Junior Cadet Regulations 1917*, A. J. Mullett, Government Printer, Melbourne, 1917.

Department of Defence Australia. *Training, Musketry and Rifle Exercises 1917*, A. J. Mullett, Government Printer, Melbourne, 1917.

Department of Defence Australia. *Regulations and Orders for the Australian.*

Education Department of Victoria. *Education Gazette and Teachers' Aid*, 1910, 1912, 1913, 1914, 1915, 1916, 1918, Minister of Public Instruction, Melbourne.

Education Department of Victoria. *The School Paper*, grade 4 – 1902, 1910; grades 3 and 4 – 1916; grades 5 and 6 – 1900, 1901, 1904, 1910, 1917, 1918; grades 7 and 8 – 1912, 1913, 1914, 1915, 1917, 1918.

Immanuel (Lutheran) College Archives. Adelaide.

Lutheran Archives. Bowden, South Australia.

Melbourne High School Archives. South Yarra, Victoria.

Military Forces and the Senior Cadets. Government Printer, Melbourne, 1927.

Parliament of South Australia. *Act to Amend the Education Act of 1915*, 16 November 1916.

Parliamentary Papers. House of Representatives, W. M. Hughes 'Military Conscription', 31 July 1901.

'Report of the Minister for Defence on the Progress of Universal Training'. 30 June 1912.

'Report of the Minister for Public Instruction, Victoria'. 1909–10, 1910–11.

Pamphlets

Australian Freedom League. 'Compulsory Military Training: An Analysis and an Exposure', Sydney, 1914.

Candy, Phillip, C., *Victorian Cadet Movement*, 1969.

Campbell, J. B. 'The Rifle Club Movement'. Melbourne: Fraser & Jenkinson, n.d.

Dancy, George. *The Teachers College War Memorial 1914–1918.*

Hamilton, Terry. 'German Immigrants/Settlers in New Zealand and links to German Schools in World War I'. Notes prepared for the author, September 2012.

Herbig, D. 'Schooldays at Friedensberg'. Lutheran Archives, South Australia, 1995.

International Arbitration and Peace Association. 'The Defence System of New Zealand'. 1913.

Lewis, Charles. 'Melbourne Teachers' College War Memorial 1914–1918'. Melbourne, 2006.

Military History Society. 'Australian Imperial Forces 1914–1920 Data'. Military History Society, ACT Branch, 1972.

Powell, Damien. 'Honour in the Field: Melbourne High School Cadets'. Ben Munday Memorial Lecture, 2001.

Rollins, Reverend W. S. 'The Defence System of New Zealand'. 1913.

Newspapers

Advertiser. Adelaide. 2 August 1916, 11 September 1916, 15 December 1916, 10 October 2004.

Adelaide Register. 23 October 1912.

The Age. 'Voice' Supplement. The University of Melbourne, 12 December 2011 – 8 January 2012.

The Age. Melbourne, 9 July 1906, 19 October 2005.

The Argus. Melbourne, 26 August 1910, 16 March 1912, 3 October 1911, 6 July 1914, 12 October 1914, 10 May 1918.

The Bulletin. Sydney, 1 July 1915.

Christchurch Press. 16 May 1912.

Daily Telegraph. Sydney, 6 February 1913, 13 September 1913.

Freedom. 24 June 1912

The Herald. Melbourne, 4 September 1912, 18 December 1915.

London Economist. 5 June 1915.

Maoriland Worker. New Zealand Federation of Labour, 9 February 1912.

The Mirror. Sydney, 7 June 1916.

The New York Times. 29 July 1915.

Parramatta Mercury. 9 September 1877.

The Socialist. Melbourne, 25 August 1911, 3 January 1913, 5 December 1913.

Weekly Times. Melbourne, 4 November 2011.

Weekend Australian Magazine. 19–20 April 2003.

Books

Adam-Smith, Patsy. *The Anzacs*. West Melbourne: Nelson, 1978.

Allan, James Alexander. *The Old Model School: Its History and Romance 1852–1904*. Melbourne: Melbourne University Press, 1934.

Anchen, J. O. *Frank Tate and His Work for Education*. Melbourne: Australian Council for Educational Research, 1956.

Austin, A. G. and Selleck, R. J. W. *The Australian Government School 1830–1914*. Melbourne: Pitman, 1975.

Barcan, Alan. *A History of Australian Education*. Melbourne: Oxford University Press, 1980.

Barcan, Alan. *A Short History of Education in NSW*. Sydney: Martindale Press, 1965.

Barcan, Alan. *Two Centuries of Education in NSW*. New South Wales University Press, 1988.

Barrett, John. *Falling In: Australians and Boy Conscription 1911–1915*. Sydney: Hale & Ironmonger, 1979.

Bate, Weston. *Light Blue Down Under: The History of Geelong Grammar School*. Melbourne: Oxford University Press, 1990.

Bean, C. E. W. *Here, My Son: An Account of the Independent and Other Corporate Boys' Schools of Australia*. Sydney: Angus & Robertson, 1950.

Bean, C. E. W. *In Your Hands, Australians*. Melbourne: Castle, 1918.

Bean, C. E. W. *Official History of Australia in the War 1914–18*. vol. 1, Sydney: Angus & Robertson, 1937.

Beasley, A. W. *The Light Accepted: 125 Years of Wellington College*. Wellington, NZ: Wordset Enterprises, 1992.

Beaumont, Joan (ed.) *Australia's War 1914–18*. Sydney: Allen & Unwin, 1995.

Bell, A. D. (ed.) *An Anzac's War Diary*. Adelaide: Rigby, 1980.

Bennett, Scott. *Pozieres: The Anzac Story*. Melbourne: Scribe, 2011.

Bessant, Bob (ed.) *Mother State and Her Little Ones*. Melbourne: Centre for Youth and Community Studies, 1987.

Blainey, G., Morrissey, J. and Hulme, S. E. K. *Wesley College: The First Hundred Years*. Melbourne: Robertson & Mullins, 1966.

Blake, Leslie (ed.) *Vision and Realisation: A Centenary History of State Education in Victoria*. vol. 1, Education Department of Victoria, 1973.

Blankfield, Allan and Corfield, Robin. *Never Forget Australia: Australia and Villers-Bretonneux 1918–1993*, Melbourne: The Villers-Bretonneux 75th Anniversary Pilgrimage Project Committee, 1994.

Boy's Own Annual. 1913–14, 1914–15, 1915–16, 1917–18, London: Boy's Own Paper Office.

Bowe, Mary. *Padua College: A College by the Sea*. Mornington, Victoria: Padua College, 1998.

Braniff, Br. V. *The Quest for Higher Things: History of Marist Brothers 100 years at Kilmore*. Richmond: Micron Press, 1992.

Broadbent, Harvey. *The Boys Who Came Home: Recollections of Gallipoli*. ABC Books, 1990.

Brodribb, T. *Addresses 1909: No. 2 — Military Training for Our Schoolboys*. Melbourne: Imperial Federation League, 1909.

Buckland, B. and Pollard, P. (eds.) *One School Two Stories 100 Years On: Hamilton Boys High School, Hamilton Girls High School*. Auckland: Imprint Graphics, 2006.

Carlyon, Les. *The Great War*. Sydney: Macmillan, 2006.

Caughey, C. (ed.) *Remuera Primary School 125 years 1873–1998*. 1998.

Charlwood, Don. *Marching as to War*. Hawthorn: Hudson, 1990.

Clapham, Marcus, ed. 'Anthem for Doomed Youth', by Wilfred Owen in *Selected Poetry of the First World War*, Wordsworth Editions, U.K., 1999

Cleverley, John (ed.) *Half a Million Children*. Sydney: Longman Cheshire, 1978.

Coates, A. and Rosenthal, N. *The Albert Coates Story*. Melbourne: Hyland House, 1977.

Cockerill, A. W. *Sons of the Brave: The Story of Boy Soldiers*. London: Cooper, Secker & Warburg, 1984.

Crawford, John and McGibbon, I. (eds.). *New Zealand's Great War: New Zealand, the Allies and the First World War*. Auckland, NZ: Excile Press, 2007.

Crotty, Martin. *Making the Australian Male: Middle Class Masculinity 1870–1920*. Melbourne University Press, 2001.

Crowley, F. K. *Modern Australia in Documents 1901–1939*, Melbourne: Wren, 1973.

Dawes, J. N. and Robson, L. L. *Citizen to Soldier: Australia Before the Great War: Recollections of members of the First AIF*. Melbourne University Press, 1977.

Denning, G. and Kennedy, D. *Xavier Portraits*. South Melbourne: Graphic Print, 1993.

Denny, Captain W. J. *The Diggers*. London: Hodder & Stouton, n.d.

Dixon, William H. *The Switzers*. London: Hurst & Blackett, 1872.

Donovan, P. and O'Neil, B. *In the Marist Tradition: Sacred Heart College Adelaide 1897–1997*. Somerton Park, South Australia: Sacred Heart College, 1997.

Donson, Andrew. *Youth in the Fatherless Land: War Pedagogy, Nationalism and Authority in Germany 1914–1918*. Massachusetts, US: Harvard University Press, 2010.

Edwards, Cecil. *John Monash*. Melbourne: State Electricity Commission, n.d.

Fitchett, Reverend William Henry. *Deeds That Won the Empire*. London: Smith Elder & Co., 1897.

Fitchett, Reverend W. H. *Fights for the Flag*. London: George Newnes, 1900.

Fletcher, J. P. and Hills, J. F. *Conscription Under Camouflage: An Account of Compulsory Military Training in Australasia Down to the Outbreak of the Great War*. Glenelg, South Australia, 1919.

Fletcher, J. and Burnswood, J. *Sydney and the Bush: A Pictorial History of Education in New South Wales*. Sydney: Government Printer, 1980.

Forward, R. and Reece, B. (eds.) *Conscription in Australia*. Brisbane: University of Queensland Press, 1968.

Garden, Don. *The Melbourne Teacher Training Colleges 1870–1982*. Melbourne: Heinemann, 1982.

Gammage, Bill. *The Broken Years: Australian Soldiers in the Great War*. Melbourne: Penguin, 1974.

Gibbs, Ronald, R. *A History of Prince Alfred College*, South Australia: Peacock Publications, 1984.

Giddings, Robert. *The War Poets*. London: Bloomsbury, 1988.

Greenwood, G. (ed.) *Documents on Australian International Affairs: The Kitchener Report*, 1910.

Grey, Jeffrey. *A Military History of Australia*. England: Cambridge University Press, 1990.

Hamilton, Bruce. *The History of Kings College (NZ) 1865–1995*. Auckland: AGM Publishing, 1995.

Hamilton, Bruce and Hamilton, Don. *Never a Footstep Back: A History of Wanganui Collegiate School 1854–2003*. Wanganui, NZ: Wanganui Collegiate Board of Trustees, 2003.

Hamilton, John. *The Price of Valour*. Sydney: Macmillan, 2012.

Hansen, Ivan. *By Their Deeds: A Centenary History of Camberwell Grammar School 1886–1986*. Melbourne: Globe Press, 1986.

Hansen, D. V. and Hansen, I. V. *With Wings: A Centenary History of Immanuel College, Adelaide 1895–1995*. Adelaide: Open Book Publications, 1995.

Hannan, Agnes. *Victoria Barracks Melbourne: A Social History*. Australian Defence Force Journal Publication, n.d.

Hill, Anthony. *Soldier Boy: The True Story of Jim Martin the Youngest Anzac*. Melbourne: Penguin, 2001.

Hillcourt, William. *Baden-Powell: The Two Lives of a Hero*. London: Heinemann, 1964.

Hocking, J. *The Story of Melbourne High School 1905–1921*. Melbourne: Specialty Press, 1922.

Hodge, B. *The Last Shilling: Australians in the Great War*. Sydney: Hicks Smith & Sons, 1974.

Holloway, David. *The Inspectors: An Account of the Inspectorate of the State Schools of Victoria 1851–1983*. Melbourne: Institute of Senior Officers of the Victorian Education Services, 2000.

Horan, Ronald S. *Fort Street: The School*. Sydney: Honeyset Publications, 1989.

Hutchinson, G. (ed.) *Eyewitness: Australians Write from the Front Line*. Melbourne: Black Inc., 2005.

Inglis, Ken S. *The Australian Colonists: An Exploration of Social History 1788–1870*. Melbourne: Melbourne University Press, 1974.

Jeal, Tim. *Baden-Powell*. London: Hutchinson, 1989.

Jauncey, Leslie. *The Story of Conscription in Australia*. Sydney: MacMillan, 1968.

Jones, Sir George. *From Private to Air Marshall: The Autobiography of Air Marshall Sir George Jones*. Richmond: Greenhouse, 1988.

Kane, K. D. *The History of Christian Brothers' College*. Melbourne: John Sands, 1972.

Kater, Michael. *Hitler Youth*. London: Harvard University Press, 2004.

Keneally, Thomas. *Australians: Eureka to the Diggers*. vol. 2, Sydney: Allen & Unwin, 2011.

Kent, Jaqueline. *In The Half Light: Life as a Child in Australia 1900–1970*. Sydney: Angus & Robertson, 1988.

King, Jonathan. *Gallipoli: Our Last Man Standing — The Extraordinary Life of Alec Campbell*. Milton, Queensland: John Wiley & Sons, 2003.

Koch, Hannsjoachim Wolfgang. *The Hitler Youth: Origins and Development 1922–45*. London: Macdonald & James, 1975.

Kuring, Ian. *Redcoats to Cams: A History of Australian Infantry 1788–2001*. Canberra: Army History Unit, Defence Department, 2004.

Kyle, Roy. *An Anzac's Story*. Melbourne: Viking, 2004.

Lake, Marilyn and Reynolds, Henry. *What's Wrong with Anzac? The Militarisation of Australian History*. Sydney: University of NSW Press, 2010.

Legg, Frank. *The Gordon Bennett Story*. Sydney: Angus & Robertson, 1965.

Lewis, Brian. *Our War: Australia During World War I*. Melbourne: Melbourne University Press, 1980.

Loh, Dr Michael. *Lutherans and the War*, an address given at the Lutheran Teachers College, Adelaide, November 6, 1969

Lynch, Edward, P.F., *Somme Mud: The Experiences of an Infantryman in France 1916–1919*, Sydney: Random House, 2006

Mackenzie, John M. *Propaganda and Empire*. Manchester University Press, n.d.

Main, J. M. *Conscription: The Australian Debate 1901–1970*. Australia: Cassell, 1970.

Maxwell, Joseph. *Hell's Bells and Mademoiselles*. Sydney: Angus & Robertson, 1939.

McKernan, Michael. *Australian Churches at War 1914–18*. Sydney/Canberra: Catholic Theological Faculty and Australian War Memorial, 1980.

McKernan, Michael. *The Australian People and the Great War*. Melbourne: Nelson, 1980.

McKinlay, Brian. *School Days: Looking back on Education in Victoria*. Melbourne: Market Street Press, 1985.

McKinlay, Brian. *Young Anzacs: The Contribution of Victorian Schools to the Gallipoli Campaign 1915*. Victoria: Ministry of Education, 1990.

McKinnon, Karen, *The Gold and Blue: Maryborough High School (NZ) 1900–2000*.

McMullin, Ross. *Pompey Elliott*. Melbourne: Scribe Publishing, 2008.

McQuilton, John. *Rural Australia and the Great War*. Melbourne: Melbourne University Press, 2001.

Meany, N. *The Search for Security in the Pacific 1901–1914* , Sydney, 1976.

Meyer, Felix. *Adamson of Wesley*. Melbourne: Robertson & Mullens, 1932.

Mordike, John. *An Army For a Nation: A History of Australian Military Developments 1880–1914*. Melbourne: Allen & Unwin, 1992.

Musgrave, P. W. *To be an Australian?: Victorian School Textbooks and National Identity 1895–1965*. Colloquium on Textbooks, Schools and Society, Melbourne: Monash University, 1996.

Naughtin, P. C. *History and Heritage: St Patrick's College Ballarat 1893–1993*, Richmond, Victoria: Spectrum, 1993.

Notman, G. C. and Keith, B. R. *The Geelong College 1861–1961*. Blackburn, Victoria: Specialty Press, 1961.

Nye, Reverend Edward. *The History of Wesley College 1865–1919*. Melbourne: McCarron Bird, 1921.

O'Brien, Gregory. *A Nest of Singing Birds: 100 Years of the New Zealand School Journal*. Wellington, NZ: Learning Media, 1961.

Oliver, Bobbie. *Peacemongers: Conscientious Objectors to Military Service in Australia 1911–1945*. Western Australia: Fremantle Arts Centre Press, 2003.

O'Neill, Elizabeth. *Battles For Peace: The Story of the Great War Told For Children*. London: Hodder and Stoughton, 1918.

O'Neill, Elizabeth. *The War 1915–16, For Boys & Girls*. London: TC & EC Jack Ltd, 1916.

Pash, J. and Treloar, J. *Adelaide High School 75th Anniversary 1908–1983: Souvenir Book*. Adelaide: Adelaide High School Council Incorporated, 1983.

Perry, Roland. *Monash: The Outsider Who Won a War*. Sydney: Random House, 2004.

Penrose, Helen. *Red, Black and Khaki: Cadets at Xavier College*. Melbourne: Eldon Hogan Trust, 1995.

Penrose, Helen. *The Way to the Stars: 150 Years of the Geelong College*. Melbourne: Australian Scholarly Publishing, 2011.

Powell, Damien. *Honour in the Field: Melbourne High School and the Military in the Century of Federation*, Melbourne University Press, 2003.

Rankin, D. H. *The History of the Development of Education in Victoria 1836–1936.* Melbourne: Arrow, 1939.

Ray, W. R. *Pulteney Grammar School 1847–1972: A Record*, South Australia: Council of Governors of Pulteney Grammar School Incorporated, 1973.

Reeves, C. *A History of Tasmanian Education.* Melbourne, 1935.

Retallack, James (ed.) *A Short History of Germany: Imperial Germany 1871–1918.* London: Oxford University Press, 2010.

Roberts, Phillip. *Duty Always: The History of Ballarat High School 1907–1982.* Maryborough, Victoria: Dominion Press, 1982.

Robson, L. L. *Australia and the Great War.* Melbourne: Macmillan, 1969.

Robson, L. L. *The First AIF: A Study of its Recruitment 1914–18.* Melbourne: Melbourne University Press, 1970.

Royal School Series. *Highroads of History.* London: Thomas Nelson & Sons, 1911.

Royal School Series. *The Royal Readers.* Book 5. London: Thomas Nelson & Sons, 1912.

Scott, Ernest. *Official History of Australia in the War of 1914–1918.* vol. 11. Sydney: Angus & Robertson, 1936.

Selleck, R. J. W. *Frank Tate: A Biography.* Melbourne: Melbourne University Press, 1982.

Silver, Lynette. *Marcel Caux: A Life Unravelled.* Melbourne: Wiley, 2006.

Stockings, Craig. *The Torch and the Sword: A History of the Army Cadet Movement in Australia.* Sydney: University of New South Wales Press, 2007.

Sweetman, E., Long, C. and Smyth, J. *A History of State Education in Victoria.* Education Department of Victoria, 1922.

Synan, Ann and Synan, Peter. *Sale High School Centenary Memories.* Sale, Victoria: Sale College, 2007.

Tanner, Thomas. *Compulsory Citizen Soldiers.* Sydney: Alternative Publishing Co-operative, 1980.

Thiele, Colin. *Grains of Mustard Seed: A Narrative Outline of State Education in South Australia.* Education Department of South Australia, 1975.

Thomas, G. *100 years from 1904 to 2004: the Hastings District High School, the Hastings Technical High School, the Hastings High School, the Hastings Boys' High School*, 2004.

Thomson, Alistair. *Anzac Memories: Living With the Legend.* Melbourne: Melbourne University Press, 1994.

Trembath, K. A. *Ad Augusta: A Centennial History of Auckland Grammar School.* Auckland: Wilson & Horton, 1969.

Triolo, Rosalie. *Our Schools and the War.* Melbourne: Australian Scholarly Publishing, 2012.

Turney, Cliff. *William Wilkins: His Life and Work.* Sydney: Hale & Ironmonger, 1992.

University of Melbourne, *Record of Active Service in the European War 1914–1918.* Melbourne: H. J. Green, Government Printer, 1926.

Valder, John. *Anzac.* London: New English Library, 1970.

Verhey, Jeffrey. *The Spirit of 1914: Military Myth and Mobilisation in Germany.* Cambridge University Press, 2000.

Welborn, Suzanne. *Lords of Death: A People, A Place, A Legend.* Western Australia: Fremantle Arts Centre Press, 1982.

Wallace, Gilbert. *How We Raised the First Hundred Thousand: an account of two years' work (1915–1916) for the Education Department's War Relief Fund*, Education Department of Victoria War Relief Fund, 1917.

Wilcox, Craig. *For Hearths and Homes: Citizen Soldiering in Australia 1854–1945.* Sydney: Allen & Unwin, 1998.

Wilcox, Craig. *Red Coat Dreaming: How Colonial Australia Embraced the British Army.* Cambridge University Press, 2009.

Wilson, Mark. *My Mother's Eyes: The Story of an Australian Boy Soldier.* Sydney: Lothian Children's Books, 2009.

Williams, John. *German Anzacs and the First World War*. Sydney: University of New South Wales Press, 2003.

Wordsworth Poetry Library. *Selected Poetry of the First World War*. London: Bibliophile Books, n.d.

Wright, Matthew. *Western Front: The New Zealand Division in the First World War.*,

Wyeth, E. R. *Education in Queensland*. Melbourne: Australian Council for Educational Research, n.d.

Zainuddin, Ailsa. 'Reverend William Henry Fitchett (1841–1928)', *Australian Dictionary of Biography*. National Centre of Biography. Australian National University, published in hardcopy 1981.

Zainuddin, Ailsa. *They Dreamt of a School: Centenary History of Methodist Ladies College, Kew*. Melbourne: Hyland House, 1982.

Articles

Alves, Geoff. 'The Department and the Great War', *The Educational Magazine*, vol. 39, no. 5, 1982.

Bessant, Bob. 'British Imperial Propaganda in Australian Schools 1900–1930', in *Working Papers in Australian Studies*, University of London, 1996.

Bessant, Bob. 'Empire Day and all that …', *The Education Magazine* (Vic.), vol. 30, no. 5, 1973.

Collins, Lieutenant C. R. 'The Training of Junior Cadets', *The Lone Hand*, 1 March 1913.

Crawford, Keith. 'When the British Began to Hate: The Manufacture of German Demonisation in British School History Textbooks 1900–1930', *History of Education Review*, vol. 38, no. 1, 2009.

Daley, Major Charles. 'Some Educational Reminiscences', *The Victorian Historical Magazine*, vol. 16, May 1936.

Daley, Major Charles. 'The Story of the Victoria Junior Cadet Corps', *The Victorian Historical magazine*, vol. 20, no. 1, 1943.

Evans, Raymond. 'The Lowest Common Denominator: Loyalism and School Children in War Torn Australia 1914–1918', *Queensland Review* (Special Edition), n.d.

Finch, Lynette. 'Young in a Warm Climate', *Queensland Review* (Special Edition), n.d.

French, E. L. (ed.) 'Recollections of Charles Long', *Melbourne Studies in Education*, 1963.

French, Maurice. 'One People One Destiny: A Question of Loyalty. The Origins of Empire Day in NSW 1900–1905', *Journal of the Royal Australian Historical Society*, vol. 61, part 4, December 1975.

Hentschke, Beth. 'The Compulsory Closures of South Australia's German Speaking Schools in World War I', *Pivot: Journal of the South Australian Education Department*, vol. 1, no. 2, 1973.

Hollingworth, Jacqueline. 'The Cult of Empire: Children's Literature Revisited', *Mother State and Her Little Ones*, Melbourne: Centre for Youth and Community Studies, 1987.

Ken S. Inglis, 'Conscription in Peace and War 1911–1945' in R. Forward and B. Reece (eds.), *Conscription in Australia*, p. 23.

Jones, David. 'Cadets and Military Training 1872–1914', *Mother State and Her Little Ones*, Melbourne: Centre for Youth and Community Studies, 1987.

Malone, E. P. 'The New Zealand *School Journal* and the Imperial Ideology', *New Zealand Journal of History*, vol. 7, no. 1, 1973.

McGeorge, C. 'Military Training in New Zealand Primary Schools', *Journal of the Australian and New Zealand History of Education Society*, vol. 3, no. 2, 1974.

Merrett, D. T. 'The School at War: Scotch College and the Great War', *Melbourne Studies in Education*, 1982.

Meyer, Charles. '"What a terrible thing it is to entrust one's children to such heathen teachers": State and Church Relations Illustrated in Early Lutheran Schools of Victoria, Australia', *History of Education Quarterly*, vol. 40, no. 3, 2000.

Meyer, Charles. 'Lutheran Schools in Victoria at the Time of the Great War 1914–1918: Religion, Ethnic Background and Treatment', *History of Education Review*, vol. 27, no. 1, 1988.

Meyer, Charles, 'Religion and Ethnic Background — A Study of Lutheran Schools in Victoria at the time of the Great War 1914–1918, in *Orthodoxies and Diversity: Conference Papers of the Australian and New Zealand History of Education Society*, Sydney, New South Wales, July 1995.

Openshaw, Roger. 'Patriotism in the Primary School Curriculum 1900–1930', *Delta*, Palmerston North, New Zealand: Massey University, 24 June 1978.

Stockings, Craig. 'Khaki in the Classroom', *History of Education Review*, vol. 37, no. 1, 2008.

Weitzel, R. L. 'Pacifists and Anti-Militants in New Zealand 1909–1914', *New Zealand Journal of History*, vol. 7, no. 2.

Theses

Firth, S. G. 'Schooling in New South Wales 1880–1914', MA Thesis, Australian National University, 1970.

Fraser, E. M. 'New Zealand Military Policy from the Boer War to the Great War 1900–1914', MA Thesis, University of Auckland, 1938.

Hannon, Anthony. 'Patriotism in Victorian State Schools 1901–1945', MA Thesis, Latrobe University, 1977.

Hollingworth, Jacqualine. 'The Call of Empire: Being the Study of Imperial Indoctrination of Australian School Children 1890–1910', PhD Thesis, Latrobe University, 1993.

Jones, David. 'The Military Use of Australian Schools 1871–1914', PhD Thesis, Latrobe University, 1991.

Milburn, James Dalton. 'New Zealand's First Experiment With Compulsory Military Training 1900–1914', MA Thesis, Victoria University College, Wellington, New Zealand, 1954.

Murray, Brendon John. 'Citizenship and Schooling: A Study of the Citizenship Ethos and Schooling in Victorian State and Catholic Systems 1910–1918', MA Thesis, Monash University, 1981.

Meyer, Charles. 'The Lutheran Congregational Schools of Victoria 1854–1930: A History', PhD Thesis, Monash University, 1995.

Roberts, Deborah E. 'The Role of Victorian State Education in the Development of a National Identity 1872–1918', PhD Thesis, Monash University, 1999.

Schaefer, Trevor. 'The Treatment of Germans in South Australia 1914–1924', BA (Honours) Thesis, Department of History, University of Adelaide, 1982.

Triolo, Rosalie. 'Our Schools and the War: Victoria's Education Department and the Great War 1914–1918', PhD Thesis, Monash University, 2008.

Volk, Valerie. 'The Closing of Lutheran Primary Schools in South Australia During the First World War', in partial fulfilment for the BEd, University of Melbourne, 1962.

Index

The Author

Dr Max Waugh is a former Victorian Government primary school teacher, school principal, and later lecturer in the History of Education at Deakin and Monash Universities. Currently retired, he has an honorary position as an Adjunct Research Fellow in the Education Faculty at Monash University in Melbourne. As a teenager, Max was a cadet in the Air Training Corps, North Melbourne Squadron, and completed his National Service training at the RAAF Base in Laverton, Victoria, during 1955 and 1956.